"*Mexican American Religions: An Introduction* wants to understand the history of Mexican religious beliefs, traditions, and practices interact with broader cultural, political, and historical themes. An invaluable resource for teachers, students, and general readers alike."

Kristy Nabhan-Warren, University of Iowa, USA.

"*Mexican American Religions: An Introduction* provides the most comprehensive and accessible treatment of this subject to date. Spanning Indigenous pre-conquest religions to the present, as well as the plurality of religious traditions Mexican Americans practice, it also encompasses insightful thematic chapters that collectively address major issues in the study of these religions."

Timothy Matovina, University of Notre Dame, USA.

"This textbook deftly examines a broad history of Mexican American religions *and* engages complex racial and ethnic issues with attention to the built environment as well as the politics of knowledge transmission. Moreover, the author's commitment to revealing how practice fits into different historical periods and political contexts productively expands how we can think about the study of religion."

Elaine Peña, George Washington University, USA.

Mexican American Religions

Mexican American Religions is a concise introduction to the religious life of Mexican American people in the United States. This accessible volume uses historical narrative to explore the complex religious experiences and practices that have shaped Mexican American life in North America. It addresses the religious impact of U.S. imperial expansion into formerly Mexican territory and examines how religion intertwines with Mexican and Mexican American migration into and within the United States. This book also delves into the particularities and challenges faced by Mexican American Catholics in the United States, the development and spread of Mexican American Protestantism and Pentecostalism, and a growing religious diversity. Topics covered include:

- Mesoamerican religions
- Iberian religion and colonial evangelization of New Spain
- The Colonial era
- Religion in the Mexican period
- The U.S.-Mexican War and the racialization of Mexican American religion
- Mexican migration and the Catholic Church
- Mexican American Protestants
- Mexican American Evangelical and Charismatic Christianity
- Mexican American Catholics in the twentieth and twenty-first centuries
- Curanderismo
- Religion and Mexican American civil rights
- Pilgrimage and borderland connections
- Mexican American Judaism, Islam, Mormonism, and Secularism

Mexican American Religions provides an overview of this incredibly diverse community and its ongoing cultural contribution. Ideal for students and scholars approaching the topic for the first time, the book includes sections in each chapter that focus on Mexican American religion in practice.

Brett Hendrickson is Associate Professor of Religious Studies at Lafayette College in Easton, Pennsylvania, USA.

Religion in America

Mexican American Religions
An Introduction
Brett Hendrickson

For more information about this series, please visit: https://www.routledge.com/
Religion-in-America/book-series/RIA

Mexican American Religions

An Introduction

Brett Hendrickson

 Routledge
Taylor & Francis Group

LONDON AND NEW YORK

First published 2022
by Routledge
2 Park Square, Milton Park, Abingdon, Oxon OX14 4RN

and by Routledge
605 Third Avenue, New York, NY 10158

Routledge is an imprint of the Taylor & Francis Group, an informa business

British Library Cataloguing-in-Publication Data
A catalogue record for this book is available from the British Library

Library of Congress Cataloging-in-Publication Data
A catalog record has been requested for this book

ISBN: 978-0-367-25014-0 (hbk)
ISBN: 978-0-367-25013-3 (pbk)
ISBN: 978-0-429-28551-6 (ebk)

DOI: 10.4324/9780429285516

Typeset in Bembo
by Taylor & Francis Books

In memory of Grant VanVeldhuizen

Contents

Figures

Acknowledgments

Writing a book is often a solitary affair, particularly in a time of global pandemic. Yet, like all books, this one benefited immensely from the help of others, a testament to the collectivity of academic work, even when we are isolated physically from one another. As an introduction to Mexican American religious history and practice, this book's debts to other scholarship run deep. Indeed, the fact that a book like this can be written points to the maturation of the field of Latino/a religious studies and religious history. In the past two decades, many excellent scholars have produced dozens of monographs about Latino/a religion, and I am grateful to them. In this, I would like to echo the great historian David Weber, who wrote in the preface to his *The Mexican Frontier, 1821–1946*, "this overview depends heavily on the research of other historians. My intellectual debts to them should be apparent in the notes to each chapter."[1] So it is with *Mexican American Religions: An Introduction*.

At my home institution of Lafayette College, I am grateful for a sabbatical leave during which much of this book was researched and written. I would like to thank my writing group for their ongoing camaraderie: Laurie Caslake, Mary Roth, and Angelika von Wahl. Thanks also must go to the students in my fall 2020 Latino/a Religions course for workshopping this book in manuscript form.

Lafayette College's libraries continue to be the jewel in our crown; I would like to especially thank librarians Ben Jahre and Thomas Lannon. Outside of Lafayette College, my thanks go to staff at the Archdiocese of San Antonio Archives, the Corrales (NM) Historical Society, the Flower Pentecostal Heritage Center, and the Archives of Labor and Urban Affairs at Wayne State University.

At Routledge, I have enjoyed the prompt and encouraging editorial work of Rebecca Shillabeer and Amy Doffegnies. Many thanks to them. The anonymous readers of this manuscript provided a great deal of helpful and nuanced feedback, and I thank them.

I made many inquiries to colleagues during the writing of this book to draw on their expertise. In particular, I would like to thank Lloyd Barba, Jessica Carr, Mark Goldberg, Kristy Nabhan-Warren, and Arlene Sánchez Walsh. As always, much love to my Young Scholars cohort (now, realistically, middle-aged scholars), with special thanks to Angela Tarango for her help and support. Thanks also to several people who helped with photo illustrations for this book: Rev. John Feagins of La Trinidad United Methodist Church in San Antonio, Fr. Rafael Garcia at Sacred Heart Parish in El Paso, Rev. Rob Woodruff of Second Presbyterian Church in Albuquerque, Julia Young, and my dear friends Rachel Srubas and Ken McAllister.

Above all, I remain so grateful for the generous love and support of my family. My kids—Tom, Elizabeth, and David—are becoming young people whom I admire so much. And as far as I am concerned, Alex hung the moon.

Note

1 David J. Weber, *The Mexican Frontier, 1821–1846: The American Southwest under Mexico* (Albuquerque, NM: University of New Mexico Press, 1982), xxii.

Introduction

Jesus, wearing a crown of thorns and a forlorn but resolute expression, carries his heavy cross down 18th Street in Pilsen, a Mexican American neighborhood in Chicago. Jesus himself is Mexican American, as are the centurions, disciples, weeping women, and other characters in the Via Crucis, the Way of the Cross. In the week before the Christian celebration of Easter, neighborhood residents take to the streets to re-enact Jesus's final moments leading up to his crucifixion and death. Many of the onlookers who line the street are likewise Mexican American, though the crowd is diverse like the city of Chicago itself. For over four decades, this particular expression of Mexican American religion—the public and embodied commemoration of Jesus's passion story—has helped to define a place and a people. The Via Crucis procession makes a religious claim on the neighborhood and the city, linking the stations of the cross with places on the street where flesh-and-blood people have lived out the joys and troubles of Mexican American daily life. The procession likewise makes a Mexican American claim on Catholicism and, going deeper, on the story of Jesus itself. The passion narrative that roots the faith of billions around the world becomes in this place and in these bodies a story of Mexican American resiliency and new life.[1]

This is but one example of the vibrant, heterogeneous expression of Mexican American religions. Religion—especially Christianity—has played an integral role in the historical trajectory of Mexican Americans from the Spanish colonial period through the western expansion of the United States and to the present day. One of the principal claims that runs throughout this book is that religion holds a central place in the history and contemporary lives of Mexican Americans. A corollary of this theme is that religion and ethnic identity are tightly interwoven; as such, a study of Mexican American religions illumines much about Mexican American ethnic identity formation and maintenance. But this is not just a story for or about Mexican Americans. Another central claim of this book is that Mexican American religious history is an intrinsic and indispensable part of U.S. religious history in general. To learn about Mexican Americans and their religion requires constant and critical attention to the multifaceted context of the United States. This must include engagement with questions of racial prejudice and economic and

DOI: 10.4324/9780429285516-1

political exclusion as well as with opportunities for creative flourishing. To return to the Via Crucis in Chicago as a metaphor: it is a complex scene of suffering and scapegoating, to be sure. But it is also a defiantly public manifestation of hope and faith. The study of Mexican American religions must lead through this very terrain.

Religion and Mexican American ethnic studies

Since the civil rights movement, scholars in the fields of history, sociology, literature, cultural studies, public health, and demography have produced important research in the relatively new fields of Chicano studies, Mexican American studies, and Latino studies (see the "A note on terms for people" section below). This ethnic studies scholarship has done much to uncover the lives, histories, and cultural production of Mexican Americans in the United States while simultaneously holding up a critical lens to economic, political, and social structures that have often overtly and covertly tried to suppress just these kinds of histories and experiences. In general, however, religious studies has not been, until recently, a prominent component of Mexican American studies. Despite this, there is little doubt that religion— as an institutional force, as a corpus of community traditions, and as an articulation of what could be called a worldview or cosmovision—is a key component of Mexican American life. In response to this fact, recent years have seen an outpouring of scholarship on many aspects of Mexican American religious life. This book introduces the reader to this now thriving field of study.

A core assumption at play in this book is that religion and ethnicity are co-constitutive.[2] To put that another way, one's religion informs and helps construct one's ethnic identity and vice versa. Here, religion does not merely mean a statement of beliefs, often having to do with God or some other supernatural power. Rather, religion, as an intrinsic part of ethnicity, is comprised not only of beliefs but also of rituals, traditions, ethical stances, personal and communal emotional orientations, and shared senses of history. For example, a Catholic Christian almost certainly believes that Jesus is the son of God and the redeemer of humankind from its sin. However, these beliefs, important as they are, occur in the larger context of the rhythm of the Mass, family traditions around holidays and life transitions, certain kinds of foods, the tenor of relationships with fellow Catholics near and far, moral decision-making, and so on. Since so many of these aspects of religion overlap heavily with what makes up ethnicity, it is inevitable that religion and ethnicity work hand in hand in the way that people understand and identify themselves. In fact, even if an individual in an ethnic community decides to stop believing in the tenets of the community's religion, the individual is nonetheless still deeply implicated in what might be called the ethnoreligious practices of the community. Of course, this is not true only for Mexican Americans, but in this book, Mexican American religion and ethnicity are the focus.

Mexican Americans in U.S. religious history

Paying attention to Mexican American religious history is essential for an overall understanding of U.S. religious history. In 2018, there were 37 million Mexican Americans, around 11 percent of the entire U.S. population.[3] This fact alone necessitates learning about Mexican American history, culture, and religion. However, demographics are hardly the only reason to study Mexican American religions. Since the Louisiana Purchase in 1803, the United States as a political entity has shared a border with Mexico (though it was still part of New Spain at the time). The United States' first major war of colonial expansion was the U.S.-Mexico War in 1846–1848, which resulted in the cessation of most of northern Mexico to the U.S. This not only incorporated the lands of California and what is now known as the U.S. Southwest into the nation but also immediately created large numbers of Mexican Americans, the people who were living in northern Mexico when it was annexed to the United States. Since a sizable portion of the current United States in fact *used to be Mexico*, it is important indeed that Mexican American religions be understood as an indelible part of U.S. religions.

Moreover, the study of Mexican American religious history highlights some of the most salient themes in U.S. religious history, particularly in relation to questions of race, immigration, and religious diversity. Mexican Americans have entered the brutal racial calculus in the United States in various ways, challenging the central Black/white dichotomy. How Mexican Americans have entered into existing religious communities in the United States has often related to the efforts of white missionaries as well as white church judicatories. Waves of Mexican immigration to the United States—as well as the relative ease of transnational flows between adjacent countries—have likewise illuminated various religious responses, from nativist rejection to hospitality and solidarity. And, as Mexican Americans and other Latinos/as have grown to become the United States' largest minority population, their impact on religious institutions, especially the Catholic Church, is enormous. In this century, the membership of the U.S Catholic Church will become more than half Latino/a, even as Latinos/as comprise a growing position of prominence in many other religious groups and traditions in the United States.

A note on terms for people

What is a "Mexican American"? For the purposes of this book, a Mexican American is anyone who lives in the United States who traces ancestry to Mexico. This could mean a person who has newly immigrated from Mexico or someone whose family has lived in the United States for many generations. Of course, Mexican Americans have diverse backgrounds. Some trace their ancestry to particular regions of the current United States. For example, *tejanos* and *nuevomexicanos* have long histories in Texas and New Mexico, respectively. Others may continue to identify with their family's places of origin in Mexico, whether this be Puebla, Veracruz, Mexico City, or Tamaulipas. Some Mexican Americans identify strongly with Indigenous people from the Americas, while others are comfortable with a more pan-Latino/a ethnic identity. Some Mexican Americans proudly claim their African heritage and connection to ancestral Afro-Mexican populations. This book, following most contemporary usage, opts to leave out the hyphen in "Mexican American."

For the most part this book does not use the terms "Chicano" or "Chicana" for Mexican Americans in general, though these words were once common. While some people still prefer these terms, many now associate them specifically with the political projects of the Chicano Movement, a branch of the civil rights movement (see Chapters 9 and 11).

Other ethnic or racial groups are discussed in this book. White people, meaning people who trace their ancestry to Europe, are simply called "white" or sometimes "Anglo," as is the custom in much of the U.S. Southwest and West when comparing white people to Mexican American or Indigenous people. This book generally avoids the words "Indian" or "Indians" for Native Americans and also capitalizes "Indigenous" and "Native" as a marker of ethnic and racial heritage.

Finally, while this book is above all about Mexican Americans, other people who have Latin American and Caribbean ancestry are also discussed at times. This book uses the terms "Latino/a" and "Latinos/as" for this umbrella group. "Hispanic" has been eschewed as too linguistically and historically restrictive. While the terms "Latinx" and "Latinxs" are growing in popularity and have the considerable benefit of not being gender specific, it is hoped that "Latino/a" and "Latinos/as" will be understood in this book as referring to people of all genders despite the gender binary nature of the Spanish language.

Looking ahead

The great majority of Mexican Americans, in terms of religion, have practiced Christianity, particularly Catholicism. Therefore, this book takes a "Christianity-plus" approach, acknowledging the overwhelming predominance of Catholic Christianity for Mexican Americans while remembering that Catholicism is not the entire story. Nonetheless, Catholicism's centuries-long history in Mexico and among Mexican Americans has left an indelible stamp on Mexican American life, even for those who are not Catholic. This means that a careful study of Mexican American Catholicism is essential for comprehending Mexican American religious identity, even when it departs dramatically from Catholic Christianity. Of course, stopping with Catholicism would distort the considerable diversity of Mexican American religious experience. Protestantism, especially its charismatic and Pentecostal variations, has been growing for decades among Mexican Americans and is now an important segment of the Mexican American religious landscape. There is also a significant population of Mexican Americans who are not Christians; they are adherents of other religions or of no religion at all.

To get at this variegated and fascinating story, this book is divided into two parts. The first and longer part, "The history of Mexican American religion," takes a chronological approach. Beginning with the "Mexican" part of "Mexican American," the book delves into the religious history of Mexico from the time of the Spanish Conquest early in the sixteenth century. In addition to examining Indigenous Mexican religious traditions and Spanish evangelization, the religious life of people in the far north of New Spain and Mexico is described. After the Treaty of Guadalupe Hidalgo (1848) in the wake of the U.S.-Mexico War, the book turns decisively to Mexican American life north of the international border. Topics include Mexican American inclusion—and alienation—in the U.S. Catholic Church, the spread of Protestantism, and the immense growth of Mexican American and other Latino/a populations in the contemporary period. The second part of the book, instead of following a historical trajectory, focuses on "Traditions and movements in Mexican American religion." These chapters dive into specific topics across time, including religious healing, civil rights, pilgrimage, transnational flows, immigration, and religious diversity.

The study of religion, especially when approached from a historical vantage point, often focuses on events, institutions, and prominent individuals. Why is this? The historical record—which is to say written or recorded artifacts that are preserved in archives, libraries, and other sorts of collections—preserves some things while obscuring others. Public figures and major occurrences are remembered; lesser-known people and day-to-day life can seem to disappear, as if they never existed. The same is true for religious history. The daily devotions, the maintenance of relationships, and the experience of emotions do not always find their way into archives. Nevertheless, it is the responsibility of historians and religious studies scholars not to forget these quotidian religious practices, even when little of them remains in the historical record. In this book, each chapter ends with a short section entitled "Religion in practice" in which the focus turns, as much as possible, to the daily religious lives of Mexican Americans and their forebears. It is hoped that these short sections remind us that Mexican American religions happen, so to speak, in the lives of people. To be sure, the big events and prominent people also have an important role to play in the history of Mexican American religion. Mexican American women and men have a rich religious heritage that reveals so much about who Mexican American people are as well as the complex religious history of the United States.

Notes

1 Deborah E. Kanter, *Chicago Católico: Making Catholic Parishes Mexican* (Urbana, IL: University of Illinois Press, 2020), 123–28; Karen Mary Davalos, "'The Real Way of Praying': The Via Crucis, Mexicano Sacred Space, and the Architecture of Domination," in *Horizons of the Sacred: Mexican Traditions in U.S. Catholicism*, ed. Timothy Matovina and Gary Riebe-Estrella (Ithaca, NY: Cornell University Press, 2002), 41–68.

2 Rebecca Y. Kim, "Religion and Ethnicity: Theoretical Connections" *Religions* 2 (2011): 312–329.
3 "Hispanic or Latino Origin by Specific Origin," *United States Census Bureau*, 2018, https://data.census.gov/cedsci/table?lastDisplayedRow=30&table=B03001&tid=ACSDT1Y2018.B03001&hidePreview=true.

Part I

Mexican American religious history

1   Indigenous religions

Mesoamerica and the North

The story of Mexican American religions begins in Mesoamerica, the stretch of land comprising most of central Mexico and Central America. Today, this region is home to millions of Indigenous people including many whose ancestors lived in the great Maya and Aztec Empires. The story continues among the peoples of what is now northern Mexico and the southwestern United States. Like people around the world, the various nations and groupings of Indigenous people of the Americas had and have complex cultural, ethical, and ritual practices that help define who they are as people, connect them to deities, and make sense of their lives. The religions of the Aztecs and of the many peoples extending northward from central Mexico not only persist today as living traditions, they also contributed in profound ways to the mestizo culture of Mexico.

Indeed, the combination of living traditions, both Indigenous American and European colonial, create the unique circumstances in which Mexican American religions emerge. Chapter 2 will take up the role of Iberian Catholicism in the colonization and evangelization of Indigenous people. In this chapter, the focus remains on the cosmologies and religious activity of Indigenous people in what is now the nation of Mexico and several states of the U.S. Southwest. Particular attention is paid to the religion of the Aztec Empire because this powerful and numerous people had an enormous impact on Spanish evangelization and the eventual character of Mexican Catholicism. Moreover, as an imperial force themselves, the Aztecs had an important influence on other Indigenous peoples throughout much of Mexico. The chapter also examines the religions of a sampling of Indigenous nations from what is now the southwestern region of the United States in order to explore how these groups encountered and interacted with Spanish colonists and missionaries.

It is important to note that much of the historical information about pre-Hispanic Indigenous Mesoamericans is mediated through the voices of Spanish colonizers. In fact, a great many of the earliest historical accounts were written by Catholic priests and friars and, therefore, inevitably reflect their biases. Two points can be made concerning this situation. First, one must take care to read Spanish Catholic histories of Indigenous religions critically, remembering that the authors of these histories were a conquering force. Second, Spanish

DOI: 10.4324/9780429285516-3

histories, one-sided and oppressive as they may be, nevertheless reflect the five-century reality of the Americas: a place where European colonialism, which includes evangelization, has changed everything permanently. The story of Mexican American religions, thus, starts not only with Indigenous Mesoamericans but also with the colonial collision of Native peoples with Europeans.

Aztec origins and migration

The Mexica people migrated to the central valley of Mexico from their ancestral home located somewhere to the north, a place they called "Aztlán," which is translated variously as "place of whiteness" or "place of the herons." The name by which the Mexica are often known—the Aztecs—means the "people of Aztlán." Aztlán is sometimes also associated with an origin site known as Chicomoztoc, "Place of Seven Caves," the place of emergence of the Nahuas, a family of tribes that included the Mexica and several other groups important to the history of central Mexico. Neither the Mexica themselves or archaeologists can locate with certainty this ancestral homeland, but there is a likelihood that the place lay somewhere in northern Mexico or the U.S. Southwest. (This last possibility—that the Aztec originated in what is now the United States—has been an important source of pride for many Mexican Americans today; see Chapter 11.) Aztlán was reputedly a land surrounded by water and imbued with divine guidance, and it served as the archetype for the island city of Tenochtitlán.[1]

The Mexica began their exodus from the north in the twelfth century C.E. Their main god, Huitzilopochtli, had promised them a rich land, and they eventually arrived on the shores of Lake Tetzcoco in 1318 C.E to claim their divine inheritance. Over the next two centuries, the Aztec Empire grew to encompass much of central Mexico, through both treaty and military occupation. At the core of the empire was the so-called Triple Alliance with the Acolhua and Tepaneca peoples, who like the Mexica, spoke Nahuatl and traced their history to a northern homeland. The Aztec capital, Tenochtitlán, today known as Mexico City, was then and continues to be one of the largest cities in the world. It grew as an island city, connected by easily defended causeways and water routes to the surrounding area. Heavy tributes from vassal states and robust trade made it a wealthy metropolis.[2]

Scholars have pored over surviving Aztec codices as well as early accounts by Spanish colonizers to gain an understanding of the religious beliefs, practices, and community structures of the people of central Mexico. As was the case with the Spanish, the Aztec religion played a central role in authorizing the power of the Aztec Empire even as it regulated many aspects of life. In what follows, various features of this religion are discussed, including its cosmology, calendar, pantheon, primary rituals and their functions, and the Aztec conception of the human being. While many serious differences existed between the religion of the Mexica and that of the invading Europeans, there were also several features that allowed for comparison with Spanish Catholicism.

Cosmology and calendar

The Aztecs conceived of space as multilayered. Above the earth were thirteen levels of heavens where various deities resided as well as the natural elements of the sky, such as the sun, planets, stars, rain, and birds. In the highest heaven lived Ometéotl, the creator deity and god of duality. Below the earth layer were nine levels of underworld, a place known as Mictlan. The majority of those who died entered Mictlan and proceeded through many trials and challenges to reach the ninth and last level, where they ceased to exist. Exceptions to this oblivion were few and reserved for those who had died in specific ways, including in battle, in childbirth, and from particular diseases. These people, instead of entering Mictlan, went to other realms created and overseen by specific deities, where the deceased enjoyed honor and joy.[3]

The Aztec terrestrial realm was symbolically tied both to their principal deities and to their conceptions of the human. At the center was the capital city of Tenochtitlán, which itself reflected in its location and layout the mythical northern land of Aztlán. The Great Temple sat in Tenochtitlán, where the Aztecs made worship and offerings to the great gods Huitzilopochtli and Tlaloc. In Aztec and other Mesoamerican cosmovisions, this center itself represented a direction, a place that anchored and oriented the rest of space. Radiating out from this center were four quadrants, each associated with a particular color and characteristic. Sources vary as to the names and features of these directions, but Davíd Carrasco, a historian of Mesoamerican religions, describes the Aztec directions this way: East was called Tlacopan and was the yellow home of fertility and the dawn. Mictlampa was in the red north, and it was known for barrenness. In the west, Cihuatlampa, was the humid, bluish green region of women. The thorny south, known as Huitlampa, was associated with the color white. The fifth direction, the center, Tlalxico, was the black navel of the world.[4] In Mexica cosmology, each of these directions represents a cosmic force as well as a child of the god Ometéotl. Their struggle for supremacy explains the conflicts and tensions rampant in the earthly realm.[5]

These cosmic conflicts and wars played out in the somewhat predictable cycles of Aztec timekeeping. The Aztecs employed three calendars. The first was a 260-day cycle in which numbers and the names of animals were matched in ways that yielded divinatory insights. This calendar was used to compile a sacred almanac of auspicious days and times for various events. A second, solar calendar counted the 365 days of the solar year and marked agricultural seasons as well as ritual observances. These two calendars interlocked into the third calendar, a 52-year cycle. The completion of such a cycle was a momentous event that could augur the end of the world. Indeed, the Aztecs believed that the world had already been destroyed four times before, and each fulfillment of the 52-year cycle created another opportunity for their current world to come to its end. These worlds were commonly referred to as "suns," and so the Aztec considered that they lived within the time of the Fifth Sun, and most of their mythology unfolds within this vast period.[6]

Major Aztec deities

Like other Mesoamerican peoples, the Aztecs engaged with many gods. These often represented natural forces or features, such as the sun, the moon, and rain, and they were related to each other as a large family of brothers, sisters, and other relations. The myths associated with the gods helped explain the rhythms as well as the vagaries of the natural world. They, likewise, supplied the basis for Aztec ritual life and political structures. There were dozens of deities, many of whom had been absorbed into the Aztec pantheon as the empire expanded to include new people and their respective deities. However, it is clear that some gods were of central importance due to their function, their prominence in Aztec ritual life, and their representation in major temples in Tenochtitlán.[7]

Atop the Great Temple in the center of the Mexica capital sat two altars, one to Huitzilopochtli and the other to Tlaloc, architecturally signifying the importance of these two deities to the Aztecs. Huitzilopochtli was known as the Hummingbird of the South, associated with the sun, and was the Aztecs' patron god. Besides being a great warrior, he led the people southward from Aztlán to central Mexico.

Tlaloc, in contrast to Huitzilopochtli, ruled over rain, mountains, and other natural phenomena. He preceded the arrival of the Mexica and had been a central deity for the earlier Mesoamerican civilization at Teotihuacán. His worship at the Great Temple focused on sustenance and agriculture, and his followers relied on his care even as they feared his might as it was expressed capriciously in natural disasters and floods. Together, these altars knit together Aztec military might and domination of the natural world.

Two important female deities were Coatlicue and Coyolxauhqui. Coatlicue was the mother of Huizilopochtli and, as such, was revered as a patroness of fertility and motherhood. Her daughter, Coyolxauhqui, was the goddess of the moon. Huitzilopochtli went into battle against her, decapitated her, and mutilated her body, thus establishing his dominance as well as the sun's daily conquering of the night.

Rarely depicted but revered was Ometéotl, the creator force and the progenitor of all gods and humans. Ometéotl was the Lord of Duality and contained both male and female, known respectively as Ometecuhtli and Omecihuatl. Ometéotl presided over the highest heaven, which was known as the "place of duality." Some commentators see in this dual god a kind of theological unifying force for the many different aspects and figures in Aztec cosmology.[8]

Another ancient deity that was common throughout Mesoamerica, well before the arrival of the Mexica, was Quetzalcoatl, the Feathered Serpent. He is the god of wind. In some early sources, Quetzalcoatl is considered to be the creator of humankind, in concert with the dual powers of Ometéotl.[9] Nahuatl philosophers believed that Quetzalcoatl, in an act of self-sacrifice, brought the time of the Fifth Sun into being. He also was frequently associated with a pre-

Aztec cultural hero known as Ce Acatl Topltzin Quetzalcoatl, who embodied the concept of man-god and savior of civilization. The Aztecs, like other Mesoamericans, believed that Quetzalcoatl would someday return to usher in a new cosmic era.[10]

Rituals

Aztec religious rituals were held throughout the year to observe festivals and auspicious days, often in relationship to the agricultural cycle. Many rituals featured sacrifice of one kind or another, including frequent human sacrifice, to re-enact the gods' sacrificial maintenance of the cosmos and to appease these gods and thus receive their favor. For the Aztecs, carrying out regular sacrifices was of utmost importance in order to insure the proper functioning of the world itself. They believed that, without their ritual sacrifices, the sun would cease to rise in the east. In this sense, the Mexica's sacrifices were the linchpin of life itself, and they considered it their solemn duty to maintain the world. And, so, sacrificial rituals occurred monthly to honor various deities, to achieve seasonal agricultural needs, and to sustain life all over the world.

For some of the rituals, the human victim would spend a set amount of time prior to the sacrifice impersonating a deity. This would allow people to interact with their god in human form in a series of re-enactments and pageants that retold the story of the deity. For instance, an important renewal ceremony known as "Toxcatl" honored, among others, the gods Huitzilopochtli and Tezcatlipoca (the powerful god of the smoking mirror, patron of rulers and of the earth). A well-proportioned and strong young man would play Tezcatlipoca for a full year prior to the rite, interacting with people throughout the city. On the day of the sacrifice, he would dance and make food offerings before he ascended the temple. There, the priest would remove his still-beating heart from his chest, decapitate him, and the body would be lowered back down the temple. According to Carrasco, this ceremony showcases "the Aztec conception of the perfect life and ideal death of the warrior displayed for all to see as he parades, sings, plays music, and is sacrificed in public."[11] The deeper meanings associated with this act include the lesson that even the mighty and prosperous are ultimately brought to their end by the gods.

While human sacrifice is the most well known of Aztec rituals, and the most essential for its role in maintaining life itself in the universe, it was not the only ritual act. Many ceremonies had to do with order, beauty, theological musings, and lofty rhetoric. Indeed, in addition to priests who carried out sacrificial rites, some of the most important holy people in Aztec society were the "tlamatinime," specially trained rhetoricians and philosophers. The expert on Nahuatl cultures, Miguel León-Portilla, described the work of the tlamatinime as practitioners of "the metaphysico-poetical approach."[12] They were responsible for educating nobles, and their poetical methods invited listeners to discover the ultimate duality of Ometéotl. One ancient codex describes the tlamatinime as a "wise man" who "himself is writing and wisdom … He is the path, the true way for others."[13] In this sense, he communicates truth and wisdom not only with his words but also with the example of his life.

Aztec religious conceptions of the human

The religious anthropology of the Aztecs, which is to say, how they understood the very nature of the human being within the cosmos, revered the body as a repository of divine forces. For example, the human sacrifices discussed above demonstrate that a sacrificial victim could take on the identity of a deity, and the spilling of human blood had the immense and essential power to sustain the world itself. In a sense, the body and blood of humans and gods symbolized the entire cosmos. The Codex Fejérváry-Mayer—one of the few pre-Hispanic manuscripts to survive the Spanish conquest—features the fire god, Xiuhteuctli. Blood flows out of him to the four directions, each represented by a sacred tree. The god Tezcatlipoca is dismembered, and his body parts flow out on the streams of blood to help constitute the four regions of the Aztec world.[14]

Figure 1.1 Page 1 of the Codex Fejérváry-Mayer, 15th century. In public domain.

The Aztecs believed that the human body contained diverse forces that historian Alfredo López Austin has called "animistic entities." The first of these is the "tonalli," which resided in the person's head. The tonalli connected the person to the gods. Transgressions and injuries could dislodge the tonalli from the body and thus cause illness. Restoring one's tonalli, in these cases, was an aspect of Mexica health care. Another entity, the "teyolia," lived in a person's heart. The teyolia governed one's intellect and emotions, and it was the part of the self that went to live in Mictlán, the region of the dead, after one's bodily death. The final entity was the "ihiyotl," which was centered in the liver, had a gaseous quality, and was associated with one's vigor and passions. These three entities, in the healthy and moral person, were in equilibrium. The person who was ill or who deviated from correct social norms was thought to be experiencing some disturbance in his or her animistic entities.[15]

Aztec religion and the Spanish

More will be said on this subject in the next chapter, but it is important to note that Aztec religion—among many other features of Aztec life—was not completely annihilated by Spanish Catholic evangelization. To be sure, Indigenous social and cultural structures were assaulted and, in some cases, destroyed by colonization, but Mesoamerican norms and convictions about the gods, the cosmos, and the self continued to influence how Indigenous people understood the new world brought on by the Spanish invasion.

While the Spaniards often accused the Mexica of devilry and savagery, many areas of Aztec religion corresponded legibly with Iberian Catholicism. For instance, Christian ideas of "spirit" and "soul," although not identical, have some characteristics in common with "tonalli" and "teyolia." The Aztec pantheon, while quite distinct from Christian monotheism, was at least theistic, and there were considerable overlaps with the host of powerful saints that Iberian Catholics prayed to for a variety of blessings and needs in their lives. Even human sacrifice, though thoroughly condemned by the Spanish, nonetheless echoed in certain ways the sacrificial death of Jesus on the cross for the salvation and maintenance of human life.

With that said, it must be acknowledged in no uncertain terms that the Spanish created a catastrophic rupture for Indigenous Mesoamericans. The Spanish destroyed Aztec temples and other sacred places and put an end to human sacrifices. Without these fundaments of their religious and ritual system, the Aztecs and others could not continue to maintain their cosmos as they perceived it, and space and time as they knew it was irreversibly altered.

Indigenous peoples of the North

When considering the history of Mexican Americans, the cultural and religious heritage of the Aztecs looms large. It was they and their neighbors in central Mexico who had perhaps the biggest impact on the Spanish conquest.

However, after establishing their control of Tenochtitlán, Spanish soldiers and Catholic friars fanned out to subdue and convert many other people groups in what came to be known as New Spain. It took them some years to get all the way to the regions that are now the states of the U.S. Southwest, and throughout this vast territory, the Spanish encountered thousands of people with diverse languages, cultures, and religious customs. Just as the Aztec religion and worldview helped to shape the new world dominated by Europeans, so, too, did the religions of other people that the Spanish conquered. These religions existed and continue to exist side-by-side with European settlers. Given the vast diversity of Indigenous people in this region, it would be impossible to examine all of them; instead, a representative selection of Indigenous groups and their religious customs are discussed below. These include the Coahuiltecan peoples of what is now central and south Texas, the Pueblos of the northern Rio Grande Valley in New Mexico, and the people who lived near the San Francisco Bay in California. Only the briefest of snapshots can be offered here of these complex and comprehensive religious and cultural systems.

Indigenous peoples of South Texas

Small, autonomous bands of Indigenous people populated the vast territories of what is today south and central Texas. Now often referred to as "Coahuiltecans," these hunter-gathers existed in autonomous bands that did not consider themselves as part of a shared regional society. The bands contained anywhere from one hundred to five hundred people, and the number of such groups likely fell between three hundred and one thousand. At one time, anthropologists and archaeologists believed that this entire population shared the Coahuiltecan language (or dialects of that language), but more recent scholarship suggests that a wide variety of languages were spoken, adding to the independence of each band.[16] Indeed, while it is a long-standing convention to refer to all these people as Coahuiltecans, it is important to remember that this is a name in some ways imposed on diverse peoples who shared a shared geographic area rather than a monolingual Indigenous culture.[17]

Relatively little is known about the religious and ritual customs of the Coahuiltecans, and all of what is known is mediated through non–Native accounts or sifted out of archaeological remains. Like other hunter-gathers in the region, it is likely that the Coahuiltecans associated many aspects of the natural world with spirits, and the emphasis of their ritual life had to do with maintaining harmony with their environment in order to survive. To this end, it seems that bands relied on shamans to cure illnesses, interpret dreams, communicate with spirits, and restore order when social rules or taboos were broken. The earliest account of these activities comes from Álvaro Núñez Cabeza de Vaca, who, with several companions, was stranded in what is now Texas and northern Mexico in the early sixteenth century. Cabeza de Vaca reported that one mechanism by which he and his party survived was to become shamans and healers themselves among the Coahuiltecans and others.[18] Other rituals included dances and religious festivals that the Spaniards called "mitotes." These events, which could last for days, involved feasting and the ingestion of peyote in order to enter trance states. Almost nothing is known of Coahuiltecan deities or myths.[19]

It was not until the eighteenth century that Coahuiltecan people came into significant contact with Europeans. Early in the 1700s, Spanish Franciscans began to construct compound-like missions in the area around San Antonio, where they gathered Coahuiltecan bands into sedentary agricultural villages. This, of course, was an immense departure from the people's nomadic hunting and gathering way of life, but the Franciscans combined instruction in Christian doctrine with a mandate to "civilize" the bands into new patterns of housing, dress, and livelihood. According to the U.S. National Park Service, which now operates the former Franciscan missions as a historic park, the Coahuiltecans, at this moment in their history, were weakened by European diseases and under threat from stronger Native peoples from the north. As such, they were somewhat willing participants in the Franciscan missions as a form of defense and self-preservation.[20] Over time, Coahuiltecans assimilated completely into the mestizo people of central and south Texas.

Pueblos of New Mexico

The Pueblo homeland is located in what is now northern New Mexico and northeastern Arizona. The name "Pueblo" is the Spanish word that means "town" and refers to the distinctive Pueblo dwellings, apartment-like adobe and stone houses, that distinguished them from many of the nomadic peoples in the region. The Pueblos, however, are not unified but rather exist in linguistic and geographic groupings. These include the Hopi, Zuni, several Keres-speaking Pueblos, and a variety of eastern Pueblos who speak related languages known as Tiwa, Tewa, and Towa. While there is no such thing as one pan-Pueblo religion, there are some shared features of cosmology, ceremonial life, and emphasis across the Pueblo peoples. Ceremonies are often focused on agricultural cycles, Pueblo origin stories generally feature an emergence from the underworld into this world, and ritual observances—which are not differentiated from other aspects of life—are normally carried out by communal religious associations.[21]

Perhaps the best-known feature of Pueblo religion is the famous katsinas. Katsinas are seasonal deities who come to visit the Hopi between December and July to ensure water for the crops. Offerings are made to please the katsinas at shrines around Hopi lands and farther west in the San Francisco Peaks.[22] The katsinas come to Hopi dances, where they interact with people, hear their intercessions, receive their gifts, and maintain the well-being of both the spirit world and this world. The katsina dances are an essential part of Hopi life since they insure the coming of the rains to irrigate the crops. The dancers themselves wear elaborate and symbolic katsina masks that depict specific katsinas.

Boys who enter the katsina associations are entitled to own a mask, which they treat as a highly sacred living being. In the Hopi language, people use the word for "friend" instead of "mask" to refer to these objects. During the dances, the katsina dancers are thought to lose their own identities and fully embody their katsinas.[23]

The Tewa-speaking Pueblos of northern New Mexico have a complex understanding of the world around them. Alfonso Ortiz, a Tewa anthropologist from Ohkay Ohwingeh Pueblo (formerly known as San Juan), explains that the Tewa world is a series of tetrads anchored by physical locations in their homeland. The first tetrad is comprised of four high mountains that fall roughly at the cardinal points of the compass, between fifteen and sixty miles from Ohkay Owingeh. The second tetrad are four flat-topped hills within the circle

Figure 1.2 The mask of Kachina (Hopi Indians "rain maker"), village of Shonghopavi, Arizona. Photograph by Underwood and Underwood, 1900, New York Public Library. In public domain.

of the first tetrad. Ortiz notes that, "Each of these hills is sacred because it is particularly dark and foreboding; each has a cave and/or tunnels running through it."[24] These mythological caves and tunnels connect the Tewa Pueblos and are the homes of supernatural beings. A final tetrad represents the dance plazas in Ohkay Owingeh, where various religious associations carry out their respective rituals. At the very center of the world, within Ohkay Owingeh Pueblo itself, lies the "Earth mother navel middle place," the principal opening place between this world and the underworld whence all life emerged.[25]

The sometimes explosive relationship between the Pueblos and the Spanish in New Mexico is covered in more detail in Chapter 3. Like the Aztecs far to the south, the various Pueblo peoples relied on their ritual activities both to structure their societies and to maintain the proper functioning of the world itself. The disruption brought by Spanish missionaries thus presented an existential threat to the Pueblos that galvanized Indigenous resistance to Spanish colonization. Today, Pueblo people around New Mexico and Arizona continue to maintain their sacred dances even as many Pueblos, to varying extents, practice Catholicism.

Native peoples of Central California

The first sustained Spanish settlement of what is now the U.S. state of California did not occur until 1769, and so the Indigenous peoples of California lived relatively free of non-Native interference significantly longer when compared to Texas and New Mexico. California's extraordinarily fertile environment made it possible for there to be over 300,000 inhabitants at the time of Spanish entry, even though they lived as hunter-gatherers. In general terms, men hunted, fished, and traded while women gathered and processed many plant-based foods and stored them in baskets.[26] These shared social and economic characteristics belie an astounding diversity. Anthropologists and linguists have counted at least six unique linguistic stocks in California that included between sixty-four and eighty mutually unintelligible languages.[27]

In this context, it can be difficult to generalize about religious and ritual practices, although shamans often played important roles. In addition to working as healers, they communicated with the dead and with other spirits. In south-central California, shamans and others among the Chumash, southern Yokuts, and a variety of coastal tribes ingested processed *Datura*, a hallucinogenic plant, in order to gain strength and sometimes to encounter "dream helpers," often in the form of animal guardians. For example, a rite of initiation for adolescents involved the taking of *Datura* in the hopes of encountering a life-long animal dream helper, such as a coyote or hawk. The helper would guide the recipient in hunting and other pursuits and serve as a protector.[28] Farther north, among the Miwoks, Pomos, and other bay-area peoples, the ingestion of *Datura* was less common; instead, they often followed what anthropologists have called "Kuksu religion" after a prominent deity. Like the Hopis and the Aztecs, Kuksu practitioners belonged to hereditary societies that carried out proscribed rituals, including impersonating the deities.[29]

The bands, nations, and peoples in what is now the U.S. Southwest had a decisive impact on Spanish Catholicism and colonization and influenced Spanish and Mexican religion in important ways. First, Indigenous people often violently resisted missionization efforts. Pueblo and Native Californian revolts doubtlessly slowed Spanish settlement. Second, Franciscan missionaries had to try to interpret Catholicism in ways that made sense to Natives. This required at least rudimentary language acquisition and a kind of proto-ethnography. This process of religious translation created opportunities for Indigenous culture to subtly color the Christian message. Finally, through both intermarriage and sexual violence, mestizo families were created and eventually came to characterize Mexican identity.

Religion in practice

The Hopi, similar to other Pueblo people, encounter katsinas and other spirits in shrines that are spread throughout the landscape, on mountains, in fields, and in settlements. Hopi towns feature at least two areas of ritual practice: the plaza and the kiva.[30] The plaza is a gathering place where dances and feasts occur. Hopi kivas tend to be rectangular, underground rooms that are reserved for the use of specific ceremonial societies. Abandoned pre-Hispanic Hopi kivas in Arizona contain elaborate murals that include depictions of warriors and anthropomorphized animals. Archaeologist Patricia Vivian suggests that these "anthropomorphized beings in many of the murals appear to be artistic manifestations of the personality and humanized form which the Pueblo" assigned to elements of the natural world. She continues, "We know that kachinas, or masked spirits, in ceremonialism today reflect that same humanism."[31] In essence, Hopi ritual spaces reflect the undifferentiated nature of humans and nature in the Hopi worldview.

In contemporary times, Hopi kivas work as communal gathering places where ceremonial societies gather to spend time together and to prepare for ritual events. For example, the Soyala ceremony marks the winter solstice. Two weeks before the solstice itself, different clans and ritual societies begin to gather in their kivas to practice their songs and carry out preliminary rituals. Men take their meals and often sleep in the kivas. Soyala welcomes the katsinas back to the Pueblo and sets a course for the coming year.[32]

Another common feature of Hopi ritual space, often within kivas, is the *sipapu*, an indention or pit in the dirt that symbolizes the place of emergence from the underworld into this world. (A cognate is the Tewa Pueblo "earth navel" found at the center of Ohkay Owingeh.) The *sipapu* is often covered with removable wooden planks or a stone plug, which can be removed to initiate contact with the personages of the underworld.[33]

Notes

1 Manuel Aguilar-Moreno, *Handbook to Life in the Aztec World* (New York: Oxford University Press, 2006), 28–29; Davíd Carrasco, *Religions of Mesoamerica*, 2nd ed. (Long Grove, IL: Waveland Press, 2014), 35–37.

2 Aguilar-Moreno, *Handbook to Life in the Aztec World*, 31–36, 59–60.

3 Aguilar-Moreno, 138, 162–66.

4 Carrasco, *Religions of Mesoamerica*, 92.

5 Miguel León Portilla, *Aztec Thought and Culture: A Study of the Ancient Nahuatl Mind*, trans. Jack Emory Davis (Norman, OK: University of Oklahoma Press, 1963), 46–48.

6 Aguilar-Moreno, *Handbook to Life in the Aztec World*, 140, 290–98.

7 Aguilar-Moreno, 144–45.

8 A fairly comprehensive description of the Aztec gods can be found in Rafael Tena, "La religión mexica: catálogo de dioses," *Arqueología Mexicana* 30 (2009): 6–94.

9 León Portilla, *Aztec Thought and Culture*, 107–13.

10 For more on the multitudinous figure of Quetzalcoatl, see Enrique Florescano, *The Myth of Quetzalcoatl* (Baltimore, MD: Johns Hopkins University Press, 1999), especially Chapter 2; Carrasco, Davíd, *Quetzalcoatl and the Irony of Empire: Myths and Prophecies in the Aztec Tradition* (Chicago, IL: University of Chicago Press, 1982).

11 Carrasco, *Religions of Mesoamerica*, 111–12. See also Aguilar-Moreno, *Handbook to Life in the Aztec World*, 154.

12 León Portilla, *Aztec Thought and Culture*, 80.

13 From the *Códice Matritense de la Real Academia de la Historia*, quoted in León Portilla, 10.

14 Carrasco, *Religions of Mesoamerica*, 86–87.

15 Alfredo López Austin, *The Human Body and Ideology: Concepts of the Ancient Nahuas*, trans. Thelma Ortiz de Montellano and Bernard Ortiz de Montellano (Salt Lake City, UT: University of Utah Press, 1988), 203–36.

16 William W. Newcomb, *The Indians of Texas, from Prehistoric to Modern Times* (Austin, TX: University of Texas Press, 1967), 30; David La Vere, *The Texas Indians* (College Station, TX: Texas A&M University Press, 2004), 64–65.

17 Thomas R. Hester, "'Coahuiltecan': A Critical Review of an Inappropriate Ethnic Label," *La Tierra, Journal of the Southern Texas Archaeological Association* 25 (1998): 3–7.

18 La Vere, *The Texas Indians*, 44–48; Alvar Núñez Cabeza de Vaca and Enrique Pupo-Walker, *Castaways: The Narrative of Alvar Núñez Cabeza de Vaca* (Berkeley, CA: University of California Press, 1993), 68–73.

19 Newcomb, *The Indians of Texas*, 52–54.

20 National Park Service, *San Antonio Missions, National Historic Park* (U.S. Department of the Interior, n.d.).

21 An early but influential anthropological survey of Pueblo religion is Elsie Clews Parsons, *Pueblo Indian Religion*, vol. 1, 2 vols. (Chicago, IL: University of Chicago Press, 1939). The general sketch of Pueblo religion in this paragraph is gleaned from Parsons.

22 Fred Eggan, "The Hopi Cosmology or World-View," in *Kachinas in the Pueblo World*, ed. Polly Schaafsma (Salt Lake City, UT: University of Utah Press, 2000), 7–16.

23 Louis A. Hieb, "The Meaning of Katsina: Toward a Cultural Definition of 'Person' in Hopi Religion," in *Kachinas in the Pueblo World*, ed. Polly Schaafsma (Salt Lake City, UT: University of Utah Press, 2000), 28; E. Charles Adams, *The Origin and Development of the Pueblo Katsina Cult* (Tucson, AZ: University of Arizona Press, 1991), 6–12.

24 Alfonso Ortiz, *The Tewa World: Space, Time, Being, and Becoming in a Pueblo Society*, (Chicago, IL: University of Chicago Press, 1969), 19.

25 Ortiz, 18–21.

26 Albert L. Hurtado, *Indian Survival on the California Frontier* (New Haven, CT: Yale University Press, 1988), 1, 18–19.

27 James A. Sandos, *Converting California: Indians and Franciscans in the Missions* (New Haven, CT: Yale University Press, 2004), 15.

28 George Harwood Phillips, *Indians and Intruders in Central California, 1769–1849* (Norman, OK: University of Oklahoma Press, 1993), 23–24; Richard B. Applegate, "The Datura Cult Among the Chumash," *The Journal of California Anthropology* 2, no. 1 (1975): 12; Lowell John Bean and Sylvia Brakke Vane, "California Religious Systems and Their Transformations," in *California Indian Shamanism*, ed. Lowell John Bean (Menlo Park, CA: Ballena Press, 1992), 43–46.

29 Sandos, *Converting California*, 32; Quincy D. Newell, *Constructing Lives at Mission San Francisco: Native Californians and Hispanic Colonists, 1776–1821* (Albuquerque, NM: University of New Mexico Press, 2009), 12.

30 For a discussion of the historical relationship between ritual in enclosed kivas and public plazas, see Adams, *The Origin and Development of the Pueblo Katsina Cult*, 103–9.

31 Patricia Vivian, "Anthropomorphic Figures in the Pottery Mound Murals," in *Kachinas in the Pueblo World*, ed. Polly Schaafsma (Salt Lake City, UT: University of Utah Press, 2000), 91.

32 Parsons, *Pueblo Indian Religion*, 2: 556–70.

33 Parsons, 1:309–10.

2 Iberian religion and colonial evangelization of New Spain

Chapter 1 could only hint at the rich variety of Indigenous religions and ritual traditions present in the Americas before and during the cataclysm of Spanish conquest and colonization. The Aztecs and all other Indigenous peoples had to contend in many ways with the radical new circumstances that the Spanish brought. There were major disruptions in political and economic structures, and the cosmovision of Native peoples was greatly challenged by often violent Catholic evangelization. The Spanish who arrived intended not only to conquer and exploit the vast territory of the Americas, they also aimed to make the millions of Native people into Christian subjects. This yoked project of subjugation and evangelization would have long-lasting ramifications for Mexican religious life and eventually for Mexican American religions as well.

The Spanish who came to conquer and convert the Americas bore with them a particular history of religious conflict back on the Iberian Peninsula. They also carried with them their own long-standing cosmovisions and ritual traditions that linked political and religious power in specific ways. Beholden both to the Spanish kings and queens as well as to the divine dictates of the Catholic Pope, the conquistadors and missionaries that arrived in what would soon be known as New Spain imposed a totalizing regime of state and religious control. This chapter examines the state of Iberian Catholicism at the time of the American conquest and shows how it worked in the context of the so-called New World. Representatives of the Spanish Crown and the Catholic Church took power over the Aztec Empire and began a centuries-long process of shaping New Spain. The chapter also explores religious debates about Indigenous personhood, and it concludes with a discussion of Spanish and Catholic expansion into the territory of what is now the U.S. Southwest.

The Reconquista and Iberian Catholicism

For centuries, the kingdoms of the Iberian Peninsula had been some of the most religiously diverse areas of western Europe. Christianity had arrived very early to Spain as part of the Mediterranean world (Spain is even mentioned in the Christian New Testament as an early mission field).[1] However, Muslim forces took control of the region early in the eighth century and remained in

DOI: 10.4324/9780429285516-4

power over much of the peninsula for the next seven hundred years. During the era of Muslim control, Spain flourished as a land of relative toleration for religious diversity, a haven for Jews, and a center of learning. Gradually, Christian strongholds in the Spanish north won back more and more control until an alliance brought about by the marriage of King Ferdinand and Queen Isabella allowed the Christian forces to retake the entire peninsula early in 1492. Whereas the Muslims had generally allowed Christians and Jews to practice their religions, the Spanish Christian monarchs often made conversion to Christianity a condition of residency, and they organized massive expulsions of Jews and Muslims. The so-called Reconquista, or "re-conquest," of Spain loomed large in the experiences of the soldiers and Christian colonists who would soon depart for the Americas. A pattern of enforced Christian conversion and the linking of political and religious expansion guided Spanish colonialism.[2]

An essential part of the Spanish Reconquista that would likewise have ramifications in Latin America was the Spanish Inquisition. The Inquisition itself was not limited to Spain but a guarantor of Catholic doctrinal integrity throughout Catholic Europe, but its Spanish permutation was especially widespread and brutal. While large numbers of Jews and Muslims were expelled from Spanish territory, those who remained were often forced to convert to Christianity. As converts, or *conversos*, they were liable to be tried by the Inquisition to judge the sincerity of their conversion. If found wanting, *conversos* could undergo a battery of punishments from jailing to torture and execution. This suspicious and dangerous context for non-Catholics had multiple impacts on the Spanish settlement and evangelization of the Americas. First, it was not uncommon for Jews to flee to remote areas of the new territories to attempt to escape the Inquisition. Because of this, there are still Jewish communities throughout Latin America, including among Mexican Americans, who can trace a Jewish ancestry to the time of colonization and, in some cases, even retain a Jewish faith.[3] Second, the forced conversion of millions of Indigenous people occurred under the ongoing threat of the Inquisition; incomplete or suspect conversions could lead to violent reprisals against Natives, including, in some cases, their enslavement or death. Inquisitorial trials were rarely used against Indigenous people, but the context of forced conversion continued to undergird Spanish evangelization.[4]

Another feature of Iberian Catholicism that would have far-reaching effects on religion as well as state formation in Latin America was a series of agreements between the Spanish monarchs and the Pope. These agreements are known as the *Patronato Real*, or "Royal Patronage." In the multiple and evolving arrangements of the *Patronato*, the Pope granted certain ecclesiastical powers to the monarchs in exchange for their promise to make the new territories Catholic. For example, while it was normally the papal prerogative to name bishops, this right was passed on to the Spanish crown. In this way, Spain's political rulers were able to set up religious leadership that accorded with their plans for the new territories. Another important power passed to the monarchs was to oversee tithing to the Church. In addition, the *Patronato* dictated how much of these tithes would remain in the royal treasuries. This profound entanglement between state and religious power and economy would leave an indelible mark on the way the Catholic Church functioned throughout Latin America.[5]

Hernán Cortés and the conquest of Mexico

After Columbus's initial arrival in 1492, it did not take long for Spanish forces to begin to establish a permanent presence on several islands in the Caribbean, including Cuba. It was from there that a series of Spanish forays to mainland Mexico would take place, culminating in the bellicose arrival of Hernán Cortés and his men in what is now Veracruz in April of 1519. By this point, Cortés had already defeated some coastal Maya populations farther south, which had allowed him to capture a woman named Malintzin, known by the Spaniards as Malinche. She quickly learned Spanish and played a pivotal role in Cortés's success, serving as his translator.

The widespread and powerful Aztec Empire held control of its far-flung tributaries by force and taxation. In this context, it did not take long for Cortés to make alliances with people who the Aztecs had conquered, including the Cempoalans and the powerful Tlaxcalans. By the time Cortés arrived in the great city of Tenochtitlán, thousands of Indigenous fighters had joined the Spanish to confront the Aztecs. In a brazen move, Cortés took the Aztec emperor, Motecuhzoma II, as his hostage. Mexica military leaders fought back, inflicting serious casualties on the Spaniards and their allies, but Cortés was ultimately victorious. Tenochtitlán was taken in August of 1521, and the ancient land of millions was christened "la Nueva España," New Spain, with Cortés as its first governor.[6]

There is reason to think that Mesoamerican myths had at least some role in the Spanish Conquest. The emperor Motecuhzoma likely thought that Cortés was the priest-king and deity Quetzalcoatl. A prophecy had predicted that Quetzalcoatl would one day return from the east, defeat the Aztec tutelary deity Huitzilopochtli, and reconquer the lands ruled by the Aztecs. Moreover, the complex Aztec calendar likewise indicated that 1519 was, in fact, a propitious year for Quetzalcoatl's return. Some speculate that this conviction contributed to Motecuhzoma's seeming inability to oppose Cortés himself, instead leaving defense of the empire to other Aztec elites.[7] No doubt, it quickly became clear that Cortés was no Quetzalcoatl, but the Spanish onslaught and eventual victory was, by this time, well underway.

Arrival of the friars and early conversions

Scholars have often used the language of "spiritual conquest" to refer to the evangelistic wing of the Spanish takeover of Mexico. The finality of the phrase, however, obscures the generations-long process of accommodation, contestation, and creativity that characterize the slow and never complete Christianization of the Indigenous people of the Americas. With that said, the violent connotations of "conquest" accurately represent the interwoven nature of Catholic missionization with military and political subjugation. Cortés himself justified his brutal overthrow of Tenochtitlán as a just war as long as it meant the conversion of the Mexicans. One of his first acts after landing in Veracruz was to celebrate Mass and call upon a Franciscan friar in his company to explain Christian doctrine to the mystified Natives, and during his march toward the Aztec capital, he caused images of Indigenous deities to be replaced with ones of the Virgin Mary.[8]

As Cortés continued to complete the military conquest of central Mexico, he called on King Charles V in Spain to supply him with missionaries to oversee the religious conversion of the Indigenous masses. He asked specifically for missionary friars rather than diocesan priests since the latter would be more costly to maintain in the yet unstructured Spanish-controlled areas of the new territory. Moreover, the mendicant orders, such as the Franciscans and the Dominicans, already had a primary commitment to educate their flocks and to spread the Catholic faith. Famously, the group of Franciscans who arrived in 1524 numbered twelve, reminiscent of Jesus's twelve apostles. A similar contingent of twelve Dominicans arrived in 1526 and were followed by seven Augustinians in 1533. Within the first three decades of their labor in New Spain, they scattered throughout central Mexico, constructed over 100 convents, and multiplied their own numbers to over 800 friars, mostly through the arrival of new recruits from Europe.[9]

As mentioned above, the European context influenced the friars' initial evangelistic strategies. After the Muslims were defeated and mostly expelled from Spain, the Catholic Church, through the Inquisition and by educational means, had committed itself to reinforcing Catholicism in the Iberian Peninsula. During this same period, the Protestant Reformation was breaking out and challenging Catholic hegemony throughout much of Europe. This upheaval and perceived need to defend Catholicism against heresy informed the friars' interactions with the Aztecs and other Native groups. Their first impulse was to root out what they considered to be idolatry, destroy Native religious art and architecture, and prohibit any non-Christian ritual activity. It was at this time that the common practice began of erecting Christian churches on top of destroyed Indigenous temples and holy places, as a twin effort to blot out and replace. In a tragic loss to history, the friars also destroyed a great number of Indigenous monuments, art, and manuscripts. This erasure of Aztec sites, in addition to promoting the proselytizing efforts of the friars, contributed to Spanish political domination since many of the temples had been symbolic centers of Aztec might.[10]

Destruction was not the friars' only early strategy, however. The convents that were spreading across the land frequently included schools, and it was in these locations that they carried out a catechetical campaign among the Native children, particularly of elite Indigenous families. Operating as residential schools, these institutions instructed the young in the Catholic religion as well

as reading and writing. This had the dual function of Christianizing a generation as well as training a tier of local leadership that was familiar with Spanish
language and customs.[11]

For larger sectors of Native society, the friars used another tactic: brief
instruction in the rudiments of Catholicism followed by mass baptisms. Within

Figure 2.1 Fray Toribio de Benavente, known as Motolinía. In public domain.

fifteen years of the arrival of the Spanish, there may have been as many as six million people baptized. There are frequent accounts of groups of clergy baptizing tens of thousands in one day, using a truncated rite. In one sense, these massive baptisms indicated an intention on the part of the clergy to continue to instruct the new converts in Catholic doctrine. However, it is clear that it was important to them to amass and be able to report large numbers of converts to their European superiors within a short amount of time.[12] Even at the time, there were those who questioned the sincerity of such conversions as well as the advisability of this method. Fray Toribio de Benavente, known as Motolinía, was one of the original twelve Franciscans. In his account of their work, he acknowledges, "Now the friars were thinking that everything was done because idolatry had been abolished in the temples of the devil and the people were coming to learn Christian doctrine, and be baptized." But they soon "discovered the most difficult thing of all," namely, that the new Native Christians continued to practice their own ceremonies and celebrations, eventually learning to keep them hidden from the Spanish.[13]

It should be noted that the Spanish and the Indigenous were not the only two populations in New Spain. Enslaved Africans as well as free Black servants arrived with the Spanish forces. The number of creoles, Black people born in the Americas, grew rapidly, and by the middle of the 1600s there were over 100,000 creoles and approximately 35,000 enslaved Africans.[14] The friars employed some of the same strategies on the creole and enslaved populations as they used to evangelize and control the Indigenous people. For instance, instruction in doctrine and the imposition of Catholic ecclesiastical oversight was extended into creole communities. Historian Herman Bennett has noted that, for "the growing African and creole populations, Christian conversion brought both obligations and rights," including the right to marry.[15] However, conversion also opened creoles to judgment in the form of the Inquisition; unlike their Indigenous neighbors, who generally avoided Inquisitorial verdicts, those descended from Africans were considered by the courts as part of the "Old World" and thus not exempt from harsher scrutiny.[16]

The encomienda system and evangelization

The legal justification for the entire Spanish Conquest of the Americas was an explicit promise to spread Christianity. By claiming the new lands not only for Spain but also for Christ and the Catholic Church, the Spaniards established the moral and legal necessity of their control. The conquistadors themselves, however, had generally committed themselves to the Conquest out of more worldly than religious motives, and they expected to receive a living, if not wealth, from their sacrifices. Even before Cortés's arrival in Mexico, the Spanish courts had established the *encomienda*, a system in which a parcel of land and all its inhabitants were granted to a Spanish subject. In exchange, the *encomendero* committed to pacifying his new Indigenous indentured workers, making them productive, and providing them with religious education. By law, *encomenderos* were required to employ a priest or a religious brother to catechize the all-but-enslaved residents of the *encomienda*. For the most part, this task fell to friars in the aforementioned mendicant orders.[17]

The legal act that the Spaniards carried out to justify this blatant theft of land and virtual enslavement was called the *Requerimiento*. The *Requerimiento*, which was read aloud to Native people, explained the most basic rudiments of the Christian religion and that it was the right of the Spanish monarchs, as empowered by the Pope, to take possession of their land. In the act of hearing these legal words read, the Indigenous people were given no choice but to accept their new lords and masters or face the legally-sanctioned—and violent—consequences. In practice, the *encomiendas* enslaved all Natives whether or not they accepted Spanish rule and the Catholic faith.[18] Essentially, Catholic instruction and conversion took place in the early years of colonization in locations of religious and secular reorganization of society, namely, the friars' convents and the elites' *encomiendas*. In both institutions, catechization and forced integration into the Spanish political economy were utterly intertwined. While many Indigenous people were brought into the *encomienda* system, not all were. Some were able to avoid or resist Spanish incursions, often by retreating to isolated and remote locations.

The role of disease and death in conversion

Making matters exponentially worse for the Natives were the massive waves of sickness and death caused by the introduction of European diseases.[19] Small pox, measles, typhus, malaria, and other diseases hitherto unknown in the Americas had devastating consequences on Indigenous people. In central Mexico, which contained the highest and most concentrated populations in New Spain, millions of people perished. By 1575, more than half of the inhabitants had died; by 1590, the Native population had decreased by 90 percent due to European and African diseases. Disease and death accompanied the Spaniards in their advance toward the north, often preceding them. This meant that as colonizers entered lands never before seen by Europeans, they often encountered weakened and ailing Native people already in crisis.[20]

The tragic epidemics paradoxically pushed Indigenous populations toward Christian ritual life and mission communities. Inhabitants of smaller villages that had been decimated by disease often had little choice but to move to mission communities in order to survive. In the Franciscan, Dominican, and Augustinian missions in central Mexico as well as newer Jesuit missions in what is now northwest Mexico, Catholic missionaries addressed the spread of epidemics with modest care for the sick and baptism. While their health-care methods saved few lives, the friars were able to draw on long-standing Christian rituals of care for the dying, developed over centuries of European epidemics. When Native religious and healing specialists, such as shamans, were unable to stem the tide of death and had no ritual response to disease-caused societal crisis, many Indigenous sought out the ritual cleansing of Christian baptism. When the friars and other religious could convince a Native leader to convert and be baptized, this often led to baptism of entire villages. Of course, these deathbed conversions did not necessarily reflect a complete religious reorientation, but the remaining populations found themselves more and more connected to the patterns of life and faith promulgated by the missions. In this way, disease itself contributed to the Catholicization of Native peoples.[21]

Catholic debates concerning indigenous personhood and worth

From a contemporary vantage point, Spanish conquest and control of the Americas and their subjugation of Native peoples seems almost inevitable, but it is important to remember that European legal and ecclesiastical debates as well as economic interests guided, and sometimes limited, Spanish colonization and evangelization. Despite the destruction of Indigenous communities and the coercive environment in which many conversions took place, there was at least some Spanish resistance to the injustices being committed against the Native people. These viewpoints remain important because they set the stage for later debates between the Catholic hierarchy, governing forces, and popular traditions and theologies. They also underscore that the Catholic Church, even from the beginning of colonization, has contained within itself diverse voices and orientations toward the poor and oppressed.

At the outset of European contact with the Americas, questions quickly arose concerning the right of Spanish and Portuguese explorers and conquistadors to take control of vast and well-populated lands. Catholic legal traditions relied on their conceptions of natural law, the observable order of things as ordained by the Creator. Theologians developed this natural law into the *ius gentium*, the law of nations, a perceived common law that governed all peoples. This legal tradition, however, did little to justify territorial expansion and the appropriation of other people's lands. A Spanish Dominican theologian, Fr. Melchor Cano, proposed an answer to this conundrum: the *ius predicando*, the law of preaching. The *ius predicando* established the right of a Christian nation to take over a pagan nation as long as the conquerors preached the Christian Gospel to the ones being conquered. This cohered with Catholic conceptions of natural law in the sense that Christian peoples were, if not naturally superior, in a position to rule over and nurture peoples who had yet to accept Christianity. The *ius predicando* thus provided an internally cogent theological rationale for the Conquest, but it also mandated that the Spanish monarchy maintain the missionary efforts of the Catholic Church. This meant that, for better or worse, the economic expansiveness of the Spanish Empire relied on active Catholic preaching and proselytism for its legal justification.[22]

While these legal theologies provided the reasoning behind the *encomienda* system, the friars who were carrying out the conversion campaigns occasionally condemned the dehumanizing abuses of forced labor that treated the Natives less as souls in need of the Gospel and more as chattel. As early as 1511, a Dominican on the island of Hispaniola named Antonio de Montesinos began to question the brutal treatment of Indigenous Caribbeans. In his remarks, he insisted that the Natives were human, pointing out that their mistreatment was often based on the opposite assumption, namely, that they were sub-human. In southern Mexico and Central America, another Dominican, Bartolomé de las Casas, gained some notoriety among Church and governing elites for his resistance to the *encomienda* system and, in time to slavery in general, whether it be of Native Mesoamericans or Africans. His influential writings and advocacy eventually resulted in some legal checks on the *encomiendas* as well as support for non-coercive conversion methods. In 1550–51, he and theologian Juan Ginés de Sepúlveda carried out an official debate in Valladolid on the justification of war against the Natives to subdue and convert them. Where Las Casas condemned war and land theft and promoted peaceful conversion, Sepúlveda argued for the natural inferiority of the Indigenous people and thus their need to be conquered and subjugated by the naturally superior Catholic Europeans.[23] Las Casas, although influential, was unable to bring an end to the *encomiendas*. However, he did make a lasting impact when, in 1537, Pope Paul III, attentive to Las Casas's arguments, issued the papal bull *Sublimis Deus*, which declared the Natives to be fully human, outlawed their enslavement, and granted them the full rights of membership in the Catholic Church.[24] In practice, these precepts and rights would not always be observed, but this was a doctrinal breakthrough for a more justice-oriented sector of the Church.

These early papal recognitions of Indigenous personhood, however, hardly meant equality. In fact, by the sixteenth century, New Spain and the rest of Spanish America was organized in a complex *sistema de castas*, or "casta" system, based in precise calculations of an individual's "blood" heritage. At the apex of the castas were the Spanish themselves. Mixtures with Africans, Indigenous people, and small populations of Asians in New Spain led to a complicated and highly stratified classifications of castas. "*Limpieza de sangre*," or "blood purity" gauged the amount of white blood that one had, with important effects on one's social standing. Historian Ben Vinson explains, "miscegenation could produce both positive and negative outcomes, enabling people to move up or down the somatic scale, expressing different characteristics and qualities as they traveled along the continuum."[25]

Northern expansion

It took years, sometimes centuries, for the Spanish to extend their settlement and evangelistic efforts northward into the part of the continent that is now northern Mexico and the U.S. Southwest. In theory, the Spanish monarchy had already made claim to all this territory, but Indigenous resistance significantly slowed both civil and religious advances. The next chapter covers in more detail the eventual founding of missions as well as Spanish towns and churches in this region; here, the focus is on initial forays followed by permanent, if sometimes precarious, Spanish settlement. The *ius predicando* continued to require that evangelization accompany Spanish territorial expansion, but the

Spaniards' initial exploration of the region was often acquisitive in nature; they were looking to expand sources of imperial wealth.

The earliest European contact with Native peoples in the area was not an intentional exploration mission but rather the wanderings of a group of ship-wrecked men. Their leader, Álvar Núñez Cabeza de Vaca (1490–1559), would eventually write a chronicle of the adventures and mishaps of the survivors and describe the Indigenous people they encountered and their customs. As part of their bid for survival, the European and African crewmembers underwent episodes of captivity and also posed as shamanic healers. Between 1528 and 1536, their travels brought them through various parts of the present-day U.S.-Mexico border region, much in Texas. Eventually, they found their way back to a Spanish settlement in what is now Sinaloa, Mexico.[26]

One of the men in Cabeza de Vaca's party was an enslaved African known as Estevanico (c. 1500–1539). Because of Estevanico's relative familiarity with the territory north of Spanish settlement, a Franciscan friar, Marcos de Niza (1495–1555), partnered with him on a fact-finding and evangelistic mission in 1539. Reaching modern Arizona, Niza and Estevanico made contact with Pueblo people, and Estevanico was reportedly killed in a Zuni town. Before returning to central New Spain, Niza claimed to have learned of a series of prosperous Pueblos that he called the "Seven Cities of Cibola." This report inspired a conquistador, Francisco Vázquez de Coronado (1510–1544), to organize an expedition to find these cities, claim them for Spain, and exploit their wealth. With Niza as something of a guide, Coronado and his men entered the region in 1540, and they passed through what is now Arizona, New Mexico, and Texas. Disappointed by the relative poverty of the people, Coronado pressed on to a final mythical source of wealth, a place known as Quivira in modern Kansas. He returned to New Spain in 1542, and his lack of success put a damper on further northern exploration and settlement for a time.[27]

The first expedition that would lead to eventual permanent European settlement in the area did not occur until more than half a century later, under the leadership of Juan de Oñate (1550–1626). Oñate was granted the right to conquer and govern the province of New Mexico, and he entered the territory with four hundred settlers and a host of Franciscans in 1598. After making alliances with Tewa Pueblo people in the northern Rio Grande Valley and ruling for some years from the San Juan Pueblo (now known as Ohkay Owingeh), he established the provincial capital of Santa Fe in 1610. During his tumultuous tenure, Oñate was known for his cruelty. An infamous example has to do with Acoma Pueblo. In 1599, the Spanish forces conquered the highly fortified Pueblo in a protracted battle. As a punishment for their resistance, Oñate distributed Acoma's children to Franciscan missions, assigned the youths and the elderly to servitude, and sentenced each warrior to have one of his feet cut off.[28] This heavy-handed brutality marked the Spanish entry into New Mexico and would eventually fuel a major Indigenous revolt (see Chapter 3).

Almost one hundred years after Oñate's often violent settlement in New Mexico, a small Spanish party entered central Texas. Led by the Franciscan

Fray Damián Massenet and a military contingent led by Domingo Terán de los Ríos, the missionary expedition settled briefly on the banks of the Yanaguana River, which they renamed the San Antonio River since they encountered the area on the feast day of St. Anthony of Padua. They did not stay long by the river and continued eastward.[29] Permanent Spanish settlement in the region did not occur until 1718 when Martín de Alarcón, the governor of the province of Texas, established a military outpost, or presidio, at San Antonio de Béxar as well as a Franciscan mission. This would serve as the hub for more missions and Spanish settlements in the region. A civilian town was soon founded near the presidio, called San Fernando de Béxar, which was made up principally of Spanish immigrants from the Canary Islands.[30]

Spanish settlements in California and Arizona happened even later. Permanent Spanish colonization of what was then known as Alta California followed a similar pattern to that in Texas. A military and political governor, Gaspar de Portolá (1716–1786), established a presidio in San Diego in 1769 to protect civilian colonists and the Franciscan missionaries. Fray Junípero Serra (1713–1784) accompanied Portolá and would go on to found many missions along the California coast.[31] Southern Arizona was known as the Pimería Alta after the Pima people in the area, who are known today as the O'odham. Unlike in most of the rest of the northern missions, which the Franciscans ran, the Jesuits operated the missions in the Pimería, and Spanish settlements were mostly small mining operations. A permanent military presence did not occur until 1752, when a presidio was built in the village of Tubac. The presidio was later moved to Tucson in 1776.[32] In contrast to New Mexico, Texas, and California, the Arizona area did not have a sizeable non-Native population until after annexation by the United States.

Religion in practice

For some women in New Spain, the decision to enter religious life in a convent offered new opportunities not only for religious devotion but, paradoxically, for some degree of autonomy. Although nuns, to be sure, followed a regimented schedule of daily prayer and labor, there were, at least in some cases, opportunities for study, reflection, and even socializing, all of which would have been hard to come by outside the walls of the convent. The first convent for women was established in Mexico in 1540, less than twenty-five years after the Conquest. Over the next two hundred years, almost forty other convents were founded in the populated center of New Spain. By fiat of the Catholic Church, only Spaniards, *criollas* (Spanish women born in New Spain), and occasionally *mestizas* (women with mixed Spanish and Indigenous heritage) were permitted to become nuns—Indigenous women were excluded. And, in most cases, religious life in the convents was limited to the upper classes since the majority of convents required that novices' families pay a significant dowry to underwrite their kinswoman's life in the cloister. Historian Susan Socolow explains, "Having a daughter or granddaughter in a convent formed part of a family strategy, identifying the family as part of an elite that shared deeply religious values while reflecting on the wealth and honor of the family."[33] Given these economic and ethnic limitations, the first convent for Native women in New Spain was not established until 1724.[34]

In the majority of convents, which housed such elite women, daily religious life was rigorous but not to the extent that there was no time for personal pursuits. Nuns' vows of poverty were lenient enough to allow them to keep personal property, including cash, jewelry, and even enslaved servants, and they often lived in relatively lavish quarters. When they were not engaged in the daily prayers, nuns had time for reading and socializing. Sor Juana Inés de la Cruz (1648–1695) famously made use of her time in the convent to engage in a life of the mind, often against the wishes of her male confessors. Her poetry and voluminous correspondence occupied time not spent on religious duties, and her education and conversational skills kept her busy with many visits from Mexico City's elite.[35]

Other convents of discalced nuns—that is, those who went barefoot or wore only sandals—observed a more austere religious life. Discalced orders, in contrast to the less stringent orders, relied less on costly dowries and therefore were more of an option for Mexican women of lower social classes. Awakened for prayer at midnight, these nuns would arise again at 5:00 a.m. to begin another cycle of prayer followed by manual labor to maintain the convent. Their diets, which included frequent fasting, consisted entirely of fish and vegetables, and their cells were simple. Free time, such as it was, was dedicated to penance and personal reflection.[36]

Notes

1 See Romans 15:23–24.
2 John Frederick Schwaller, *The History of the Catholic Church in Latin America: From Conquest to Revolution and Beyond* (New York: New York University Press, 2011), 13–22.
3 For examples of writing on Mexican American "crypto-Jews," see Cary Herz, Ori Z. Soltes, and Mona Hernandez, *New Mexico's Crypto-Jews: Image and Memory* (Albuquerque, NM: University of New Mexico Press, 2009); Ilan Stavans and Steve Sheinkin, *El Iluminado: A Graphic Novel* (New York: Basic Books, 2012). Most Jews in Latin America, it should be noted, can trace their past to immigrants in the nineteenth and twentieth centuries.
4 Patricia Lopes Don, "Franciscans, Indian Sorcerers, and the Inquisition in New Spain, 1536–1543," *Journal of World History* 17, no. 1 (2006): 27–49.
5 Schwaller, *The History of the Catholic Church in Latin America*, 35.
6 Manuel Aguilar-Moreno, *Handbook to Life in the Aztec World* (New York: Oxford University Press, 2006), 380–84. See also Ross Hassig, *Mexico and the Spanish Conquest*, 2nd ed. (Norman, OK: University of Oklahoma Press, 2006).
7 Aguilar-Moreno, *Handbook to Life in the Aztec World*, 382; Davíd Carrasco, *Religions of Mesoamerica*, 2nd ed. (Long Grove, IL: Waveland Press, 2014), 78–79.
8 Robert Ricard and Lesley Byrd Simpson, *The Spiritual Conquest of Mexico: An Essay on the Apostolate and the Evangelizing Methods of the Mendicant Orders in New Spain, 1523–1572* (Berkeley, CA: University of California Press, 1966), 15–18.

9 Ricard and Simpson, 21–23.

10 Ricard and Simpson, 36–38.

11 Christian Duverger, *La conversión de los indios de la Nueva España*, Collección 500 Años 18 (Quito, Ecuador: Abya-Yala, 1990), 121–22. Regarding the early convents, see Beverley Spears, *Early Churches of Mexico: An Architect's View* (Albuquerque, NM: University of New Mexico Press, 2017).

12 Duverger, *La Conversión de los indios de la Nueva España*, 126–28.

13 Toribio Motolinía and Elizabeth Andros Foster, *Motolinía's History of the Indians of New Spain* (Westport, CT: Greenwood Press, 1973), 53.

14 Herman L. Bennett, *Africans in Colonial Mexico: Absolutism, Christianity, and Afro-Creole Consciousness, 1570–1640* (Bloomington, IN: Indiana University Press, 2003), 27.

15 Bennett, 193.

16 Bennett, 53–54.

17 Alberto Martínez Boom, "Evangelización e instrucción pública en el orden colonial español," *Revista Española de Educación Comparada*, no. 31 (2018): 62.

18 Martínez Boom, 58; John Lynch, *New Worlds: A Religious History of Latin America* (New Haven, CT: Yale University Press, 2012), 25.

19 For a comprehensive account of the role of disease in the Spanish Conquest, see Noble David Cook, *Born to Die: Disease and New World Conquest, 1492–1650* (New York: Cambridge University Press, 1998).

20 Daniel T. Reff, *Plagues, Priests, and Demons: Sacred Narratives and the Rise of Christianity in the Old World and the New* (New York: Cambridge University Press, 2005), 127.

21 Reff, 162–63, 172–73, 179.

22 Schwaller, *The History of the Catholic Church in Latin America: From Conquest to Revolution and Beyond*, 40–41.

23 Lynch, *New Worlds: A Religious History of Latin America*, 31–37.

24 Schwaller, *The History of the Catholic Church in Latin America: From Conquest to Revolution and Beyond*, 45. See also Bartolomé De las Casas and Stafford Poole, *In Defense of the Indians: The Defense of the Most Reverend Lord, Don Fray Bartolomé de Las Casas, of the Order of Preachers, Late Bishop of Chiapas, against the Persecutors and Slanderers of the Peoples of the New World Discovered across the Seas* (DeKalb, IL: Northern Illinois University Press, 1992).

25 Ben Vinson III, *Before Mestizaje: The Frontiers of Race and Caste in Colonial Mexico* (New York: Cambridge University Press, 2018): 48. See also María Elena Martínez, *Geneaological Fictions: Limpieza de Sangre, Religion, and Gender in Colonial Mexico* (Stanford, CA: Stanford University Press, 2008).

26 Alvar Núñez Cabeza de Vaca and Enrique Pupo-Walker, *Castaways: The Narrative of Alvar Núñez Cabeza de Vaca* (Berkeley, CA: University of California Press, 1993).

27 Joseph P. Sánchez, Robert L. Spude, and Art Gómez, *New Mexico: A History* (Norman, OK: University of Oklahoma Press, 2013), 16–21.

28 Sánchez, Spude, and Gómez, 40–41.

29 Thomas S. Bremer, *Blessed with Tourists: The Borderlands of Religion and Tourism in San Antonio* (Chapel Hill, NC: University of North Carolina Press, 2004), 11, 19.

30 Jesús F. de la Teja and John Wheat, "Béxar: Profile of a Tejano Community, 1820–1832," in *Tejano Origins in Eighteenth Century San Antonio*, ed. Gerald E. Poyo and Gilberto M. Hinojosa (Austin, TX: University of Texas Press, 1991), 2–3.

31 Donald A. Nuttall, "Gaspar de Portolá: Disenchanted Conquistador of Spanish Upper California," *Southern California Quarterly* 53, no. 3 (1971): 185–98.

32 Rex E. Gerald, *Spanish Presidios of the Late Eighteenth Century in Northern New Spain*, Museum of New Mexico Research Records 7 (Santa Fe, NM: Museum of New Mexico Press, 1968), 16.

33 Susan Migden Socolow, *The Women of Colonial Latin America*, 2nd ed. (Cambridge: Cambridge University Press, 2015), 98.

34 Mónica Díaz, *Indigenous Writings from the Convent: Negotiating Ethnic Autonomy in Colonial Mexico* (Tucson: University of Arizona Press, 2010), 7–8.
35 Socolow, *The Women of Colonial Latin America*, 106, 110; Cruz Juana Inés de la, Electa Arenal, and Amanda Powell, *The Answer / La Respuesta, Including a Selection of Poems* (New York: Feminist Press at the City University of New York, 1994), 6–7.
36 Socolow, *The Women of Colonial Latin America*, 105–6.

3 The colonial era in northern New Spain

After their initial exploratory forays and the first permanent settlements in the vast territories of northern New Spain, the Spaniards began to build their own towns and churches in the region, even as newly constructed Catholic missions punctuated the landscape in an effort to convert the Native inhabitants. The exact time spans of Spanish control vary by the date of entry and colonization in the various regions of the north. In New Mexico, the site of earliest European habitation, there were over two hundred years of Spanish rule. In contrast, the Spanish did not settle and evangelize the California coastline until the late 1700s, only a few decades before Mexico gained its independence. This chapter looks at the proliferation of missions in northern New Spain as well as the somewhat slower establishment of Catholic parishes and dioceses in the region.

Why cover northern New Spain in a history of Mexican American religion? First, this is the part of the Spanish Empire—and later, Mexico—that would be captured and annexed by the United States in the middle of the nineteenth century. In this sense, the region itself is literally "Mexican American." Second, although many Mexican Americans' families did not migrate to this area until after the U.S. takeover, cultural and religious patterns persisted. This means that, for instance, religious customs begun in New Mexico in the eighteenth century remain relevant for Mexican Americans (and others) in that state today, even if they cannot trace a New Mexican ancestry from the time of Spanish settlement. Finally, demographic realities mean that a large majority of Mexican Americans live today in the border states.[1] The U.S. West and Southwest, formerly the northern frontier of New Spain and Mexico, are the Mexican American heartland, and the historic patterns of religious life there set the scene for many later developments.

Secular and regular clergy

Since the beginning of the Spanish Conquest, different kinds of Catholic clergy have played essential roles in the establishment and practice of Christianity in the Americas. Therefore, it is important to understand the authority structures that oversee different kinds of clergy as well as their varying functions.

DOI: 10.4324/9780429285516-5

In the simplest of terms, there are two kinds of associations of Catholic clergy and religious. The so-called regular clergy belong to religious orders, such as Franciscans or Jesuits. The word "regular" here refers to the "rules" that regulate these orders. Not all members of religious orders are priests; some do not seek priesthood ordination and are simply brothers of the order. An important term for many orders active in Mexico is "friar," the title of a member of one of the mendicant orders, such as Franciscans, Dominicans, and Augustinians. (The Spanish title for a friar is "fray," such as Fray Bartolomé de las Casas.) Members of the regular clergy report to the leader of their order rather than to a bishop or other ecclesiastical overseer. The heads of orders report directly to the pope in Rome. This means that ordered clergy often have more latitude than other priests, and they can often dedicate themselves to particular vocations, such as evangelization, education, or care for the sick. Women religious, or nuns, generally belong to religious orders that may or may not be connected to male orders.

The other type of Catholic priests are secular clergy. This counter-intuitive name does not connote a lack of religion; instead, it points to ministry in the secular world rather than in a monastery. Unlike regular, ordered clergy, who answer to the leaders of their order, secular priests operate in a geographically organized hierarchy. The local unit is the parish, which gathers Catholics from an area into a congregation that the priest serves. A diocese is comprised of several parishes; its leader is a bishop. Groups of dioceses form a province, and the bishop of one of the included dioceses is appointed as archbishop of the whole province; his particular diocese is referred to as the archdiocese. Generally speaking, the primary task of a secular priest is to see to the needs of his parish by leading worship, administering the sacraments, and providing pastoral care.

Both regular and secular clergy were part of the earliest moments of the Spanish colonization of Mexico. The Franciscans, as discussed in Chapter 2, were tasked with forming missions for the Indigenous people and carrying out massive conversion campaigns. The secular clergy, even before the official establishment of parishes and dioceses in New Spain, were responsible for seeing to the religious needs of the Spanish colonists by establishing churches in the new territory.[2] One of the premises behind this division was that, as the religious orders converted the Native people to Christianity, the ordered clergy and their missions would be replaced by parishes, secular clergy, and new dioceses. This process is referred to as "secularization."

Under the powers that the pope granted to the Spanish monarchy in the *Patronato Real*, the monarchs held significant power over secular clergy, including having a hand in naming bishops to their positions. Regular clergy, although not governed by the crown-appointed bishops, were not entirely free from monarchical influence, especially since the monarchy funded the missions. Given the more direct control it had over the secular clergy, the Spanish crown had a stake in secularization and tried at various times to compel it. In reality, the process of secularization often took decades, if not centuries. The reasons for the slow pace of secularization include a reticence on the part of regular clergy to concede their missions, an acknowledgement that Native conversion was often gradual and multi-generational rather than sudden, and a shortage of diocesan priests in some areas due to low numbers of educated young men willing to enter the priesthood.[3]

What this all meant for northern New Spain is that, for most of the colonial period, the missionary orders—especially the Franciscans—were the primary, and often only, official representatives of the Catholic Church. The history of their missions, their interactions with Native people, and their de facto care for Spanish and mestizo Catholic populations constitute the bulk of Catholic institutional life on New Spain's northern frontier. As explained in Chapter 2, Spanish settlement of Indigenous lands was legally contingent on Native evangelization. This meant that the first permanent Spanish incursions into the north were both military and religious in nature. It also meant that the first waves of Catholicism were led by the religious orders; if diocesan priests were on hand during colonization, it was to serve as chaplains to Spanish soldiers and colonists in their new towns. Only later did New Spanish dioceses extend their control over Catholic parish life. In what follows, the various areas of colonization and missionization are explored; different geographic contexts, Indigenous communities, and time periods all had an impact on how Catholicism spread to the north.

New Mexico: Settlement, revolt, resettlement

Franciscans accompanied Juan de Oñate and the six hundred Spanish settlers that entered New Mexico in 1598. Following the patterns of conquest dictated by law and now buttressed by a century of colonization, Oñate had the *Requerimiento* read aloud to the Pueblos, admonishing them to embrace the Catholic faith or face military consequences. It is doubtful that this act itself led to any conversions, but the Franciscans did achieve some initial evangelistic success, especially with the Tewa-speaking Pueblos. These Pueblos likewise had been somewhat more accommodating of the newcomers, and the earliest Spanish settlements were in or adjacent to their towns. Oñate, later in 1598, reiterated his demands to Pueblo leaders that they must accept the Franciscans' religious instruction and obey Spanish rule, and he threatened them with total destruction.[4] In this bellicose atmosphere, the Franciscans went about building mission churches up and down the northern Rio Grande Valley and carried out the massive baptisms that were the custom in early New Spain. By 1630, Fray Alonso de Benavides made a rosy report to his superiors:

> All the Indians are now converted, baptized and well ministered to, with 33 convents and churches in the principal pueblos and more than 150 churches throughout the other pueblos. … Here where scarcely 30 years earlier all was idolatry and worship of the devil, without any vestige of civilization, today they worship our true God and Lord.[5]

As in central Mexico, it is highly unlikely that the reported number of baptisms reflected a total and lasting religious reorientation of nearly the entire Pueblo population. Rather, the numbers indicated the extent of Franciscan contact and disruptive insertion into Native lives, in what would soon spark a major backlash.

Although the various Pueblos had never in their history come together—in fact, they had often engaged in open conflict—the crisis brought about by the Franciscan missions united them under the leadership of a Tewa man named Popé. It is little wonder that the Pueblos were in a revolutionary mood. Over the course of the seventeenth century, Pueblo populations had plummeted due to disease and Spanish violence from somewhere between 60,000 to 100,000 inhabitants in 130 Pueblos to only seven thousand gathered in just thirteen remaining Pueblos. Franciscans had forbidden Pueblo ritual practices, such as katsina dances, and had troubled their kinship networks by forcing them to adopt Spanish family structures.[6] The friars used cruel corporal punishments to exact obedience to Catholic religious and cultural customs. In response, Popé and other Pueblo leaders organized a secret rebellion that exploded in August 1680. In just a few days, the Pueblos, who radically outnumbered the Spanish, destroyed every Catholic mission and killed twenty-one of the thirty-three Franciscan missionaries in New Mexico. Their wrath against the civilian population was somewhat more subdued—375 of 2,350 colonists were killed, and the remaining Spanish were forced to flee south to El Paso. Spanish efforts to retake the area were unsuccessful for twelve years.[7]

Eventually, under the command of a new governor, Diego de Vargas, the Spanish retook New Mexico in 1692. The Franciscans also returned and began to rebuild their destroyed missions. However, the Pueblo Revolt had lasting consequences on the missionaries' methods. They adopted a more educational approach to Christianization and never again claimed that they had definitively converted the entire Pueblo population. They also curtailed their raids on Pueblo ceremonies and their attacks on the katsina dances, and they stopped enforcing required Mass attendance.[8]

The Franciscans also found other duties to occupy their time in the post-Revolt period. Throughout most of the eighteenth century, there were no secular clergy in New Mexico, and so it fell to the Franciscans to meet the religious needs not only of the Natives but of the growing population of colonists. Villa churches, that is, churches in non-Native settlements, grew in various places, including Santa Fe, Santa Cruz, and Albuquerque, and Franciscans served all these congregations like parish priests. In 1767, the missions and all other churches in New Mexico were officially secularized, but in name only, as no diocesan clergy made their way to the region for another thirty years. In the interim, an aging and declining number of Franciscans were stretched thin to meet all of New Mexico's Catholics' needs. Finally, the Diocese of Durango began to send secular priests to New Mexico in 1797, but by the end of the Spanish colonial era, the entire territory was served by only nine Franciscans and five secular priests.[9]

Figure 3.1 Statue of Po'pay by Jemez Pueblo sculptor Cliff Fragua, located in the U.S. Capitol Visitor Center. With permission of the Architect of the Capitol.

After the enforced secularization of the Franciscan missions, but prior to Mexican independence in 1821, the bishop of Durango, José Laureano Antonio Zubiría y Escalante, sent official representatives to New Mexico to assess the state of Catholicism in the region. These observers took a multi-faceted inventory of New Mexico's churches and missions, ostensibly in preparation for the placement of diocesan priests under Bishop Zubiría's command. Despite centuries of Franciscan outreach to both Native and non-Native populations, Zubiría's men were unimpressed with New Mexican Catholicism. Shortly after Mexican independence, a government investigator named Antonio Barreiro reported the following:

> Spiritual administration in New Mexico is in a truly doleful condition. Nothing is more common than to see an infinite number of sick die without confession or extreme unction. It is indeed unusual to see the eucharist administered to the sick. Corpses remain unburied for many days, and children are baptized at the cost of a thousand hardships. A great many unfortunate people spend most of the Sundays of the year without hearing mass. Churches are in a state of near ruin, and most of them are unworthy of being called the temple of God.[10]

To be sure, priests then as now are a necessary part of much Catholic worship since many rituals, such as those mentioned in Barreiro's report, cannot be completed without them. Catholic and governmental officials often interpreted a lack of priests, then, as a sign of religious degradation. However, this dearth of clergy made New Mexico an ideal location for the flourishing of popular and durable Catholic traditions that had no need of priests. Household and village Catholicism melded Spanish and Indigenous traditions in ways that met peoples' needs for worship, pastoral care, rites of passage, and even the settling of disputes. In this sense, the negative tenor of official reports belies the vitality and autonomy of New Mexican popular religiosity at the end of the Spanish colonial period. The Penitente Brotherhood, a famous exemplar of this religiosity, is discussed later in this chapter.

Missions, presidios, and villas in Spanish Texas

Significant settlement and missions did not occur in Texas until well after colonization was well under way in New Mexico and was sparked by French incursions into the territory in the late 1600s. Accordingly, the first efforts to install a mission presence was in east Texas, near the border with French Louisiana. Franciscans from Querétaro and Zacatecas founded short-lived missions near the present-day city of Nacogdoches in 1716. When they had to leave the area in 1719 due to hardships and ongoing conflicts with the French, they joined other Franciscans, who had begun a more successful mission enterprise on the banks of the San Antonio River just the year before.[11] Mission and settlement in the San Antonio area followed a typical pattern, where a

Franciscan mission to the Indigenous inhabitants was accompanied by a military presidio as well as a civilian village. After some initial success for the mission nearest the presidio, Mission San Antonio de Valero (later known as the Alamo), several other missions were established down the San Antonio River.[12]

As mentioned in Chapter 1, the Native inhabitants of the region, though often referred to collectively as "Coahuiltecans," were nomadic hunters and gatherers who spoke dozens of languages and did not share a common identity. They were under intense pressure for a number of reasons, including population decline caused by European diseases, Spanish takeover of their lands, and warfare and rivalry among Native groups, especially frequent attacks from Apaches. The missions provided at least some protection against these challenges, even if they created others. On the one hand, the missions achieved economic success. In the fort-like confines of the mission grounds, both Natives and colonists carried out agriculture and various trades, such as weaving and smithing. This allowed the missions to be not only self-sufficient but also to produce a wide variety of surplus goods for trade. The nearby presidio as well as the enclosed and fortified nature of the missions made them relatively safe against external attacks. They also functioned fairly well as centers of religious education. Since the Indigenous groups gathered in the missions rarely shared a language, the acquisition of Spanish as a common tongue contributed to the pace and success of Catholicization. Despite these aspects of mission life, the constant threat of disease often led to deadly epidemics as well as the decision to flee the missions for healthier environs. As a result, the Franciscans, with the aid of Spanish military forces, were often on the hunt for new Native populations to replenish mission labor forces.[13]

As in New Mexico, the missions were eventually ordered to be secularized; in Texas, the process began in 1793. The remaining Franciscans stayed on to assist the transition as their erstwhile missions were transformed into village parishes. Shortly after Mexico gained independence, the parishes—still under Franciscan guidance—were transferred to the oversight of San Fernando Church, the principal non-mission parish in the region. A lack of Franciscan persistence to prop up the missions combined with the distribution of mission land to its long-time occupants soon meant that missions ceased to have any religious function.[14]

Meanwhile, the non-Native colonists of San Antonio relied on their Catholic identity to provide structure and cohesion to their community. Shortly after the establishment of the first mission and the military garrison, civilian immigrants from the Canary Islands arrived in the area in 1731 and founded the Villa de San Fernando. Father José de la Garza accompanied them and helped establish the first parish to serve the settlers as well as the soldiers in the presidio. They built the first parish church soon after and gave it the same name as their villa. Both Spanish civilians and military personnel used the church, and marriages in the church between Canary Islanders and military men contributed to the social integration of the town. Yearly celebrations in early San Antonio followed the Catholic calendar closely and relied on cooperation between laypeople and clergy to organize. Years later, San Fernando Church would go on to become San Fernando Cathedral, the oldest Catholic cathedral sanctuary in the United States.[15]

Jesuits missions in Arizona

Franciscans led the earliest Christian missions to the territory now known as Arizona. They were part of Oñate's settlement of New Mexico and founded missions among the Hopis in the early seventeenth century. However, these missions were destroyed in the Pueblo Revolt and never rebuilt. The next missions would be built far to the south by Jesuits under the leadership of an Italian priest named Father Eusebio Kino. He entered the area, then considered part of the New Spanish province of Sonora, in 1699 after spending some time farther south among O'odham people, known then as the Pima. In what would eventually be Arizona, Kino founded the missions of San Xavier del Bac, San Miguel, Tumacácori, and Guevavi.[16] Deviating from the patterns set near Franciscan missions in New Mexico and Texas, a military presidio did not accompany these Jesuit outposts. Kino insisted that the Pimas were friendly and receptive to the missions, and, indeed, the early Jesuits and Pimas rarely encountered the mobile unit of Spanish forces that had been stationed well to the south of Kino's northern missions. After Kino's death in 1711, the O'odham people around the missions had, at best, infrequent visits from Jesuit priests until the 1730s.[17]

Eventually, the Jesuits tried again to operate the missions in their northern territory, but they encountered frequent resistance from a variety of Indigenous peoples, including the O'odham, Yaquis, Seris and Apaches. During this same time, priests and Natives alike continued to suffer the devastating effects of disease. The situation was so dire that, between the years of 1755 and 1760, the Jesuits produced a series of reports ominously entitled a "Brief Review of the Disasters of Sonora." In addition to Native resistance and disease, the Jesuit missions languished for financial and administrative reasons as well. The slow pace of secularization of successful Jesuit missions farther south meant that diocesan priests were not replacing Jesuit missionaries, thus locking them into continued service. This meant that too few missionaries were available to expand into the rugged and often hostile north. Behind all this was a general lack of funding from the Spanish government for frontier missions.[18]

The Jesuits haltingly cared for the various missions among the O'odham in southern Arizona for the next few years until they were expelled from all Spanish territories throughout the Western Hemisphere in 1767. (Their removal had nothing to do with Jesuit activities in northern New Spain but resulted, rather, from distant ecclesiastical and political disputes in Europe.) After their expulsion, Franciscans came to take their places in the missions, building up some, such as San Xavier del Bac and Tumacácori, and letting others, like Guevavi, fall into ruin. As in other areas of New Spain's northern frontier, the Franciscan presence in Arizona was more or less synonymous with the Catholic presence until the U.S. takeover in the middle of the nineteenth

Figure 3.2 Postcard of Mission San Xavier del Bac, ca. 1902, the Miriam and Ira D.
Wallach Division of Art, Prints and Photographs: Photography Collection,
New York Public Library Digital Collections. In public domain.

century. The friars served the declining missions and the small numbers of non-
Native farmers and miners who inhabited this least populous part of northern
New Spain.

Coastal missions and Catholicism in California

Compared to most of New Spain's northern expanses, settlement and missionization in California occurred late. It was not until 1769 that Spanish military forces
and Franciscan missionaries under the leadership of Fray Junípero Serra arrived in
Alta California, the territory known today as the U.S. state of California. The
relatively dense Indigenous population of the region, approximately 300,000
people, lived in small settlements and spoke dozens of mutually unintelligible
languages. The livelihood as well as the cultural patterns of Native groups reflected
the variety and abundance of California's natural resources, with a majority of
people living in California's vast and rich central valley.

Under Serra, the Franciscans focused their efforts on the California coast,
establishing twenty-one missions from San Diego to Sonoma between 1769 and
1821. By this date, the pattern of Franciscan missions was well-practiced: Indigenous converts were gathered into enclosed or semi-enclosed communities
where they were instructed not only in Catholic doctrine but in European modes
of dress, housing, family relationships, and economic structures. Nearby presidios
and colonial settlements provided both military protection and markets for mission

residents. During the relatively brief California mission era, 81,000 people were baptized as new Christians in the missions.[19]

Daily life in these missions was strictly regimented. Mission bells woke people to morning prayer and breakfast. Labor in the missions' fields followed for most of the adults; children underwent catechetical education and also participated in agricultural labor. The day was further punctuated by daily Mass, other required times of prayer, and meals. In addition to fieldwork, the missions also trained Native craftspeople, who constructed buildings and other objects for daily life. Indigenous women in the missions were at the bottom of the social hierarchy, often far below where they had functioned in their own communities prior to enclosure among the Franciscans. Before marriage, girls and women were kept in locked quarters, meaning that virtually the only way to gain any autonomy was through marriage. Even then, Natives were not allowed to leave the missions, and if they defected, they were often brought back by force.[20]

The Franciscans who ran the missions varied in terms of their benevolence toward the Indigenous people, but the friars most certainly considered the Natives to be child-like and in need of constant education and reproof. Shirking work or skipping religious obligations were offenses that the Franciscans disciplined with corporal punishment. Serra himself argued that it was the job of the fathers to flog the Native "children" when they disobeyed. This abuse led to conflict and occasional rebellion. In 1775, Kumeyaay people in Mission San Diego, Serra's first mission in California, rose up, killed the priest in charge of the mission, and burned it to the ground.[21]

A few Indigenous men and women in the missions were elected to positions of leadership and supervision under the Franciscans, where they had some influence on the impartation of Catholic ideology. These people were often baptized as young children and had grown up in the missions and therefore likely had strong Spanish language skills and a more complete understanding of Catholic teaching. Historians have speculated that such Native leaders may have assisted the Franciscans with mediating and translating Christian instruction to make it comprehensible to new converts. Being thus positioned between Franciscan oversight and their ancestral communities, these Native Californian mission officials helped interpret Catholic concepts in ways that resonated creatively with their own systems of meaning.[22] Another site of this creative mixing of Christian and Native occurred in sacred art. As part of their evangelistic campaign, the Franciscans had distributed thousands of prints of saints to mission residents as tokens of instruction and devotion. In short order, Native artists began painting their own depictions of Catholic saints, and historians have noted that many of these images both record Catholic imagery and expand upon it using Indigenous symbols of holiness and power. For instance, one Native-painted image of St. Raphael the Archangel features the saint in a traditional Chumash cape holding a talisman in the shape of a killer whale. This icon represented a Chumash dream helper used by shamanic healers.[23]

Given the relatively late date of Franciscan missionization in California, levels of Spanish civilian settlement remained low compared to New Mexico and

Texas. Some civilians settled in towns in Los Angeles, San José, and what is now Santa Cruz, but most of the non-religious and non-Native inhabitants of California were soldiers associated with military presidios up and down the coast. As in other parts of northern New Spain, the Franciscans often did double duty, serving both the missions and the Spanish military and civilian outposts. Some of the presidios had chapels for religious services; the one at the presidio in Monterey eventually was selected as the site of the first cathedral in California. The growing impetus in New Spain to secularize all the missions on the northern frontier was felt in California, but no significant changes to the missions and their administration occurred until after Mexican independence. Eventually, most of the secularized missions were sold, and their lands were given to Mexican settlers.[24]

Religion in practice

Among the northern territories of New Spain, New Mexico stands out as the place of longest Spanish and Catholic settlement as well as the largest colonial population. During the founding decades of the territory, there were often dozens of Franciscans at work, both in missions to the Pueblos and in colonial towns. However, in the eighteenth century, the Spanish government began to scale back the scope of the missions by calling for their secularization and reducing their funding. Few new friars came to replace the aging Franciscans, and diocesan priests—despite the orders to secularize—were slow to arrive in remote New Mexico. A Catholic lay order arose to meet this shortage of official religious leadership. The name of the order, which continues into the present in New Mexico and southern Colorado, is the Fraternidad Piadosa de Nuestro Padre Jesús, or the "Pious Brotherhood of Our Father Jesus," more commonly known as the Penitentes.

The precise origin of the Penitentes is unclear—they may have evolved from the Third Order Franciscans, a lay organization that had been active in several New Mexican villages in the 1700s. The members of the Brotherhood gathered in simple buildings called *moradas* to transact their business and carry out their rituals. In partnership with women in the villages, Penitente brothers met a variety of secular needs: helping the poor and hungry, providing care to the sick, and maintaining order. Each chapter had an *hermano mayor*, or "head brother," who oversaw the brothers under his care as well as his local community. Other Penitente officers included the *celador*, "warden/discipline keeper"; *enfermero*, "medical caretaker"; *picador*, "bloodletter" during acts of penance; *rezador*, "prayer leader"; and *pitero*, "flute player" during ritual processions.[25]

In terms of religious practice, the Penitentes maintained a liturgical calendar of observance with particular focus on penitential practices during Lent—hence their name—in preparation for Holy Week and Easter. Outside observers have perhaps dwelt too much on their practices of self-flagellation, long pilgrimages through New Mexico's high desert, and even re-enactments of Christ's crucifixion. In fact, when Bishop Zubiría learned of the Penitentes, he condemned them for what he called their "butchery," and he commanded, futilely, that they be suppressed.[26] His and other opposition did force the Brotherhood to maintain secrecy for many years, but they remain active in many Nuevomexicano villages from Santa Fe to Taos.

Notes

1 Sharon R. Ennis, Merarys Ríos-Vargas, and Nora G. Albert, "The Hispanic Population: 2010" (U.S. Census Bureau, 2010), https://www.census.gov/prod/cen2010/briefs/c2010br-04.pdf.
2 John Frederick Schwaller, *The History of the Catholic Church in Latin America: From Conquest to Revolution and Beyond* (New York: New York University Press, 2011), 60.
3 Schwaller, 87–88.
4 "Act of Obedience and Vassalage by the Indians of San Juan Bautista" in George P. Hammond and Agapito Rey, *Don Juan de Oñate: Colonizer of New Mexico*, ed. George P. Hammond, vol. V and VI, Coronado Cuarto Centennial Publications, 1540–1940, (Albuquerque, NM: University of New Mexico Press, 1953), 344.
5 Benavides is quoted in Moises Sandoval, *On the Move: A History of the Hispanic Church in the United States* (Maryknoll, NY: Orbis Books, 1990), 14–15.
6 Ramón A. Gutiérrez, *When Jesus Came, the Corn Mothers Went Away: Marriage, Sexuality, and Power in New Mexico, 1540–1846* (Stanford, CA: Stanford University Press, 1991), 120–31.
7 Edward H. Spicer, *Cycles of Conquest: The Impact of Spain, Mexico, and the United States on the Indians of the Southwest, 1533–1960* (Tucson, AZ: University of Arizona Press, 1962), 163; Charles Wilson Hackett, *Historical Documents Relating to New Mexico, Nueva Vizcaya, and Approaches Thereto, to 1773*, vol. III, (Washington, DC: Carnegie Institution, 1937), 327–39.
8 Spicer, *Cycles of Conquest: The Impact of Spain, Mexico, and the United States on the Indians of the Southwest, 1533–1960*, 165–66.
9 Martha Weigle, *Brothers of Light, Brothers of Blood: The Penitentes of the Southwest* (Albuquerque, NM: University of New Mexico Press, 1976), 21–23. For a rosier assessment of the number of priests in colonial New Mexico, see Robert E. Wright, "How Many Are a 'Few'? Catholic Clergy in Central and Northern New Mexico, 1780–1851," in *Seeds of Struggle/Harvest of Hope: The History of the Catholic Church in New Mexico*, ed. Thomas J. Steele, Paul Rhetts, and Barb Awalt (Albuquerque, NM: LPD Press, 1998), 219–62.
10 Quoted in Weigle, 21–23.
11 William H. Donahue, "The Missionary Activities of Fray Antonio Margil de Jesús in Texas, 1716–1722," *The Americas* 14, no. 1 (1957): 47–53.
12 Thomas S. Bremer, *Blessed with Tourists: The Borderlands of Religion and Tourism in San Antonio* (Chapel Hill, NC: University of North Carolina Press, 2004), 20.
13 Bremer, 22–25.
14 Félix D. Almaráz, Jr., "San Antonio's Old Franciscan Missions: Material Decline and Secular Avarice in the Transition from Hispanic to Mexican Control," *The Americas* 44, no. 1 (1987): 2–4, 20.
15 Timothy M. Matovina, *Tejano Religion and Ethnicity: San Antonio, 1821–1860* (Austin, TX: University of Texas Press, 1995), 6; Timothy M. Matovina, *Guadalupe and Her Faithful: Latino Catholics in San Antonio, from Colonial Origins to the Present* (Baltimore, MD: Johns Hopkins University Press, 2005), 49–50. See also Gerald E. Poyo, "The Canary Island Immigrants of San Antonio: From Ethnic Exclusivity to Community in Eighteenth-Century Béxar," in *Tejano Origins in Eighteenth-Century*

San Antonio, ed. Gerald E. Poyo and Gilberto M. Hinojosa (Austin, TX: University of Texas Press, 1991), 41–58.

16 Thomas E. Sheridan, *Arizona: A History* (Tucson, AZ: University of Arizona Press, 1995), 30–31.

17 John L. Kessell, *Mission of Sorrows: Jesuit Guevavi and the Pimas, 1691–1767* (Tucson, AZ: University of Arizona Press, 1970), 32–33.

18 John Augustine Donohue, *After Kino: Jesuit Missions in Northwestern New Spain, 1711–1767*, Sources and Studies for the History of the Americas, VI (St. Louis, MO: St. Louis University, 1969), 139, 156.

19 Lisbeth Haas, *Saints and Citizens: Indigenous Histories of Colonial Missions and Mexican California* (Berkeley, CA: University of California Press, 2013), 5.

20 Alison Lake, *Colonial Rosary: The Spanish and Indian Missions of California* (Athens, OH: Swallow Press/Ohio University Press, 2006), 71, 83–84.

21 Steven W. Hackel, *Junípero Serra: California's Founding Father* (New York: Hill and Wang, 2013), 200, 206–7.

22 Steven W. Hackel, *Children of Coyote, Missionaries of Saint Francis: Indian-Spanish Relations in Colonial California, 1769–1850* (Chapel Hill, NC: University of North Carolina Press, 2005), 241–42.

23 Haas, *Saints and Citizens*, 86–89.

24 Lake, *Colonial Rosary*, 163.

25 This description of Penitente ranks comes from a nineteenth-century chapter constitution collected by a vocal critic of the Order. Alex M. Darley, *The Passionists of the Southwest, or the Holy Brotherhood: A Revelation of the "Penitentes,"* reprint ed. (Glorieta, NM: Rio Grande Press, 1968), 14–22.

26 Alberto López Pulido, *The Sacred World of the Penitentes* (Washington, DC: Smithsonian Institution Press, 2000), 41; Weigle, *Brothers of Light, Brothers of Blood*, 195.

4 Religion in the Mexican period

The Mexican Period referred to in the title of this chapter begins in 1821, when Mexico gained its independence from Spain, and ends in 1848, when the Treaty of Guadalupe Hidalgo was signed at the conclusion of the U.S.-Mexican War. As a result of that war, Mexico ceded vast portions of its territory to the United States, including most of California, Arizona, and New Mexico. The Mexican Period in Texas is shorter, as Texas gained its own independence from Mexico in 1836 before it was annexed into the U.S. as a state in 1845. While this period is little more than a quarter century, important changes in Mexican religion occurred during this time and reflect a sort of culmination of historical trends begun under Spanish rule.

The Spanish monarchs, through their proxy viceroys and other networks of control, had reigned over New Spain for three centuries. The Catholic Church, as an evangelistic force among Indigenous peoples and as a spiritual authority over the lives of all Spanish subjects, had been a partner in governance from the beginning. The relationship between "church" and "state" had not always been conflict-free, but for the most part, the people of New Spain, at every social class and of every ethnic background, would find that being Catholic and being a citizen were indelibly linked. Providing the legal structure for this linkage were the long-functioning mandates of the *Patronato Real*, which situated at least some administration of the Church in the hands of the Spanish monarchs. This long relationship between political and ecclesiastical governance helped to set the scene for Mexican independence and helps explain some of the Mexican north's vulnerability to Anglo-American encroachment.

Of course, it is well beyond the scope of this book to describe and explain all the causes and circumstances of the Mexican fight for independence and the founding of the nation of Mexico; the focus here will be on religious aspects of life in Mexico's first decades. And, as in previous chapters, most of the attention will be on Mexico's northern frontier. Given the immensity of the territory and the relative paucity of active clergy, Catholic officialdom in the north faltered during the Mexican Period. This hindered some kinds of religious practice and promoted other kinds of creative and civic religiosity among the people.

DOI: 10.4324/9780429285516-6

The Catholic Church and Mexican independence

In the years leading up to the revolution for Mexican independence, the Catholic Church was unquestionably the most powerful institution in Mexican society. Catholic and Mexican rhythms of life were almost synonymous, with the annual liturgical calendar of observances and celebrations setting the pace of life from villages to cities. Even the most humble priest in a rural parish possessed authority over the lives of his parishioners, young and old. The upper echelons of the clergy, bishops and archbishops, enjoyed not only extensive political influence but also significant wealth. In 1813, the Catholic Church owned 47 percent of the total value of all of Mexico's property. These vast holdings made the Church the landlord and lender for many citizens who paid rents and mortgages in addition to tithes.[1] The Catholic Church thus exercised influence on many levels of Mexican life from daily religious and civic observances to economic livelihood.

The vast wealth and influence of the Church, however, was hardly shared evenly throughout the secular and regular priests and nuns that made up the rank and file of local Catholic leadership. There were also national and ethnic divisions among the different strata of clergy. During the final years of New Spain, the combined annual income of the eight Mexican bishops and one archbishop was 539,000 pesos. In contrast, a village parish priest might earn only 120 pesos per year. The regular clergy in the missions generally received between 300 and 400 pesos, but this money was to be used for the maintenance of the missions as well as salary. In 1810, all but one of New Spain's bishops was a Spaniard; almost all local clergy were Mexican-born (criollos) as well as mestizos. As a result, four-fifths of criollo, mestizo, and Indigenous clergy supported the insurgency for independence against Spain and against the conservative Spanish upper echelon of the Church itself. In this context, it is not surprising that some of the most important revolutionary leaders in Mexico's struggle for independence were themselves priests, two of the most important being Father Miguel Hidalgo and Father José María Morelos. Indeed, the "Grito de Dolores" issued by Hidalgo on September 16, 1810, is considered the beginning of the revolution. Mexico finally won its independence from Spain in 1821.[2]

A major question that the new Mexican nation had to consider was what role the powerful and pervasive Catholic Church would play. During the centuries of Spanish rule, the Church had clearly held enormous power, accumulated wealth, and demanded respect and obedience at every level of society. Moreover, as noted in previous chapters, both tradition and the legal arrangements of the *Patronato Real* inserted the monarchy deep into Church affairs, with the result of entangling political and ecclesiastical authority. However, Mexican elites, like other elites around Latin America, had been profoundly influenced by the liberal ideals of the European Enlightenment, which, in part, called for curbing the power of authoritarian rule of monarchies and church leaders. These ideals helped spark the revolutions that were occurring throughout the Americas and in Europe. In highly Catholic Mexico, it would prove impossible to shunt the Church aside, and so the debate about ecclesiastical power there revolved around questions of influence over Catholic leadership and control of Catholic money.

More conservative forces during and after the fight for Mexican independence were content to continue to support the prominent position of the Catholic Church in Mexican society. Liberal voices likewise recognized the ongoing import of Catholicism for Mexico but were committed to checking Church power, principally by extracting Catholic wealth for the benefit of the new nation. Not surprisingly, the upper levels of Mexican Catholic clergy were sympathetic with the conservatives. In terms of the *Patronato Real*, Church leaders and conservative-leaning politicians argued that the *Patronato*, which was at heart an arrangement with the Spanish monarchy, had ended with independence, and its administrative powers had reverted to the pope in Rome. Only he, then, held ultimate authority over the direction of Mexican Catholicism. Ironically, the more liberal elements took what can be considered a "regalist" position in that they maintained that the rights of the *Patronato* formerly granted to the monarchy should transfer to the new, republican government. Specifically, they argued that the right to name bishops and to administer tithes for the funding of the Catholic Church should be under their purview as the new leaders of a constitutionally Catholic nation.[3]

For a brief period after independence, Mexico was ruled by Agustín de Iturbide, one of the fighters in the insurgency against Spain, who had declared himself the emperor of Mexico. But by 1823, he was deposed and sent into exile. For decades thereafter, Mexico's republican government bounced back and forth between conservative, more authoritarian presidents and liberal, more reform-minded leaders. The former generally supported an influential role for the Catholic elites, while the latter were more inclined to rein in the colonial-era excesses of the Church. But both sides never seriously questioned the Catholic identity of Mexico. This was codified into law with the Constitution of 1824, which declared unequivocally: "The religion of the Mexican nation is and will perpetually be the Roman Catholic Apostolic. The nation protects it with wise and just laws and prohibits the exercise of any other religion."[4] It was not until well after the U.S.-Mexican War and the cessation of most of northern Mexico to the United States (see Chapter 5) that the Mexican government would move away from its policy of explicit support for the Catholic Church.

The conservatives and liberals at the top of Mexico's government fought over the extent of the Catholic Church's power, but the reality for most Mexicans was that Catholicism continued to play an integral role in their lives. Priests sometimes oversaw this daily Catholicism, helping people celebrate rites of passage, such as baptisms, marriages, and funerals. Priests accompanied many in their quotidian struggles and celebrations, offering blessing and counsel. However, Catholicism imbued Mexican life in ways that had little need of priests. For example, children were named for saints, church bells provided the soundscape of marking time, and entertainments and celebrations accompanied frequent religious processions through village and city streets throughout the country. Reverence for the Virgin Mary was nearly universal, and the Virgin of Guadalupe gained immense popularity as a national symbol and caretaker. No foreign visitor would mistake Mexico for anything but a Catholic country.[5]

Independence on the northern frontier

The Mexican insurgency against Spain included proponents in Texas, including a revolutionary leader named José Bernardo Gutiérrez de Lara. The United States kept a close eye on the struggle for independence in the northern area, particularly Texas. After the Louisiana Purchase in 1803, the U.S. suddenly shared a long border with the Spanish Empire, and it was keen to maintain its control over the region. It soon became clear that, even in the first decades of the nineteenth-century, at least some in the U.S. had designs on Texas and other parts of what would soon be northern Mexico. President Monroe went so far as to offer Gutiérrez military assistance as long as the latter would agree to cede Texas to the territories of the Louisiana Purchase. Gutiérrez declined, but the episode set the stage for future Anglo-American efforts to acquire Texas.[6] With U.S. pressure from the east and revolutionary fervor rising from the south, various skirmishes broke out over Texas during the following decade, including several incursions of Anglo-Americans from the Arkansas Territory and naval battles along the Texan coast. Only in 1819 did Spain negotiate with the United States a hard border between their two territories at the Sabine River—rather than farther south and west in Texas. This line continues today to mark state boundaries between Texas and Louisiana.[7] However, as discussed below, the Sabine River border hardly kept Anglo-Americans from flowing into Mexican Texas after Mexico's independence.

Support for independence in New Mexico and California varied, and both regions saw little to no military activity during the years of the insurgency against Spain. If anything, Mexican settlements in these enormous territories became more precarious and open to attack from Native groups as Spanish forces were siphoned away to deal with the revolution. Moreover, Spain had long legally required that all trade in New Spain be concentrated in the imperial capital of Mexico City, with the result that goods from the northern territories had to be shipped long distances to the south. This meant that the entire northern region stood to make important economic gains from independence, as this would legalize and promote commercial activity with U.S. traders. After independence, the Santa Fe Trail quickly established an east-west trade route between Missouri and New Mexico, and trappers soon opened other trails to California. This commercial activity brought resources into the region, but it also served to weaken the northern frontier's connection to central Mexico.[8]

The fate of the missions

The Franciscan missions in New Mexico, Texas, California, and, to a lesser extent, southern Arizona, had been at the Catholic heart of northern New

Spain. To be sure, there was a smattering of presidio chapels and villa churches operated by secular clergy, but in many cases, even these were served by Franciscans until quite late in the colonial period. The ideal, however, had been for the friars eventually to work themselves out of a job, converting the Indigenous people to Christianity, and being replaced by dioceses and parishes served by bishops and diocesan priests. Spanish officials had promoted this vision as the government had more political and economic influence over the secular wing of the Church than over the more autonomous religious orders.

After Mexican independence, the push for secularization of the missions became even stronger for a number of reasons. First, many of the friars who remained in the northern missions were Spanish-born; as Spaniards, they chose or were forced to leave Mexico when Spain was defeated. Second, elements in the Mexican government—especially the liberals—were even more keen than the Spanish viceroys to exercise power over the Church and its resources. They desired to communicate Mexican independence from Spain by demonstrating control over the national church, and the precarious economic state of the new nation meant that access to Catholic resources was highly desirable. Finally, during the fight for independence, the Spanish government diverted the funds it had been sending to the missions to the war effort. This state of affairs continued after independence as the new nation's limited coffers were likewise used for other priorities.[9] In short, with few friars to continue to staff the missions, a government that coveted the Church's wealth, and a steep decline in funding, the secularization of the missions was accelerated.

In the San Antonio-area missions in Texas, partial secularization had begun in the 1790s, and the process was completed in 1824. Instead of replacing the mission priests with new recruits for the Diocese of Nuevo León, which covered Texas at the time, the missions' land was sold to the remaining residents as well as to other farmers in the nearby communities. By this time, there was little differentiation racially or ethnically between the Indigenous and mestizo populations of the region, and most citizens considered sale of the mission lands to be a boon for Texas's agricultural economy. The mission church buildings themselves still belonged to the Catholic Church, but they were unused for religious services. Most fell into ruin or were repurposed; for example, the Mission San Antonio de Valero was made into a military installation and renamed the Alamo.[10]

The much younger missions along the California coast, like the Texas missions, were secularized, but not until 1834, well into the Mexican period. The Franciscans were forced to cede the highly desirable coastal and agricultural land owned by the missions, but unlike in Texas, little of these properties reverted to Indigenous converts. In Texas, the slow process of *mestizaje* and assimilation of the Native people over decades had meant that mission lands, at least in part, were distributed to people with a measure of Indigenous heritage. The shorter duration of the mission period in California created a different situation with less incorporation of Indigenous people into the political economy of Spanish settlements. When the missions were finally secularized, the

Native inmates were mostly ignored, and the Mexican government granted the lands to upper-class Californians. The few Natives who remained near the missions were forced into peonage, changing in short order from religious neophytes to indentured laborers. Others returned to Indigenous-controlled lands to the east or sought their fortunes in Mexican towns. The mission churches themselves fell into disuse and ruin. In 1840, a priest wrote of the situation that, "All is destruction, all is misery, humiliation and despair."[11] In short, the Mexican period in California saw a decline in official Catholic presence and even greater levels of anomie and disenfranchisement of Native peoples.

New Mexico presented an entirely different religious environment during the Mexican period. In Texas, Arizona, and California, the regular clergy who organized the missions were laboring amid nomadic and semi-nomadic people, often drawn from dozens if not hundreds of language groups. The evangelistic strategy of imposing sedentary residential and economic patterns had to fight constantly against earlier ways of life. In much of New Mexico, the Franciscans' mission efforts were focused on Pueblos, who already gathered themselves in towns and agricultural settlements familiar to Europeans. This is not to say, of course, that the Pueblos posed no resistance to missionization—the Pueblo Revolt is but one marker of that resistance—but in general terms, the Franciscan mission model was a better fit in New Mexico than elsewhere on the northern frontier. Additionally, the Spanish and later Mexican population of New Mexico was substantially greater than in Texas, Arizona, or California, where European and Mexican populations remained in the low thousands. At the time of independence, the Mexican population of New Mexico was 42,000 and growing.[12]

Secularization of the New Mexican missions began in the late 1700s, but by 1820, only five secular priests were stationed there. More detrimental to the missions than the slow arrival of diocesan clergy was the steady decline in the number of Franciscans who were not being replaced as they aged and died. Of the few who remained, most were serving the growing non-Pueblo communities.[13] The number of secular clergy in New Mexico did grow in the Mexican period, but the era of Franciscan missions to the Pueblos had come to a close.[14]

Throughout the rest of Mexico's northern regions, the Catholicism of the missions and the scattered villa churches was under decline as Franciscans left or died, and few parish clergy came to take their place. Indigenous lands that had been stolen by the Church to create missions were parceled out to Mexican settlers, and mission church buildings sometimes fell into disuse and ruin. However, popular modes of Catholicism, sometimes inflected with Indigenous worldviews, continued to be an important feature of northern Mexican life. The official representatives of Catholicism were undoubtedly weakened during the Mexican period, but the religion of the people turned out to be a durable anchor in changing times. The following sections examine these changes and challenges in more detail in New Mexico and Texas.

Local-born clergy in New Mexico

Catholics in New Mexico, by the time of Mexican independence, were already used to scarce numbers of clergy. During the colonial era, almost all priests in the region were Franciscan missionaries, and some had been conscripted into duty as the leaders of non-mission churches in the *Nuevomexicano* towns. But this was not a long-term solution in terms of Catholic leadership; the missions had been legally secularized for years, and the Franciscan Order's long reign over New Mexican Catholicism was basically over. As discussed in Chapter 3, the Pious Brotherhood of Our Father Jesus, or the Penitentes, lent considerable religious stability to many New Mexican communities, as did day-to-day household observances of prayer and veneration of the saints. Oratories and chapels provided religious and community gathering places for the people, even if they rarely, if ever, received visits from ordained clergy.

New Mexico, in addition to its tradition of lively lay Catholicism, was also unique in northern Mexico in that its non-Native population produced a notable number of clergy during the Mexican period. In Mexico, the Diocese of Durango, which oversaw New Mexico, enjoyed fewer disruptions in leadership than many other Mexican dioceses. Due to this relative stability, Durango's seminary was able to continue to train and ordain priests throughout the 1820s, including several capable young men from northern New Mexico. One of these native priests ("native" in the sense of being from New Mexico rather than Native American) was Father Juan Felipe Ortiz, the scion of a wealthy Santa Fe family, who would go on to become the diocesan representative in New Mexico and later an important ally of Santa Fe's first bishop. Another was the famous Father Antonio José Martínez of Taos. Padre Martínez was a shrewd and ambitious man who, at times, was a staunch advocate for New Mexico's unique Catholic traditions.

Padre Martínez played a role in the increase of local secular clergy when in 1833 he was granted permission by the bishop to open a preparatory seminary in Taos to ready young men for more advanced study and ordination in Durango. Generally, Martínez would provide two years of basic education to his students before they would head south to complete their studies. While not every new priest in New Mexico matriculated from Martínez's seminary, many did, and between 1833 and 1845, eighteen local men were ordained and placed in parishes. Supplementing his influence on New Mexico and its Catholicism, Martínez also brought a printing press to the territory and produced religious textbooks for his students, catechisms, prayer books, and pamphlets in addition to a variety of other publications, including a newspaper.[15]

In 1833, Bishop Zubiría visited New Mexico from his seat in Durango, the first time a bishop had set foot in the territory for seventy years.[16] To be sure, local clergy considered this to be an honor, but the bishop's visit also occasioned some severe criticism of New Mexican Catholicism. Zubiría was dismissive of New Mexico's rich yet rustic religious art, which he labeled "misshapen" and commanded that the priests not bless such images and that the people not purchase them until they could be improved to the status of "moderately average" in appearance.[17] The bishop had even harsher words for the Penitentes, calling them a brotherhood of "butchery" due to their penitential practices, and he put them under a strict prohibition. Of course, the Penitentes, long used to autonomy from priestly oversight, took little notice of Zubiría's ban, and, significantly, Padre Martínez and other local clergy likewise did little or nothing to enforce the bishop's commands regarding New Mexican sacred art or the Penitentes.[18] It would be an exaggeration, perhaps, to say that local priests defied the bishop's orders, but it is clear that having local men in the priesthood allowed most popular religious customs to continue and even flourish.

Tejano Catholicism and Anglo–American settlement of Texas

Texas is, without a doubt, the area of northern Mexico that went through the greatest transformation after Mexican independence. The reason for this was that Emperor Agustín Iturbide, the first ruler of the independent nation of Mexico, negotiated and signed in 1823 an "Imperial Colonization Law" that permitted and promoted the establishment of Anglo-American immigrant colonies in Texas. After Iturbide was deposed, subsequent Mexican governments endorsed the law, which allowed thousands of settlers from the United States, Ireland, and other nations, to claim vast tracts of land in Texas and to establish new towns and cities. The colonists, most of whom were U.S. Anglos, agreed to become Mexican citizens, to conform their local governments to Mexican administrative forms, to pay taxes and tithes to Mexico, and to convert to Roman Catholicism, the state religion of Mexico.[19] Mexico's nascent government had compelling reasons to allow substantial Anglo colonization of Texas. Texas was sparsely inhabited by Mexicans, and large portions of the territory were under Indigenous control. Mexico reasoned that Anglo settlers could both "pacify" the Native peoples and create a buffer on the border with their powerful neighbor to the northeast, the United States. Another motivation was financial. The new nation required resources, and tax-paying immigrants would provide much-needed funds in the form of taxes. Colonists swore loyalty to Mexico and its customs and religion, and Stephen F. Austin, a leader among the Anglo Texans, was adamant about enforcing compliance to the strictures of the laws of settlement. Anglo colonization continued rapidly throughout the 1820s and 1830s. By 1836, there were over 30,000 Anglo settlers compared to only 3,470 Tejanos (Mexicans who lived in Texas at Mexican independence).[20]

The insistence that Anglo colonists convert to Catholicism influenced who would agree to settle in Texas—those who were very committed to their Protestant Christianity were unlikely to find this requirement acceptable and would therefore decline to emigrate. Colonists, then, were those who were either ambivalent about their religion, or who were sufficiently attracted by the economic promise of Texas that they were able to overlook this enforced change in their religion. For the most part, however, the conversions occurred on paper rather than in actual day-to-day life. Early in Anglo colonization, mutually beneficial marriage relationships were often contracted between upper-class Mexican women and Anglo men; in these cases, the husband's conversion often also led to considerable assimilation into Tejano society. Later on, when the Anglo population far surpassed the Mexican, Anglos had few opportunities to interact with Mexican Catholics at all, and the shortage of priests in Mexico, especially in the north, meant that many could go years with no interaction with Catholic clergy or worship. The long-term consequences of this was that when the Anglo Texans (with some Tejano allies) would later seek independence from Mexico, they quickly reverted to the Protestantism they had briefly left behind.[21]

Although outnumbered by Anglo colonists, most Tejanos continued to embrace the state Catholicism of Mexico. The largest Tejano city was San Antonio, long the site of many of Texas's most important Franciscan missions. In contrast to the Anglo settlements, which rarely if ever had contact with Catholic clergy, San Antonio had its own priest, Father Refugio de la Garza. This meant that Tejanos during the Mexican period were able to participate in the sacramental life of the Church—regular Masses, baptisms, marriages, and

Figure 4.1 San Fernando Cathedral, rear view, date unknown, by Ernest Wilhelm Raba (1874–1951). University of North Texas Libraries, The Portal to Texas History, crediting San Antonio Conservation Society.

funerals. At an even more pervasive level, public life in San Antonio was overtly Catholic, as it was in the rest of Mexico. Children's education in the grammar school was imbued with religious instruction. The school day opened and closed with prayer. Lessons in memorization featured portions of the Catholic catechism, the priest visited the school frequently to offer instruction and hear confessions, and students were required to attend Sunday Mass together as a mark of piety and good citizenship. Adult citizens in San Antonio likewise practiced a public and civic Catholicism. Special Masses and prayers marked holidays and other public observances. Town council meetings spent considerable time planning religious feasts and celebrations. Father de la Garza oversaw the observance of Mexico's Independence Day, September 15, with public addresses that promoted patriotism and religious devotion. In short, Catholicism and Mexican national identity were mostly undifferentiated among Tejanos.[22]

Religion in practice

Her devotion was already quite important during Spanish rule, but Our Lady of Guadalupe became a religious and national symbol after Mexican independence. People all over the new nation, including in the northern region, looked to Guadalupe as a guardian and mother of Mexico.

While historians argue about the dates and characters in the story, the legend of the Virgin of Guadalupe's appearance, or apparition, near Mexico City ostensibly goes back to 1531, only a decade after Cortés defeated the Aztecs. A poor, Nahuatl-speaking peasant named Juan Diego was traveling just outside the city when a brown-skinned young woman appeared to him, spoke to him in his own language, and directed him to tell the bishop that she desired that a church be built in her honor. Bishop Zumárraga, predictably, had no time for the Indigenous peasant, but Juan Diego persisted in his requests, encouraged by more apparitions of the Virgin. Finally, Mary filled Juan Diego's cloak, or *tilma*, with Castilian roses—foreign and out of season—and he brought these as a sign to Zumárraga. After Juan Diego emptied out the roses, all could see that the Virgin's image remained imprinted on the *tilma*. With this miracle, the bishop realized his folly in not believing Juan Diego sooner and ordered that, indeed, a church be built at the site to honor and venerate the Virgin of Guadalupe. Over the subsequent centuries, the Nahuatl-speaking, brown-skinned Mary would serve as an important driver of Indigenous evangelization throughout Mexico and beyond. Non-Indigenous groups in Mexico—criollos and mestizos—would also go on to adore and claim her as their own.[23]

Devotion to Our Lady of Guadalupe surged in San Antonio after Mexican independence. In fact, the insurgents against Spain had used her image on their banners, and for a short while in Texas, the Spanish governor, Manuel Salcedo, tried to limit celebrations around her December 12 feast day, acknowledging that her devotion was linked to Mexican self-determination. In the Mexican period, December 12 was a national holiday, which suited the people of San

Antonio well as the day had become the largest celebration of the year. The celebration included religious observances, such as processions, decorating the church, devotional singing, and saying the rosary. In the plaza outside the church, the people danced, feasted, and enjoyed other entertainments, such as bullfights and other spectacles. Historian Timothy Matovina notes that, although sources from the time period do not mention women's participation in the planning and execution of Guadalupan celebrations, this silence concerning women in the documentary record is not evidence of women's absence, but rather the result of gendered divisions in Texas's public life and historical memory. Later records prove that women took active leadership in many aspects of devotion to Our Lady of Guadalupe and celebration of her December feast day.[24] In later eras, Guadalupe would go on to become a symbol of empowerment for many Mexican American women.

Notes

1 Stanley C. Green, *The Mexican Republic: The First Decade, 1823–1832* (Pittsburgh, PA: University of Pittsburgh Press, 1987), 75; John Frederick Schwaller, *The History of the Catholic Church in Latin America: From Conquest to Revolution and Beyond* (New York: New York University Press, 2011), 103–4.

2 Lillian Estelle Fisher, *The Background of the Revolution for Mexican Independence* (New York: Russell & Russell, 1971), 217, 256; Green, *The Mexican Republic*, 73, 182; Ernesto de la Torre Villar, *La Independencia de México*, 2nd ed. (Mexico City: Editorial Mapfre/Fondo de Cultura Económica, 1992), 61, 85–86.

3 Michael P. Costeloe, *Church and State in Independent Mexico: A Study of the Patronage Debate, 1821–1857* (London: Royal Historical Society, 1978), 66.

4 "Constitución de 1824," *Texas Law: Tarlton Law Library*, accessed September 7, 2018, https://tarltonapps.law.utexas.edu/constitutions/mexican1824spanish/t1s1. My translation.

5 Green, *The Mexican Republic*, 72–73.

6 Carlos Castañeda, *Our Catholic Heritage in Texas*, reprint ed. (New York: Arno, 1976), VI:64, 86, 101.

7 Donald E. Chipman and Harriet Denise Joseph, *Spanish Texas, 1519–1821*, Revised (Austin, TX: University of Texas Press, 2010), 254.

8 David J. Weber, *The Mexican Frontier, 1821–1846: The American Southwest under Mexico* (Albuquerque, NM: University of New Mexico Press, 1982), 10–11, 125–35.

9 Weber, 44–46.

10 Gerald E. Poyo and Gilberto M. Hinojosa, eds., *Tejano Origins in Eighteenth-Century San Antonio* (Austin, TX: University of Texas Press, 1991), 82–83; Thomas S. Bremer, *Blessed with Tourists: The Borderlands of Religion and Tourism in San Antonio* (Chapel Hill, NC: University of North Carolina Press, 2004), 160 (n. 63); Weber, *The Mexican Frontier, 1821–1846: The American Southwest under Mexico*, 54–55.

11 Quoted in Weber, *The Mexican Frontier, 1821–1846: The American Southwest under Mexico*, 67.

12 Weber, 57, 195.

13 Weber, 59.

14 Robert E. Wright, "How Many Are a 'Few'? Catholic Clergy in Central and Northern New Mexico, 1780–1851," in *Seeds of Struggle/Harvest of Hope: The History of the Catholic Church in New Mexico*, ed. Thomas J. Steele, Paul Rhetts, and Barb Awalt (Albuquerque, NM: LPD Press, 1998), 219–62.

15 Fray Angélico Chávez, *But Time and Chance: The Story of Padre Martínez of Taos, 1793–1867* (Santa Fe, NM: Sunstone Press, 1981), 43–44, 48.

16 Fray Angélico Chávez and Thomas E. Chávez, *Wake for a Fat Vicar: Father Juan Felipe Ortiz, Archbishop Lamy, and the New Mexican Catholic Church in the Middle of the Nineteenth Century* (Albuquerque, NM: LPD Press, 2004), 29.

17 Zubiría's full comments can be found in Fray Angélico Chávez, *But Time and Chance: The Story of Padre Martínez of Taos, 1793–1867* (Santa Fe, NM: Sunstone Press, 1981), 41. My translation.

18 Chávez, 46–47.

19 The text of the Imperial Colonization Law can be found in Christopher B. Conway, ed., *The U.S.-Mexican War: A Binational Reader*, trans. Gustavo Pellón (Indianapolis, IN: Hackett, 2010), 1–6.

20 Handbook of Texas Online, "Census and Census Records," *TSHA*, June 12, 2010, https://tshaonline.org/handbook/online/articles/ulc01.

21 Howard Miller, "Stephen F. Austin and the Anglo-Texan Response to the Religious Establishment in Mexico, 1821–1836," *The Southwestern Historical Quarterly* 91, no. 3 (1988): 283–316; William Stuart Red, *The Texas Colonists and Religion, 1821–1836: A Centennial Tribute to the Texas Patriots Who Shed Their Blood That We Might Enjoy Civil and Religious Liberty* (Austin, TX: E. I. Shettles, 1924).

22 Timothy M. Matovina, *Tejano Religion and Ethnicity: San Antonio, 1821–1860* (Austin, TX: University of Texas Press, 1995), 18, 20–21.

23 The earliest written histories of this legend do not appear until the 1640s. See Luis Laso de la Vega et al., *The Story of Guadalupe: Luis Laso de La Vega's Huei Tlamahuiçoltica of 1649* (Stanford, CA: Stanford University Press, 1998); Stafford Poole, *Our Lady of Guadalupe: The Origins and Sources of a Mexican National Symbol, 1531–1797* (Tucson, AZ: University of Arizona Press, 1995). For more information on Guadalupe's resonance today among Mexican Americans, see Ana Castillo, *Goddess of the Americas = La Diosa de Las Américas: Writings on the Virgin of Guadalupe* (New York: Riverhead Books, 1996); Jeanette Rodriguez, *Our Lady of Guadalupe: Faith and Empowerment among Mexican-American Women* (Austin, TX: University of Texas Press, 1994).

24 Timothy M. Matovina, *Guadalupe and Her Faithful: Latino Catholics in San Antonio, from Colonial Origins to the Present* (Baltimore, MD: Johns Hopkins University Press, 2005), 58–60.

5 Religion and race

The U.S.-Mexican War and Mexican Americans

Only twenty-five years after Mexico won its independence from Spain, the growing United States entered into war with its young neighbor to the south. After the battles were over and the treaties signed, the northern half of Mexico was annexed by the U.S., immediately incorporating thousands of former Mexican citizens into new U.S. states and territories. The U.S.-Mexican War and its effects would have permanent repercussions for Mexican Americans.[1]

Above all, Mexican Americans, who had long been Spanish subjects, once again found themselves ruled by an imperial power, this time in the form of the expanding United States. It is not an exaggeration to say that Mexican Americans, with a brief interim of convulsive independence, moved from one colonial power to another. Indeed, with the U.S. victory over Mexico, the very notion of "Mexican American" was created, although the term itself did not come into common usage until later. Unlike other non-Native ethnic groups in the United States, Mexicans, at least at first, did not immigrate but were overtaken as the spoils of war. The initial chapters of this book have examined the religious lives of Mexicans in the New Spanish and Mexican north precisely because this heritage, as a result of the U.S.-Mexican War, is part of the continuous history of Mexican American religions.

This chapter explores the U.S.-Mexican War and its effects on Mexican American religion. Religious difference was one of the justifications for the war, as many Anglo-Americans were quick to define the conflict in terms of Protestant freedom against Catholic totalitarianism. The chapter looks at how the religious lines drawn in the war often created or reinforced perceived racial differences between Anglos and Mexicans, thus linking religion and race. A complex and often injurious outcome of the U.S. victory is that the Mexican residents of the annexed lands became religious minorities in a nation that purported to uphold religious toleration and freedom. In a matter of months, Mexican Catholics, whose religion had been roughly equated with citizenship, became Mexican American Catholics, a marginal population within a denomination often itself under attack for not being sufficiently "American." Nevertheless, many Mexican Americans found within their religious practice not only

DOI: 10.4324/9780429285516-7

spiritual sustenance but also a source of community cohesion in the face of racial and religious prejudice.

The U.S.–Mexican War

Several historians have provided accounts of the U.S.-Mexican War.[2] Here, a brief survey of the war and some of its causes is useful for understanding how religious concerns played a part in the conflict. While the U.S. was clearly the aggressor, it is important to remember that both nations and their respective political and economic contexts influenced the conflict.

Mexico's government had experienced almost no stability in the first decades of the nation's life. Competing elites, some with conservative and others with liberal tendencies, often violently clashed over the country's leadership; not counting the brief reign of Emperor Iturbide, Mexico was ruled by twenty different men in nearly fifty presidencies between 1823 and 1846. At issue were competing visions of Mexico's national identity and governance. On the one side were centralists who imagined a Mexico that was not dissimilar to New Spain. In their imagined nation, the government would work closely with the military and the Catholic Church to maintain concentrated power in the hands of elites. On the other side were the federalists who argued for a decentralization of power in Mexico. For these leaders, it was important that the states held more sway in national governance, even deploying their own militias. There were divisions among the federalists: a moderate faction continued to support at least some national alliance with the Catholic Church, and a more radical faction that wanted a secular nation, without the interference of the Church in political affairs. Between independence and the war with the United States, the presidency of Mexico bounced back and forth between centralists and federalists, not always peacefully. Various constitutions likewise were in force throughout this period, articulating different polities for the nation and making it difficult for the Mexican states to chart a clear course in terms of economic development, governance, and relationships with the Catholic Church. This was especially true in the northern region, which had already experienced long years of neglect under Spanish rule.[3]

Several forces at play in the U.S. raised tensions with Mexico. Above all, the 1845 annexation of Texas as a state intensified the relationship between the two nations. Anglo-Texans and their Tejano allies had successfully wrested Texas away from Mexico in 1836, declaring it an independent republic. However, the security of the Texas Republic against Mexican efforts to retake the territory depended in large measure on the United States, and the question of annexing Texas to the U.S. was on the table from the beginning, both in Texas and in Washington. Those elements of the U.S. government who supported annexation tended to do so in order to promote westward expansion and to increase the number of slave-holding states. Annexing Texas fulfilled both these desires. Journalist John O'Sullivan coined the phrase "manifest destiny" in 1845 in reference to the Texan annexation, and he was clear that the United States' sights were set not merely on Texas. He wrote,

> California will, probably, next fall away from the loose adhesion which, in such a country as Mexico, holds a remote province in a slight equivocal kind of dependence on the metropolis. Imbecile and distracted, Mexico never can exert any real governmental authority over such a country.[4]

Manifest destiny relied on the belief that Anglo-Americans, particularly white Protestants, had a superior civilization to that of the Mexicans and the Native people, and therefore were justified in their conquest of the western half of the continent.

Another driver of conflict was slavery. Many of the Anglo settlers in Texas brought enslaved people with them to work the land, even though Mexico had abolished slavery throughout its territory and was, on principle, opposed to slavery in Texas. Even though the Mexican government had done little to challenge the practice of chattel slavery in Texas, Anglo-American enslavers in Texas and in the U.S. South nonetheless sought Texas statehood to protect their slavery-dependent economic interests. And so, Texas was admitted to the union as a slave state amid protests from U.S. abolitionists and others in the northern states.

What finally initiated open war was an ongoing border dispute in Texas. During the years of the Texas Republic (1836–1845), Mexico and Texas never came to an agreement about the location of the border, the Texans claiming it was at the Rio Grande, and the Mexicans putting it at the Nueces River, more than a hundred miles to the north. The area between the two rivers was the site of various skirmishes, and there were even some Mexican attempts to retake San Antonio. The Texans and Mexicans had also fought over much of west Texas and the eastern half of New Mexico. In this context, one of the attractions of becoming a U.S. state was gaining the protection of the U.S. military to help settle these border disputes. Early in 1846, General Zachary Taylor stationed his troops on the Rio Grande across from the Mexican city of Matamoros, deep within the disputed territory. When Mexican forces attacked Taylor's installation, President James Polk was able to claim that Mexico had started the war by hostilely invading U.S. territory.

The war was lop-sided in that the United States won all major battles and was able to push the fighting into several regions of Mexico simultaneously. In addition to the forces in northern Mexico near Texas, the U.S. also sent large numbers of troops to the west through New Mexico and into California, where they claimed not only victory but also territory. The battles that decisively ended the war happened in central Mexico in 1847, when U.S. soldiers

PLUCKED :

THE MEXICAN EAGLE BEFORE THE WAR!   THE MEXICAN EAGLE AFTER THE WAR!

Figure 5.1 Plucked or, The Mexican eagle before the war! The Mexican eagle after the war!,
1847, Library of Congress, https://www.loc.gov/item/2002695264.

fought their way westward from where they had landed in Veracruz. In September, they captured and took control of Mexico City. It took some time to come to terms, but the Treaty of Guadalupe-Hidalgo was signed in February 1848, bringing an end to the U.S.-Mexican War. Mexico, which had already lost Texas a decade earlier, was forced to surrender the territory containing what is now the states of California, Nevada, Arizona, New Mexico, and parts of Colorado and Wyoming. Overtly religious consequences of the treaty are discussed in more detail below, but it should be clear that this transfer of land and people radically transformed both Mexico and the United States. The U.S. not only greatly increased its territory and achieved a truly transcontinental expanse, it also—by force of treaty—gained thousands of citizens who, until the war, had been Mexicans.[5]

U.S. anti-Catholicism and Mexican Catholic responses

Before discussing the aftermath of the U.S.-Mexican War and its consequences for Mexican American religion, it is important to recall the role that Anglo-Protestant anti-Catholicism played in the conflict. To be sure, manifest destiny and the slavery question were drivers of the war. However, another pervasive force that contributed to the rise of hostilities was a pernicious anti-Catholicism in the United States in the mid-nineteenth century, an anti-Catholicism that was rhetorically extended into the west as a struggle against the Catholic

Church. By the middle of the 1800s, Catholic immigration from Europe was radically changing the demographic landscape of the United States, and nativist fearmongers were warning of an anti-democratic Catholic totalitarianism that would destroy the nation. At times, their vitriol spilled into violence against Catholics.[6]

In 1835, the Presbyterian minister Lyman Beecher published *A Plea for the West*, an appeal for the quick and complete expansion of Protestant churches and Protestant people into the western half of the North American continent. He was spurred to write his *Plea* not so much because he feared the Catholicism of the Mexican lands to the west; indeed, he, like many of his contemporaries, seemed to imagine the American West as a land nearly devoid of both people and religion despite centuries of Spanish Catholicism and eons of Indigenous inhabitation. Rather, he worried that the waves of European Catholic immigrants entering from the east would roll through the United States only to conquer the west for the pope in all his anti-liberal tyranny. "The Catholicity of this nation, and its rapid increase, cannot be safely regarded as a mere insulated religion, but rather as one department of a comprehensive effort to maintain despotic government against the march of free institutions."[7] Beecher was hardly alone in his sentiments. Southern Protestants, especially Baptists, were the most active in opposing "popery" on the expanding western frontier. Other Protestant denominations were not quite as strident in their anti-Catholic rhetoric; nevertheless, nearly all church bodies helped fund a phalanx of missionary organizations whose purpose was to save the American west from what they considered to be the perils of "Romanism."[8]

Historian John Pinheiro argues that the nativist viewpoints of Lyman Beecher and his allies were a driving force behind the war between the United States and Mexico. What Pinheiro calls a "Beecherite synthesis" promoted an American Protestant norm as the bedrock of manifest destiny, denigrated Mexicans, and was a factor in army recruitment. In fact, argues Pinheiro, the anti-Catholicism of Beecher and his supporters was "the most effective tool Americans had to make sense of the war."[9] The call to make war against Mexican Catholics became a decisive symbol of Protestant nativist anxiety in a country being remade by Catholic immigrants.

In Mexico, before and during the war, there was explicit confidence that U.S. anti-Catholic nativism could create a decisive benefit for Mexico. Mexican authorities were conscious of the social and political divisions in the U.S. around the issue of European immigration and anti-Catholic riots and violence in northeastern cities. They were also aware of the fact that the U.S. army contained large numbers of immigrants, many of whom were Catholic. Even before the war officially started, Mexican General Pedro Ampudia circulated propaganda among U.S. troops gathered in Texas, calling for Europeans to desert to Mexico, where they would be welcomed.[10] The second round of Mexican propaganda came from General Santa Anna and focused much more precisely on the question of Catholic identity:

Can you fight by the side of those who put fire to your temples in Boston and Philadelphia? Did you witness such dreadful crimes and sacrileges without making a solemn vow to our Lord? If you are Catholic, the same as we, if you follow the doctrines of Our Savior, why are you seen murdering your brethren? Why are you antagonistic to those who defend their country and your own God?[11]

Whether due to this propaganda or for other reasons, hundreds of Catholic immigrants in the U.S. Army did desert to Mexico before and during the war.[12] Mexico's Catholicism thus helped spark the war and, in some ways, stoked anti-Catholic fervor within the United States. This hostility contributed to the difficult and sometimes dangerous environment for Mexican Americans after the war as they faced the challenges of suddenly living in the U.S.

The animosity against Catholics during the U.S.-Mexican War highlights the rampant nativism that was plaguing the nation during this era of immigration and expansion. A feature of this nativism was to racialize many European Catholic immigrants as a non-white, inferior race; Mexican American Catholics absorbed into the growing nation faced these pressures even more acutely.

Figure 5.2 Mexican rulers, migrating from Matamoras with their treasures, ca. 1846, F. & S. Palmer, Library of Congress, https://www.loc.gov/item/2003689270. Notice the priest accompanying the other "Mexican rulers" out of Texas.

Many Anglo-Protestants linked Mexican Americans' Catholicism and their mestizo identity to denigrate them as racially deficient and intrinsically unable to integrate into a democratic republic like the United States. The Mexican press was particularly sensitive to racial attitudes in the U.S. and often argued that such attitudes posed a serious threat to Mexico. In 1844, a reporter for *El Siglo Diez y Nueve*, a Mexican newspaper, wrote sardonically that U.S. politicians were committed in their own minds "to exterminate the odious Spanish race along with their detestable Papal religion, and seize the effigies of gold and silver from the churches which they profaned with their superstitions."[13] American Protestants often referred to Mexicans and Mexican Americans as a "mongrel race" and "medieval." Centuries of Catholic rule had ostensibly removed all their initiative and desire to better themselves.[14] While some Anglo Protestants felt that Mexicans could be rehabilitated, others felt that they were forever incapable of democratic self-determination.

European Catholic priests who entered Texas after its annexation to the U.S., while obviously not opposed to the Catholic identity of their Mexican American parishioners, nonetheless often regarded them as uncivilized and docile children in need of societal and religious reform. For example, a French priest named Emmanuel Domenech, despite speaking no Spanish at all, was stationed at a Mexican American parish near Brownsville, Texas, in 1851. His initial impressions of his flock convinced him that he must dispel their "ignorance, superstition, indifference, and immorality." He was particularly offended by their Catholic folk rituals, which had developed in areas long neglected by Spanish and Mexican clergy. He found "religious views to be modified and ceremonies to be purified from every heterogeneous alloy opposed to the solemnity of Catholic worship." Ultimately, he grew to enjoy the company of his Mexican American congregation due to their humble, charitable, and pliable nature, though his good opinion was couched in an enduring paternalism: "I soon perceived that there was a means of taming and bending all these different natures, half savage and wholly ignorant though they were."[15]

The Treaty of Guadalupe-Hidalgo and "freedom of religion"

The Treaty of Guadalupe-Hidalgo, which ended the U.S.-Mexican War in 1848, did make some provisions for the Mexican inhabitants of the conquered territory. However, in most cases, Anglo settlers generally found ways to roll back or ignore the legal protections and rights guaranteed to Mexicans in the treaty. For instance, in Article VIII of the treaty, Mexican inhabitants of the annexed lands were granted U.S. citizenship as well as property rights for the properties they owned, but the U.S. government struck out Article X, which had given more explicit property protections to Mexicans. This act foreshadowed decades of litigation and land grabs that caused much of Mexicans' properties to be taken by white settlers.[16] Chapter 6 discusses this in more detail, but U.S. authorities likewise did not always respect Mexican Americans' citizenship.

The treaty's protection of religious freedom is consistent with the rest of the language in the document in that it reflects U.S. values but leaves room for interpretations that are not entirely helpful for Mexican Americans. Article IX guarantees to Mexicans in the captured lands "the free exercise of their religion without restriction."[17] On its surface, this appears to be the extension of one of the bedrock rights granted in the Constitution to all U.S. citizens and residents, namely, that no law shall either establish the dominance of one religion or prohibit the "free exercise" of all religions. And, indeed, the Treaty of Guadalupe-Hidalgo, consistent with the First Amendment of the U.S. Constitution, ensured the religious freedom of Mexican American Catholics. This protection was an important and positive acknowledgment of Mexican Americans' rights to their religious traditions.

At the same time, the treaty did away with the Catholic establishment in the conquered lands, meaning that, for the first time since the Spanish Conquest, the Catholic Church in the region was forced to contend with Protestant newcomers. It would be misleading to suggest that this was a level playing field with open religious competition; while the United States had no state church, in contrast to Mexico, Protestantism had long held immense political and social power. As U.S. settlers, many of whom were Protestants, entered the former territories of Mexico, they moved to establish Protestant churches and to evangelize Catholic Mexicans. In the meantime, the vanishingly small number of Mexican Catholic clergy that had been in the region either headed south to stay in Mexico or had to accommodate themselves to the oversight of the U.S.

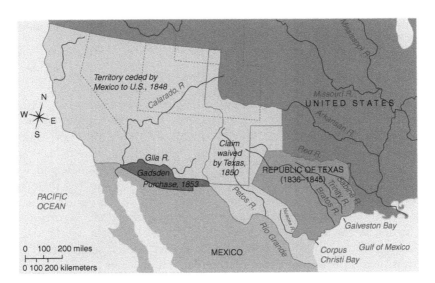

Figure 5.3 Mexican territories transferred to the United States in the 19th century.

Catholic Church. In both cases, Mexican American Catholics soon found themselves in a new religious environment, rife with Protestant prejudice and competition and new non-Mexican clergy who often did not respect their unique Catholic traditions.

Mexican Americans in the U.S. Catholic Church in the wake of the U.S.-Mexican War

The Catholic Church has always been a global church in the sense that the pope and his administration ultimately oversee Catholicism in every place in the world.[18] Yet, the Church operates within national boundaries, meaning that the Catholic hierarchy in a particular country is responsible for the care and oversight of Catholics within its national jurisdiction. Therefore, when much of Mexican territory was transferred to the United States as a result of the U.S.-Mexican War, Catholicism and Catholics in the region were affected by the remapping of dioceses to respect the new international boundary. New bishops and priests were assigned to newly formed U.S. dioceses and parishes and charged with seeing to the needs of all Catholics, including Mexican Americans, in these new states and territories.

In some ways, this was a positive development for Mexican Americans in that the Mexican Catholic Church had not always been able to provide adequate numbers of priests to the far-flung towns and villages of Mexico's far north. The Spanish missions to the Native peoples of the region were in general decline, or even abandoned, and the Mexican Church lacked the resources to meet these challenges. On the other hand, the new priests, for the most part, were unacquainted with and looked down on the Catholic traditions of Mexican Americans, oftentimes spoke no Spanish, and focused much of their efforts on European American Catholic settlers. In short, Mexican American Catholics quickly found themselves marginalized in their own land.

Texas

The annexation and statehood of Texas in 1845 helped precipitate the U.S.-Mexican War, and in some ways Texas served as a pattern for the eventual U.S. takeover of much of the rest of northern Mexico. A key difference in Texas was that Anglo-American settlement in the area had numerically dwarfed the Tejano population for several years. In 1849, Texas had approximately 200,000 inhabitants, of whom only 10 percent were Catholic. Many of these were Mexican Americans who lived in and around the Tejano city of San Antonio, though European Catholic immigrants, especially Germans, had also settled in the state.[19]

During the time of the Republic of Texas, the Vatican stationed a French priest named Jean Marie Odin in San Antonio to take charge of Texan Catholics. Once the first diocese in Texas was formed in 1847 in Galveston, Odin took over there as its first bishop. In San Antonio, Odin dismissed the last two remaining Mexican priests for corruption and ineffectiveness, an act which did not seem to bother resident Tejanos, perhaps due to the priests' Mexican nationalism. Odin made efforts to learn Spanish and instructed that all new priests in the area do the same. He participated in Tejano Catholic festivities in San Antonio, including the important celebration dedicated to Our Lady of Guadalupe. Until U.S. statehood, the Tejano and Anglo government in San Antonio helped plan and sponsor this event, and it was celebrated throughout Texas in both Tejano and Anglo communities as an emblem of pan-Texas heritage. After statehood, the city government stepped out of a planning role in this religious festival, but it continued as a popular religious and communal occasion.[20]

Tejano Catholics' religious observances, such as the Guadalupan celebration, had long existed seamlessly with public life. The Catholic establishment in Mexico—and New Spain before that—meant that there was no enforced division between religious and civic activity. On top of that, the frequent shortage of priests in the north often meant that laypeople practiced their religion as a community with an emphasis on traditions and cooperation rather than doctrinal purity. The Anglo Protestant majority in Texas often found this kind of religious practice to be superficial and not sufficiently rooted in pious reflection. One Protestant observer noted,

> Every Mexican professes to be a Catholic and carries about his person the crucifix, the rosary, and other symbols of the mother church. But religion with him, if one is permitted to judge the feelings of the heart by outward signs, is more a habit than a principle or feeling.[21]

The new Catholic clergy arriving from the U.S. and Europe sometimes agreed with the Protestants. A French priest whose Mexican American parish was near Brownsville, said,

> The ceremonies of the Church used to borrow from time and place certain peculiar features to which those people attached great interest and importance. It is much easier to go to church and join a procession than to reform one's life.[22]

Despite their deep-seated Catholic traditions, Tejanos thus had to contend with detractors both inside and outside of their church.

California

Perhaps the single most important event in nineteenth-century California was the discovery of gold at Sutter's Mill in January 1848, a month before the Treaty of Guadalupe-Hidalgo was signed. Elite Mexican Californians, or Californios, owned large portions of California's fertile land, which should have remained legally protected under the provisions of the treaty. However, as thousands of miners and other migrants flooded into the territory to establish mines and mining towns, Californios and Natives often found themselves treated as foreign minorities and pushed aside. Anglo and other immigrant populations soon far outnumbered Mexican American communities in the San Francisco Bay area and Los Angeles.

The first two bishops assigned to the U.S. state of California were Spaniards, Joseph Sadoc Alemany in the northern half of the state and Thaddeus Amat, who oversaw Santa Barbara, Los Angeles, and other parts of southern California. Alemany seems to have had a fair amount of sympathy and support for his Mexican American flock, providing them with Spanish-speaking priests. In 1875 he organized Our Lady of Guadalupe parish in San Francisco, a Spanish-language national parish, as a result of a community-sponsored petition. Things were not so welcoming in Amat's diocese. He made frequent negative comments about the "superstition" of Mexican American Catholics, and he actively suppressed folk religious practices related to healing and rites of passage. He joined with Protestant leaders to condemn Mexican American religious and civic festivals and focused his energies on the Anglo Catholic population. In many areas, Mexican Americans ceased regular Mass attendance, and as their communities became more and more segregated and impoverished, they had fewer opportunities to participate meaningfully in their ancestral Catholic faith.[23]

New Mexico

The U.S. political takeover of New Mexico, which occurred mid-war in 1847, was followed quickly by the transfer of Catholic oversight from the old Mexican diocese of Durango to a newly formed jurisdiction. The U.S. Catholic Church placed in charge a French missionary priest, Jean Baptiste Lamy, and French missionaries would remain in control of New Mexico's Catholic Church until well into the twentieth century. Lamy himself was named bishop and then archbishop of Santa Fe as the Vatican recognized the importance and size of the existing Nuevomexicano Catholic population. However, many of the priests sent to serve the new diocese, like Lamy, were foreign missionaries and did not always understand or accommodate the local customs of New Mexico's Catholics.

As mentioned in earlier chapters, much of northern New Mexico had long relied on the lay ministry of the Fraternidad Piadosa de Nuestro Padre Jesús, or Penitentes. The Penitente brothers, along with their families, ensured that popular Catholic liturgies were observed and saw to the material and spiritual needs of many in the villages of the region. Local Nuevomexicano clergy, such as Padre Martínez of Taos, understood the Penitentes and collaborated with them, and Martínez held it as a point of pride that he was the official chaplain to the Penitentes prior to the U.S. takeover. However, his relationship with the Penitentes had already begun to slip prior to the change in regime when, in 1837, a group of northern rebels linked with the Penitentes assassinated the

Mexican governor and declared an autonomous New Mexican government. Martínez's support of the Mexican government put him at odds with many laypeople. Church pressure against the Penitentes rose considerably after Lamy's arrival. Lamy, like Bishop Zubiría of Durango before him, opposed the harsh penances and self-directing nature of the Penitentes and issued decrees to bring the group under ecclesiastical control.[24]

Besides trying to reign in the Penitentes and their erstwhile supporters in the New Mexican clergy, Lamy also gained control over Nuevomexicano Catholicism by flooding his diocese with foreign priests and nuns. At the end of his career in 1885, Lamy had placed 114 French priests in the diocese, which comprised three fourths of all the clergy. He also brought in an order of nuns from Loretto, Kentucky, to establish and operate Catholic schools around the territory. Despite these efforts to impose a new order of Catholic oversight on New Mexico, he ended his tenure frustrated that he had made little headway against the Penitentes and other local Catholic customs.[25]

In summary, the transfer of territory from Mexico to the United States had sudden and lasting effects on Mexican American religious life. The Catholic customs of Mexican Americans in the region had been, in many ways, indistinguishable from civic life. Local government officials in conjunction with clergy or lay organizations often oversaw public religious processions and celebrations. Mexican citizenship and Catholicism were intertwined. While U.S. authorities guaranteed religious freedom to the Mexican American Catholics in the captured territories, they also curtailed the generations-old traditions of public, state-sponsored Catholicism. On top of this official relegation of Mexican American Catholicism to the edges of public life, anti-Catholic nativism combined with racial prejudice against Mexicans also meant that Anglo Protestants often sought ways to denigrate and suppress Mexican Americans' faith traditions. Unfortunately, some Anglo Catholics—including new clergy— joined in criticizing Mexican Americans' popular traditions, branding them as "superstitious" and backwards. Mexican Americans, in response, often embraced anew their religious practices as vital mechanisms to help them maintain their ethnic and religious identity in a new country where they were suddenly minorities. What had been the religion of the state became an important tool for many Mexican Americans to mark and celebrate their heritage.

Religion in practice

Historical archives open a window onto the past, but they can also obscure in that they often contain little or no record of certain kinds of people and their activities. In reading historical documents about the U.S.-Mexican War—and what historians have written using these documents—one could conclude that women were largely absent, not only from the major moments in the conflict but from the affected territory. This is also true of religious history, with its focus on male Catholic clergy, male debates concerning church and state, and mostly male lay organizations. Finding women in the story and discovering how religion was part of women's lives, therefore, is a crucial challenge.

Historian Amy Porter pored through dozens of Mexican women's wills to open a window onto how women lived in northern Mexico in the mid-nineteenth century. She discovered that, in addition to owning houses and other valuable goods, women so valued their religious items that they often mentioned them specifically in their wills, leaving them to loved ones and giving instructions for their use. Women in northern Mexico, including New Mexico and Texas, were far more likely to list images and statues of saints in their wills than were men; in Santa Fe, for instance, 56 percent of women mentioned their saints in their wills, while only 17 percent of men did. Most popular among these images were Our Lady of Guadalupe, images of Christ, John Nepomucene, Saint Anthony, and Saint Francis. In addition to the mention of saints' images, women also left money in their wills for charitable and religious causes, including for the maintenance of churches, public religious images, masses for the souls in purgatory, and for canonization proceedings.[26]

The wills also reveal information about women's religious activities during their lives by their explicit mention of their participation in devotional societies. Given the importance of Franciscan missions throughout the northern region of Mexico, it is not surprising that many women gave evidence of Franciscan devotion. This is most clear in that large percentages of women in Texas and New Mexico left instructions that they should be buried in the habit of the Third Order Franciscan, a lay order that was popular throughout the area. In Santa Fe, an astounding 78 percent of women in the wills that Porter studied requested burial in the Third Order Franciscan habit. These requests declined somewhat after the forced secularization of the missions, but the wills make clear that this kind of devotionalism did continue at least for a time after the Franciscans were no longer in power.[27] Porter concludes that, in their wills, "borderlands people, and especially women, reveal that their spiritual concerns were a major part of their lives and not always distinct from mundane affairs." She finds that the wills show that women followed the "gender ideals" of New Spanish and Mexican Catholicism, "which instructed them to be pious, devout, obedient, and models and instructors of spirituality to their children." But, they also reveal that women clearly stepped outsides the confines of their homes to practice their religion, supporting public charities, and participating actively in community and church organizations.[28]

Notes

1   This book joins other scholars and refers to the conflict as the "U.S.-Mexican War" rather than the "Mexican-American War" or, as it was for many years, simply the "Mexican War." The latter minimizes the binational nature of the war. The more common "Mexican-American War" invites confusion with the ethnic signifier "Mexican-American," which is a term for people, not war.

2 For example, see Peter Guardino, *The Dead March: A History of the Mexican-American War* (Cambridge, MA: Harvard University Press, 2017); Amy S. Greenberg, *A Wicked War: Polk, Clay, Lincoln, and the 1846 U.S. Invasion of Mexico* (New York: Alfred A. Knopf, 2012).

3 Timothy E. Anna, *Forging Mexico: 1821–1835* (Lincoln, NE: University of Nebraska Press, 1998).

4 Quoted in Christopher B. Conway, ed., *The U.S.-Mexican War: A Binational Reader*, trans. Gustavo Pellón (Indianapolis, IN: Hackett, 2010), 53.

5 The full text of the Treaty can be found at "Treaty of Guadalupe Hidalgo; February 2, 1848," The Avalon Project, Yale Law School, accessed April 30, 2019, http://ava lon.law.yale.edu/19th_century/guadhida.asp.

6 Maura Jane Farrelly, *Anti-Catholicism in America, 1620–1860* (Cambridge: Cambridge University Press, 2018); Jenny Franchot, *Roads to Rome: The Antebellum Protestant Encounter with Catholicism* (Berkeley, CA: University of California Press, 1994).

7 Lyman Beecher, *A Plea for the West* (Cincinnati, OH: Truman & Smith, 1835), 145.

8 Ray A. Billington, "Anti-Catholic Propaganda and the Home Missionary Movement, 1800–1860," *The Mississippi Valley Historical Review* 22, no. 3 (1935): 380–82.

9 John C. Pinheiro, *Missionaries of Republicanism: A Religious History of the Mexican-American War* (New York: Oxford University Press, 2014), 66.

10 Edward S. Wallace, "The Battalion of Saint Patrick in the Mexican War," *Military Affairs* 14, no. 2 (1950): 85.

11 Quoted in Michael Hogan, *The Irish Soldiers of Mexico*, rev. ed. (Guadalajara, Mexico: Fondo Editorial Universitario, 2011), 156.

12 The St. Patrick's Battalion is the most famous example of these Catholic deserters fighting for Mexico. See Robert Ryal Miller, *Shamrock and Sword: The Saint Patrick's Battalion in the U.S.-Mexican War* (Norman, OK: University of Oklahoma Press, 1989); Peter F. Stevens, *The Rogue's March: John Riley and the St. Patrick's Battalion, 1846–48* (Washington, DC: Potomac Books, 2005).

13 *El Siglo Diez y Nueve*, May 13, 1844, quoted in Gene M. Brack, *Mexico Views Manifest Destiny, 1821–1846: An Essay on the Origins of the Mexican War* (Albuquerque, NM: University of New Mexico Press, 1975), 122.

14 Robert W. Johannsen, *To the Halls of the Montezumas: The Mexican War in the American Imagination* (New York: Oxford University Press, 1985), 166–67.

15 Emmanuel Domenech, *Missionary Adventures in Texas and Mexico: A Personal Narrative of Six Years' Sojourn in Those Regions* (London: Longman, Brown, Green, Longmans, and Roberts, 1858), 222, 249–50.

16 Conway, *The U.S.-Mexican War*, 127–28.

17 "Treaty of Guadalupe Hidalgo; February 2, 1848."

18 A caveat is that there are some Catholic groups that do not align themselves with the papal hierarchy. See Julie Byrne, *The Other Catholics: Remaking America's Largest Religion* (New York: Columbia University Press, 2018).

19 José Roberto Juárez, "La iglesia católica y el chicano en sud Texas, 1836–1911," *Aztlán: A Journal of Chicano Studies* 4, no. 2 (1973): 222.

20 Timothy M. Matovina, *Tejano Religion and Ethnicity: San Antonio, 1821–1860* (Austin: University of Texas Press, 1995), 41–45, 52.

21 Quoted in Matovina, 40.

22 Domenech, *Missionary Adventures in Texas and Mexico*, 260.

23 Jeffrey M. Burns, "The Mexican Catholic Community in California," in *Mexican Americans and the Catholic Church, 1900–1965*, ed. Jay P. Dolan and Gilberto M. Hinojosa (Notre Dame, IN: University of Notre Dame Press, 1994), 134–37.

24 Alberto López Pulido, *The Sacred World of the Penitentes* (Washington, DC: Smithsonian Institution Press, 2000), 42–43; Martha Weigle, *Brothers of Light, Brothers of Blood: The Penitentes of the Southwest* (Albuquerque, NM: University of New Mexico Press, 1976), 53–54.

25 Nancy Hanks, *Lamy's Legion: The Individual Histories of Secular Clergy Serving in the Archdiocese of Santa Fe from 1850 to 1912* (Santa Fe, NM: HRM Books, 2000), xiii; Brett Hendrickson, *The Healing Power of the Santuario de Chimayó: America's Miraculous Church* (New York: New York University Press, 2017), 89–90.
26 Amy M. Porter, *Their Lives, Their Wills: Women in the Borderlands, 1750–1846* (Lubbock, TX: Texas Tech University Press, 2015), 77–79, 82.
27 Porter, 74–75.
28 Porter, 84–85.

6 Mexican migration and the Catholic Church, 1880–1940

Mexico and the United States ratified the Treaty of Guadalupe-Hidalgo in 1848, ceding extensive Mexican territory to its northern neighbor. This was followed up with the Gadsden Purchase in 1854 that added Tucson and the southern portions of Arizona and New Mexico to the United States, thus finalizing the current border between the two nations.[1] However, it would be incorrect to assume that the new border suddenly became a hard and impassable line. To be sure, it took many decades before border crossing was significantly monitored. Even today, the U.S.-Mexico border remains one of the most frequently crossed international boundaries on earth. Of course, the United States and Mexico, since the U.S.-Mexican War, have developed as two independent nations, but Mexican migration to the U.S. has meant that one of the largest ethnic minority populations in the United States is Mexican Americans, and a great number of Mexican Americans live in territories of the U.S. that were formerly parts of Mexico.

During the second half of the nineteenth-century and the first decades of the twentieth-century, the relatively open border allowed the U.S. West and Southwest to continue to maintain strong cultural ties to Mexico even as many Anglo-Americans limited Mexican Americans' political and social inclusion and empowerment. Nonetheless, factors in both Mexico and the U.S. meant that northern migration brought thousands of Mexicans across the border in this period. On the one hand, this influx of Mexicans kept Mexican Catholic traditions alive in the United States in ways that provided meaning and coherence to Mexican American life. On the other hand, as in previous eras, the U.S. Catholic Church often did not always do enough to welcome and include Mexican American Catholics into parish life. This period, then, was marked by massive Mexican migration, a growth of Mexican American Catholicism in numeric terms, and rampant prejudice against and exclusion of Mexican Americans that often extended into the U.S. Catholic Church.

Patterns of migration after the U.S.-Mexican War

In 1848, there were approximately 80,000 Mexicans living in the territories ceded to the U.S. after the war.[2] Only in Texas had there been significant

DOI: 10.4324/9780429285516-8

Anglo-American settlement, but the conclusion of the war opened the entire region to large numbers of U.S. migrants. The famous gold rush in California attracted thousands of newcomers from around the globe, swelling the population and creating scores of new towns and cities. The period after the U.S.-Mexican War was likewise one of increased immigration from Mexico as Mexicans sought out new opportunities in these formerly Mexican lands. By the turn of the century, there were over 103,000 Mexican-born immigrants living in the United States. That number increased to over 640,000 by 1930 and the onset of the Great Depression.[3]

Scholars who study human migration often talk of "push" and "pull" factors. The former are motivations to leave one's homeland, while the latter are the forces of attraction to a new destination. For Mexicans, political upheaval and lack of economic opportunity in Mexico constituted the principal reasons for leaving for the north. In the United States, Mexicans were attracted by the promise of work, relative stability, and educational opportunities for their children. Of course, leaving one's family and country of origin to enter a new land where Mexicans were often the targets of racial prejudice and economic oppression mitigated the decision to emigrate. Historian Gilbert G. Gonzalez has noted that such a "push-pull" analysis can obscure international forces of economic and political imperialism; considering only push and pull factors can make it seem like immigration is a "win-win" situation when, in fact, global economic inequities and explicit strategies of labor exploitation have sparked much migration between Mexico and the United States.[4]

It is nevertheless helpful to mention some of the most important events and forces that propelled thousands to seek new opportunities in the United States. One is the Chinese Exclusion Act of 1882. Anglo-American fear and racial animus toward East Asian immigrants to the American West sparked this legislation, which, as its name suggests, put strict limits on immigration from China. An unintended consequence of this was labor shortages that favored Mexican immigration.[5]

Conditions in Mexico also contributed to northern migration. During the long rule of the general and strongman Porfirio Díaz, whose presidency ran from 1876 to 1911, economic developments changed the face of Mexican labor. Vast tracts of land in Mexico were held and worked communally by Indigenous and mestizo peasants. Díaz ordered the privatization and sale of these lands, transforming the agricultural workforce of the nation into indentured servants of wealthy landowners, or moving them out of agricultural work into growing Mexican industries. In both cases, wages and living conditions often plummeted, and in northern Mexico, there were reported labor shortages as many laborers simply left to work and live in the United States.[6]

During this time period of growth of the Mexican population in the United States as well as rapid settlement of the region by Anglo-Americans and others, Mexican and Mexican American Catholics continued to find support for their community in their religious traditions. Official representatives of the U.S. Catholic Church responded in varied ways to these traditions, sometimes embracing them and the Mexican American population, and at other times rejecting or ignoring Mexican American Catholicism. Women's religious orders spread through the region to operate ministries of education and social care. While many of these nuns were Irish immigrants, others were Mexican and Spanish, and, in both cases, often spent long hours working for and among Mexican Americans. Western and Southwestern cities with significant Mexican American populations continued to stage public festivals for their patron saints, with many locales celebrating Our Lady of Guadalupe.[7] Mexican American priests in the region likewise worked to welcome Mexican newcomers.

There were also instances of pushback and repression. Bishop Lamy in Santa Fe made various efforts during his tenure to limit the activities of New Mexico's famous Penitentes. He also found himself frequently at odds with Mexican American priests over questions of discipline and tradition, especially those priests who predated Lamy's own arrival in New Mexico.[8] In 1881, near the end of his career, Lamy wrote a letter to his Vatican overseers bemoaning the deficiencies of his Nuevomexicano flock. He lamented, "Our Mexican population has quite a sad future. Very few of them will be able to follow modern progress. One cannot compare them to the Americans on the grounds of intellectual liveliness, know-how, and industry."[9] His deprecatory attitudes, unfortunately, were not unique. Not long after he arrived at his new post in Los Angeles, Bishop Thaddeus Amat suspended the remaining Franciscans for "fomenting superstition," which, in this case, meant supporting the folk religious customs of the Mexican Californians.[10]

The Mexican Revolution and Mexican immigration

Porfirio Díaz's long regime had already led to the displacement of many people in Mexico, thousands of whom had migrated to Mexico's lost territories in the U.S. After the turn of the century, forces of opposition gathered against Díaz, seeking not only to oust him from power but to change the course of the nation. The events and actors of the Mexican Revolution, as Díaz's ouster came to be called, set the course for the modern nation of Mexico. They also sparked lasting constitutional changes that would sharply limit the public role of the Mexican Catholic Church. As earlier chapters have noted, the Catholic Church in Mexico, depending on the regime, had often enjoyed oligarchical control over much of the country alongside other elites, and new limits on the Church were met with joy by some and indignation by others. The upheaval concerning the Catholic Church eventually broke into open conflict in parts of Mexico—the Cristero Rebellion—and hundreds of Mexican priests fled to the United States for their own safety.

Decades of relative peace in Mexico—enforced by President Díaz's might—began to unravel in 1910 when a wealthy northerner, Francisco Madero, issued a political challenge and call for elections. Those who had suffered under the strenuous changes of Díaz's rule, particularly the rural poor, soon joined Madero and other revolutionary leaders to topple the dictator, which they accomplished in late 1911. However, the government in Mexico City quickly fell into a violent chaos that extended through 1917 when a new constitution was drafted and a mostly orderly system of presidential succession was put in place.

The years of the Mexican Revolution were catastrophic for many Mexicans. Violence rolled across the country as various armed factions vied for supremacy. With all the upheaval, agriculture was near impossible, and food production plummeted, leading to starvation, disease, and looting. In this context, emigration was one of the only ways to escape the national crisis. As violence started to wind down in Mexico, there arose more and more need in the United States for Mexican labor. In 1917, the U.S. entered World War I, thus creating an immediate need for immigrant workers as many U.S. men left for war. Internal migration in the U.S., at the same time, was pulling many workers in the West and Southwest to higher-paying industrial jobs in the North. What started as a steady but relatively small stream of Mexican migration during Díaz's regime turned into a flood of hundreds of thousands in the 1910s and 1920s.[11]

The Cristero Rebellion

Even from the time of Mexican independence, liberal elites in Mexico's government called into question the pervasive power of the Mexican Catholic Church. Later in the nineteenth century, after a civil war (1857–1860), the liberals gained definitive power and passed extensive legislation greatly limiting the role of the Catholic Church in public life. A series of laws and a new constitution divested the Church of many of its properties, did away with ecclesiastical courts, and restricted the fees that priests could charge for services rendered. Unlike earlier constitutions, this one made no provision for the Catholic Church as the state religion of Mexico.[12] When Porfirio Díaz took power in 1876, he did not overturn these anticlerical laws but neither did he enforce them. This allowed him to maintain a level of personal control over the Church, as it depended on Díaz's good will to continue relatively unchecked.

Díaz's departure from power and the Mexican Revolution preceded the Mexican Constitution of 1917, a highly anticlerical document that greatly curtailed the Catholic Church's public activities, nationalized Church property, banned religious orders, and allowed federal and state governments to control many Church affairs. Post-Revolution leaders, like Díaz before them, did not apply these laws systematically to the Catholic Church. However, when President Plutarco Calles (1924–1928) came to power, his anticlerical tendencies prompted him to enforce the Constitution, which sparked a backlash from many Catholic clergy and laypeople throughout the nation.[13] Open war broke out between the Calles government and Catholic militants in 1926 and continued through 1929 when a truce was reached. This conflict, known as the Cristero Rebellion, or Cristero War, took the lives of 90,000 people and further weakened Mexico's economy.[14] The war also bolstered the already brisk migration of Mexicans to the United States. Historian Julia Young has called this the "Cristero diaspora," which included "tens of thousands of labor emigrants, more than two thousand exiled priests and nuns, numerous members of the Mexican [Catholic] hierarchy, and dozens of middle-class lay political activists."[15]

These religious refugees had a role to play in the United States among Mexican Americans. The U.S. Catholic Church received the exiled clergy as something of a boon to the growing ranks of Mexican and Mexican American Catholics and placed many Mexican priests and nuns in Mexican American parishes. The National Catholic Welfare Conference (NCWC) handled the logistical and financial task of resettling the exiles in churches and communities across the country, not only in the border region. Chicago's growing Mexican American population benefited significantly from the sudden influx of Mexican clergy, as did Detroit, Milwaukee, and several other Midwestern cities.[16]

As early as 1925, during President Calles's crackdown on the Mexican Catholic Church, the NCWC in the United States got heavily involved in advocating for Mexican Catholics. The NCWC's general secretary, Fr. John Burke, began a multifaceted protest movement that included appeals to President Coolidge in Washington, a publicity campaign, and the organization of protest rallies among U.S. Catholic laypeople. After some initial reticence, Coolidge's secretary of state, John Kellogg, lodged official protests with the Mexican government concerning the treatment of Catholics and the curtailing of religious liberty in Mexico.[17] In 1926, U.S. bishops issued a pastoral letter to all Catholics in the United States calling for support for their co-religionists in Mexico. They wrote that it was necessary "to show our deep sympathy with the suffering people of Mexico in the persecution now raging in that country." They noted that Mexico was "our neighbor" and

> a republic which it was intended should be modeled on lines similar to ours, and a nation with a Christian population whose devotion to the Catholic Church makes a special call upon the charity of the faithful everywhere, but more especially those of the United States.[18]

That the United States served as a refuge for Mexican Catholic clergy and laypeople in the 1920s is ironic and complex. As Chapter 5 described, Mexicans' Catholicism was a significant driver of the U.S.-Mexican War, and after annexation, the U.S. Catholic Church often shunted Mexican American Catholics to the edges of parish and diocesan life. This, of course, was one of myriad ways that Mexican Americans, in the decades after the war, were disenfranchised as a racial and cultural "other." Despite all this, several factors created a situation wherein the U.S. would serve as a haven for fleeing Cristeros. First, the legal and cultural traditions of religious toleration in the U.S.—though not consistently applied—in this case worked in the favor of Mexican religious refugees. Second, as noted above, the U.S. Catholic Church had a great need for more Spanish-speaking clergy and thus were able quickly to resettle the Mexican priests. Leaders like

Figure 6.1 Priests returning from Los Angeles to Mexico, July 5, 1929, in Julia Young's personal collection. Courtesy Julia Young.

Fr. Burke, deeply moved by the plight of their Mexican counterparts, worked assiduously to welcome the Mexican priests. Third, the anti-Catholic nativism of the nineteenth century in the U.S. had subsided somewhat by time of the Cristero War. On the Mexican side, the second half of the nineteenth century saw a decisive anti-clerical turn, which was expressed in a series of laws and constitutions that greatly limited the public exercise of Catholicism. When this combined with an already robust stream of Mexican emigration to the United States, oppressed Catholic clergy and devout laypeople joined their compatriots in the journey to the north.

The Great Depression, repatriation, and deportation

Conditions in Mexico and the ongoing need for labor in the United States kept rates of Mexican immigration high throughout the 1920s, in spite of growing anti-immigrant sentiment and legislation. Severe restrictions on Asian immigration had already occurred, and in 1924, Congress passed the Johnson-Reed Act, which imposed national quotas on many southern and eastern European immigrants. No such quotas were put in place on the nations of the Americas, and the need for inexpensive labor was accentuated by the legislation. This meant that Mexican immigration continued apace during the decade, despite the Johnson-Reed Act's insistence that the United States was, racially, a "Nordic" nation. The Act established the Border Control, but in its initial permutation, it had little to do with stopping the flow of Mexican immigration.[19] In effect, Mexicans and Mexican Americans, though they escaped racial quotas in this round of legislation, remained a highly exploited and exploitable underclass of laborers. The guarantees of citizenship and land rights expressed in the Treaty of Guadalupe-Hidalgo were, for the most part, defunct.

The onset of the Great Depression in 1929 led quickly to the end of the open border between the U.S. and Mexico. As an underclass with few legal protections, Mexican and Mexican American workers were some of the first affected and hardest hit by the economic crisis. They were scapegoated throughout the Southwest and California for not only taking jobs from "Americans," but also for creating the crisis in the first place. Congress passed yet another immigration act in 1929, this time making it a felony to enter the U.S. unlawfully; the law put in place the legal mechanism to begin deporting thousands of Mexicans and other immigrants. Depression-era Los Angeles was an epicenter of anti-Mexican rhetoric and violence due to the high concentrations of Mexican Americans in southern California. City police officials ramped up a scare campaign against Mexicans that included harassment and sweeps in Mexican American neighborhoods. Tens of thousands of people fled to Mexico "voluntarily," while many others were deported. By 1935, over 340,000 people had been deported or repatriated to Mexico. Tragically, in California over 80 percent of the people repatriated were Mexican American citizens or legal residents of the U.S. Many of these people had never lived in Mexico at all.[20]

The National Catholic Welfare Conference, which had been an active voice in support of the Mexican Catholic Church during and after the Cristero War, again stepped in to assist with advocacy for Mexican and Mexican American Catholic families that had been separated during the repatriation. According to historian Zaragosa Vargas, the deportations were catastrophic for many families when U.S.-born children were left behind or in some other way removed from their parents during sweeps. Vargas notes that a Mexican American named Cleofas Calleros, who was working with the Bureau of Immigration of the National Catholic Welfare Conference, was instrumental in helping reunite families in the 1930s. Calleros's advocacy convinced immigration officials to expand what proofs of residency and employment they would accept to let deported and repatriated Mexicans and Mexican Americans back into the U.S.[21]

Mexican American Catholics in U.S. Catholic parishes

To summarize, changing conditions in both Mexico and the United States in the second half of the nineteenth century and first few decades of the twentieth propelled Mexican migration to the U.S. in a steady stream that gained strength during and after the Mexican Revolution. With the exception of the Cristero Rebellion, which explicitly moved Catholics from Mexico across the border, little has been said so far in the chapter about what it was like to be a Mexican

American Catholic in the United States. Even though most Mexicans settled in lands that had been, for centuries, part of Spanish America, they nonetheless had to confront a new reality where they were "double minorities" in a country still dominated by white Protestants. This section fills in this gap by focusing on several examples of Mexican American Catholic experiences in this period in Texas and California. To be sure, experiences of Mexican Americans in other regions, especially those outside of the border states, varied somewhat from the following examples, but these cases provide a general overview of day-to-day Mexican American Catholic life before and after the turn of the last century. The examples discussed below focus on Texas and California, but Mexican immigrants made their way well beyond the border region, including large numbers to the Midwest and South. For instance, a great number of Mexican laborers worked in both mining and agriculture in the Mississippi Delta.[22]

Prior to the major uptick in Mexican immigration to the U.S. after the Mexican Revolution, the biggest demographic shift in much of the American West and Southwest was the arrival of Anglo-Americans and other European immigrants, who were pouring into the region on newly completed railroads. The U.S. Catholic Church dedicated itself in these years to providing priests and building churches for the Anglo migrants while, at the same time, maintaining at least some attention to Mexican American Catholics. Los Angeles is one of the cities where white Americans and European immigrants soon outnumbered the Mexican American inhabitants. In the 1880s, Los Angeles's population more than quadrupled, and it doubled in the 1890s, bringing the total population to more than 100,000. During this time period, the Mexican American population moved from around 2,000 to as many as 5,000. To keep up with this influx, the Diocese built several new churches and schools for non-Mexican American Catholics. This did not mean that Mexican Americans were neglected necessarily. La Placita parish, the traditional Mexican American congregation in the city, continued to flourish, and a new daycare and educational center was built in 1897 for Mexican American children.[23]

The Daughters of Charity, an order of nuns, were active in Los Angeles at this time and led many of the educational and charitable outreach efforts of the diocese. Most religious charitable organizations at the time, both Protestant and Catholic, spent considerable energy on immigrant communities in Los Angeles including Mexicans, Japanese, and a variety of southern and eastern European groups. The paradigm they followed was that of "Americanization," or helping immigrants to adopt English and what they considered to be typical American customs. Catholic leaders, including Bishop Cantwell in Los Angeles, supported Americanization but were aware that this model held the potential to promote Protestantism over Catholicism as more essentially "American." In this context, the Daughters of Charity were on the frontline of serving Catholic immigrants, helping them acculturate and yet remain Catholic. Mexican Americans who required charitable services in Los Angeles soon came to prefer working with the Daughters of Charity—rather than with Protestant groups like the Salvation

Army—because the nuns supported their Catholicism. After the Mexican Revolution, the families of several Mexican elites relocated to Los Angeles after their displacement in Mexico. The daughters of some of these families came together under the nuns' guidance and formed *Las Señoritas de la Caridad*, or "Young Ladies of Charity." Engaging specifically with poor Mexicans and Mexican Americans, the Señoritas taught catechism, worked in a Catholic orphanage, provided direct financial assistance, and socialized with one another.[24]

In El Paso, the situation was somewhat different. While the city also experienced Anglo settlement, the Mexican American population remained at or above half the total population in the final decades of the nineteenth-century. El Paso, significantly smaller than Los Angeles, had been the home of St. Mary's, a Catholic church building shared by all Catholics in the city. Due to rising numbers of Anglo and Mexican American residents, two new churches were built in 1893 to serve, separately, the English- and Spanish-speaking residents, Immaculate Conception and Sagrado Corazón, respectively.[25] As in Los Angeles, the Catholic Church in El Paso did not end their efforts to serve Mexican Americans but most certainly diversified their attention to accommodate English-speaking newcomers (and sometimes German- and Italian-speaking Catholics as well). Historians have debated how much this change in the Church's focus was a sensible response to demographic realities or a way to separate and sideline Mexican Americans from U.S. Catholic life.

Figure 6.2 Façade of the Parroquia del Sagrado Corazón, El Paso, Texas. Courtesy Sacred Heart Parish.

The establishment of national parishes in Texas and elsewhere—that is, parishes that served specific ethnic and linguistic communities rather than a geographic area—did not necessarily lead to equal treatment for Mexican Americans. Mexican Americans' low economic and social location, combined with racial animus, often meant that the "Mexican Church" was the only place where Mexican Catholics were welcome. Historian Roberto Treviño notes that Mexican American Catholics in Houston were often denied entry to Anglo Catholic churches or forced to sit in back pews. Separate congregations for Mexican Americans was one strategy for addressing what Catholic leaders called "the Mexican problem"—the perceived need to serve Mexicans as Catholics while lamenting their poverty, backwardness, and slowness to assimilate. Even those Catholic clergy who were sympathetic with their Mexican American flocks found it near impossible to avoid paternal attitudes and language when referring to "our poor Mexicans." The Spanish-language national parishes, in this context, often served as a mechanism for segregation. Treviño concludes, "The structures of the Catholic Church [in the 1910s and 1920s] replicated Mexican subordination in American society."[26]

In California, a successful strategy to care for the wave of Mexican immigrants was the mission church, not to be confused with the evangelistic missions of the Franciscans and other orders discussed in earlier chapters. In terms of organization, a mission is normally dependent on a parish, but in practice, many Mexican missions operated like stand-alone parishes, sometimes with their own priest. For example, the parish church of St. Boniface in Orange County founded four separate mission chapels to minister to Mexicans in the 1920s when they recognized that the rural areas of the county had experienced a massive influx of Mexican laborers. In other cases, Anglos showed little tolerance for Mexican worshipers in their parish, which led to the creation of a mission in order to keep Mexicans out of the parish church. Despite these occasional tensions, founding missions was a successful strategy. Historian Jeffrey Burns attributes this success to three factors. First, Mexican missions made it possible for Mexicans and Mexican Americans to practice their Catholicism in ways that were congruent with their traditions. Many missions, for instance, were named for Our Lady of Guadalupe or other saints popular in Mexico. Second, due to widespread poverty among Mexican and Mexican American communities, the missions enjoyed the financial support of the wider Catholic Church. Dependency on another parish, of course, could create its own problems, but this support allowed many missions to flourish. Finally, an honest assessment of the past reveals that Anglo racism often made missions necessary. Mexicans and Mexican Americans were simply not welcome in many Anglo parishes, and the establishment of Mexican missions made segregation possible. This created safe refuges for Mexican American Catholics but also served as a reminder of their "less than" status in the United States.[27]

Religion in practice

Many Mexican American Catholics, following long Mexican traditions, pray the rosary. The rosary, of course, is in no way limited to Mexican Americans, but it holds a special significance for them when prayed as a ritual marker of ethnic solidarity and community togetherness. The rosary itself is string of beads or knots that are used to mark off particular prayers and holy mysteries. The beads are grouped into "decades" of ten small beads and one larger one; the smaller beads represent one saying of the Hail Mary while the larger bead is for the Lord's Prayer. This gives the devotion a Marian quality, which is to say, it emphasizes devotion to Mary, Jesus's mother. When the rosary is prayed in community, it is often done so antiphonally, where a leader or a small group says part of the prayer, and the others gathered complete the prayer.

At the turn of the century, Mexican Americans, especially women, prayed the rosary together for various reasons, including to intercede with Mary for their families, to grieve the dead, and to sanctify the times and places in which they lived. Livia León Montiel was born in 1914 outside Tucson, Arizona, into an Arizonan family that predated the U.S.-Mexican War. In her childhood household, both her father and mother were devout Catholics, and her father made sure that the whole family prayed the rosary together every night. This tradition remained important to León Montiel throughout her life, and she prayed the rosary daily with her own children until they were in college. She admits that, when she was a young person, her father's faith sometimes seemed fatalistic to her.

> I remember, when I was in my teens, getting impatient with my father because everything was "God's will." "Si Dios dirá; Si Dios lo manda." But when you get older you realize that some things you can control and some things you can't.[28]

Catholic traditions, like the daily rosary, helped her find strength in life that was rooted in the rituals of her faith and her family.

A contemporary of León Montiel's in Tucson was Socorro Félix Delgado. She also prayed the rosary daily with her family, an experience she remembers with candor.

> My grandmother had a special devotion to the rosary, and we used to pray the rosary every night, on our knees. And after the rosary she prayed to each and every saint whose picture she had up there on her wall. So when she would say, "Let's pray the rosary," I used to think, "Oh, no!" because it would take forever! And we had to stay on our knees. If we dared to squirm or slouch she would give us "that look"—straighten up, keep still, stay quiet.[29]

Félix Delgado recalled that the rosary had an important role to play on other occasions as well. It preceded prayers and songs on the night of Christmas Eve, but above all, it provided comfort and structure to the act of mourning during a wake. Her grandmother was known in their community as a gifted leader of prayers for the dead. She would often be called out to assist with the praying the rosary and other intercessions during a deceased loved one's *novenario*, or the nine days of prayer that followed the death. The repeated and Marian prayers of the rosary, in this way, tied many Mexican American families together, empowered women's religious leadership in the home and community, and helped ease the pain of death.[30]

Notes

1 For a full history of the boundary line between the two nations, see Rachel St. John, *Line in the Sand: A History of the U.S.-Mexico Border* (Princeton, NJ: Princeton University Press, 2011).

2 Richard L. Nostrand, "Mexican Americans Circa 1850," *Annals of the Association of American Geographers* 65, no. 3 (1975): 378–90.

3 Migration Policy Institute, "Mexican-Born Population Over Time, 1850–Present," migrationpolicy.org, August 14, 2013, https://www.migrationpolicy.org/programs/data-hub/charts/mexican-born-population-over-time.

4 Gilbert G. Gonzalez, "Mexican Labor Migration, 1876–1924," in *Beyond La Frontera: The History of Mexico-U.S. Migration*, ed. Mark Overmeyer-Velázquez (New York: Oxford University Press, 2011), 30.

5 Erika Lee, "The Chinese Exclusion Example: Race, Immigration, and American Gatekeeping, 1882–1924," *Journal of American Ethnic History* 21, no. 3 (2002): 45.

6 Friedrich Katz, "Labor Conditions on Haciendas in Porfirian Mexico: Some Trends and Tendencies," *The Hispanic American Historical Review* 54, no. 1 (1974): 1, 36, n. 106.

7 Timothy M. Matovina, *Latino Catholicism: Transformation in America's Largest Church* (Princeton, NJ: Princeton University Press, 2012), 30–31.

8 See Fray Angélico Chávez and Thomas E. Chávez, *Wake for a Fat Vicar: Father Juan Felipe Ortiz, Archbishop Lamy, and the New Mexican Catholic Church in the Middle of the Nineteenth Century* (Albuquerque, NM: LPD Press, 2004); Fray Angélico Chávez, *But Time and Chance: The Story of Padre Martínez of Taos, 1793–1867* (Santa Fe, NM: Sunstone Press, 1981).

9 Quoted in Frances Margaret Campbell, "American Catholicism in Northern New Mexico: A Kaleidoscope of Development, 1840–1885" (Graduate Theological Union, 1986), 97.

10 Jeffrey M. Burns, "The Mexican Catholic Community in California," in *Mexican Americans and the Catholic Church, 1900–1965*, ed. Jay P. Dolan and Gilberto M. Hinojosa (Notre Dame, IN: University of Notre Dame Press, 1994), 135.

11 Timothy J. Henderson, *Beyond Borders: A History of Mexican Migration to the United States* (Malden, MA: Wiley-Blackwell, 2011), 22–25.

12 John Frederick Schwaller, *The History of the Catholic Church in Latin America: From Conquest to Revolution and Beyond* (New York: New York University Press, 2011), 146–47.

13 Julia Grace Darling Young, *Mexican Exodus: Emigrants, Exiles, and Refugees of the Cristero War* (New York: Oxford University Press, 2015), 23–25.

14 Henderson, *Beyond Borders*, 27.

15 Young, *Mexican Exodus*, 7.

16 Young, 42–51.

17 Richard Gribble, "Roman Catholicism and U.S. Foreign Policy, 1919–1935: A Clash of Policies," *Journal of Church and State* 50, no. 1 (2008): 84, 86.

18 Quoted in Gribble, 89.

19 Henderson, *Beyond Borders*, 41–42.

20 Henderson, 45; Zaragosa Vargas, *Crucible of Struggle: A History of Mexican Americans from Colonial Times to the Present Era* (New York: Oxford University Press, 2011), 218–20.
21 Vargas, *Crucible of Struggle*, 220.
22 Julie M. Weise, *Corazón de Dixie: Mexicanos in the U.S. South since 1910* (Chapel Hill, NC: University of North Carolina Press, 2015), ch. 2.
23 Robert E. Wright, "Mexican-Descent Catholics and the U.S. Church, 1880–1910: Moving Beyond Chicano Assumptions," *U.S. Catholic Historian* 28, no. 4 (2010): 86–87.
24 Kristine Ashton Gunnell, "The Daughters of Charity as Cultural Intermediaries: Women, Religion, and Race in Early Twentieth-Century Los Angeles," *U.S. Catholic Historian* 31, no. 2 (2013): 52–53, 60–61.
25 Wright, "Mexican-Descent Catholics and the U.S. Catholic Church," 91.
26 Roberto R. Treviño, *The Church in the Barrio: Mexican American Ethno-Catholicism in Houston* (Chapel Hill, NC: University of North Carolina Press, 2006), 87.
27 Burns, "The Mexican Catholic Community in California," 163–66.
28 Patricia Preciado Martin, *Songs My Mother Sang to Me: An Oral History of Mexican American Women* (Tucson, AZ: University of Arizona Press, 1992), 19–20.
29 Martin, 61–62.
30 Martin, 67–68.

7 Mexican American Protestants

So far, this book has focused almost exclusively on the historical development of Mexican American Catholics. But, starting in the nineteenth century, concurrent with the United States' western expansion, Protestant forms of Christianity began to make inroads into some Mexican American communities. Since then, Protestantism, especially its evangelical and Pentecostal variations, has grown steadily and sometimes rapidly among Mexican Americans and other Latinos/as. Recent surveys indicate that the percentage of the Latino/a population that is Protestant is growing. In 2007, 19 percent of Latinos/as identified as some type of Protestant. By 2014, that figure had risen to 22 percent, and some estimates suggest that the numbers of Protestant Latinos/as will continue to grow.[1] (Significant numbers of Latinos/as are also leaving both Catholic and Protestant Christianity for other religions or no religion at all, a topic that is covered in Chapter 13.) While these data discuss Latinos/as without separating out Mexican Americans, it is clear that major shifts are underway in the religious orientation of many Latinos/as, including Mexican Americans.

To understand why Protestantism has appealed to some Mexican Americans, it is important to note some of the essential differences between Catholic and Protestant Christianity. Protestant denominations—discrete historical and theological divisions within Protestantism—began to separate from the Roman Catholic Church in Europe in the early sixteenth century. Protestant reformers demanded a variety of changes in Catholic worship, theology, and leadership. Typically, Protestants have privileged Bible reading and Bible study as authoritative guides to community life over and against long-standing Catholic Church traditions. In many cases, they have challenged the hierarchical clergy structure of the Catholic Church in favor of more localized leadership and empowerment of the laity. Protestants have emphasized personal piety and private experiences of salvation over Catholic sacramental notions of salvation centered in the ritual life of the Mass. Unlike the mostly unified Catholic Church, Protestants have divided easily into thousands of branches and churches. In recent centuries, Protestant zeal for missionary activity has posed a challenge to Catholic missionaries in largely non-Christian regions as well as in countries that formerly were characterized by a near monopoly of the Catholic Church. This latter scenario has reshaped Latin America, with some countries, such as Guatemala and Brazil, moving toward Protestant majorities.[2]

DOI: 10.4324/9780429285516-9

To switch from one religion to another is freighted with meaning and social consequences. Mexican Americans in the United States who have switched to Protestantism, either in the past or today, almost always have done so after first being Catholic. Children of converts who remain Protestant nonetheless do so in extended families that include Catholics. The United States, a country that was founded by Protestants, has a history of anti-Catholic oppression and a culture that is deeply influenced by Protestantism.[3] In this context, to switch to Protestantism from Catholicism can simultaneously alienate one from one's Catholic family and help to integrate one with perceived U.S. Protestant norms. As is discussed below, this integration, however, has not been complete for many Mexican American Protestants as they struggle to gain equity in Protestant denominations and congregations, where white leaders have not always made room for non-white newcomers.

Mexican American Protestants, like other Protestants in the United States, fall principally into three overlapping groups: members of mainline denominations, evangelicals, and Pentecostals. The latter two groups are the subject of Chapter 8. This chapter explores the history of mainline Protestantism among the Mexican American community and discusses the sometimes tense dynamics of religious switching within families. Tensions also developed within Protestant denominations when Mexican American converts and their descendants encountered race- and class-based barriers to their full participation and integration.[4] Over time, Mexican Americans have made their own place at the Protestant table, though the mainline denominations remain, by some measures, the least attractive Protestant religious home for Mexican Americans.

Protestant missions in the American West

Concerns about the growth of Roman Catholicism in the United States was one of the motivating factors of the U.S.-Mexican War (see Chapter 5). When the conflict was over, missionaries poured into the newly acquired territory to ensure the continued hegemony of Protestant Christianity. The missionaries' primary focus was split between converting (and therefore, in their minds, civilizing) Native American tribes and providing religious guidance and churches to the hurly-burly western Anglo settlements. But, many Protestants also found in the Mexican American population a worthy target of proselytism, thereby putting themselves in direct competition with the U.S Catholic Church that simultaneously moved into the region.

Political and military control of the new territory was critical to the task of integrating new states and territories into the U.S., but Protestant missions also played an important role. Native and Mexican American conversion to Protestantism was seen as an essential component of "Americanization."[5] For some, the very facts of the U.S. victory over Mexico in 1848 and the immediate discovery of gold in California signaled a divine plan for the spread of Protestantism. One missionary wrote in 1853, "Why, Sir, did God preserve this whole country more than a century after its discovery, for the English race, turning the foot of the Spaniard to the sunny regions of the tropics?" He continued, "why were the immense treasures of California hidden from all the world, even from the keen-scented Spaniards, until she was annexed to this Republic? ... Is it possible not to see the hand of God in all this?"[6] In this sense, Protestant expansion was a potent ingredient of manifest destiny.

Protestant missionaries who entered formerly Mexican lands realized that the Mexican Americans they encountered were Catholics from birth, but the missionaries' low regard for both Catholicism and Mexican American religiosity motivated them in their proselytism. In his 1902 history of Presbyterian home missions, Sherman Doyle wrote of New Mexico: "The people are ignorant, superstitious, and fanatical." He noted with contempt that the Spanish Catholics had had three centuries to make good Christians of the people of New Mexico, "yet when Protestant missionaries entered, it was to find the people living in darkness, degradation, and sin." Elaborating, he remarked, "The cross, the image of Christ, the Virgin Mary, and the saints, are idolatrously worshiped."[7] Presbyterian missionaries began to have some success in New Mexico in the second half of the nineteenth century. One of their main techniques was the establishment of Protestant schools to teach New Mexican children not only reading and arithmetic but also to conform them to Anglo Protestant cultural standards. Doyle remained hopeful that this would liberate the people:

> [T]he great masses of the people are under the dominating influence of the Catholic Church and it will require both patience and time to win them away from this allegiance and to make it possible for them to appreciate and to participate in the advantages of Protestant Christianity. But from our schools will soon come a generation that will throw off this yoke of bondage, and the harvest time of souls will be here.[8]

The situation in Texas was similar to that in New Mexico with the major exception that there were far more Anglo Protestants in Texas at the conclusion of the U.S.-Mexican War. For the most part, Protestant missionaries in Texas occupied themselves with meeting the needs of these Anglo settlers. Some Baptists and Methodists even had their start when Texas was yet part of Mexico, holding prayer meetings in defiance of Mexican law.[9] Evangelizing the Anglo population got underway shortly after Texan independence, but in the words of one settler, Noah Smithwick, the missionaries were not immediately successful:

> Preachers were a little slow in getting around to look after the lost sheep, and in truth met with little encouragement when they did come. The Methodists held one camp meeting in Webber's prairie during my residence there, but the constant dread of Indians made our outdoor gatherings rather poorly attended.[10]

After annexation in 1845, more Protestant churches and missionaries entered the new state, including some who focused their efforts on Mexican American conversion. However, attitudes toward the Tejanos' capacity for religious enlightenment was not always positive. A Methodist missionary in Texas, Rev. Alexander H. Sutherland, characterized Tejanos as spiritually scarred by their centuries of Catholicism: "Age on age of darkness, duplicity, and degradation have left [them] so full of evil, so prone to evil, that the task of purification and elevation would be utterly hopeless, leaving out the divinity of the agency."[11] Eventually, and perhaps despite attitudes such as Sutherland's, some Tejanos were attracted to Protestant churches. The most successful in this regard were the Methodists, Baptists, and Presbyterians. By the 1880s and 1890s there were even some Spanish-speaking pastors, such as Rev. Arturo Castro in Gonzales, Rev. Santiago Tafolla in San Diego (Texas), and Rev. J. J. Mercado. As in New Mexico, a central strategy was the establishment of Protestant schools that educated children and identified and trained Mexican American Protestant leaders.[12]

Mexican American Protestant religious switching

Protestant missions to Mexican Americans, particularly those that included educational outreach, began slowly to bear fruit around the turn of the century, but this could hardly be considered a massive religious re-alignment. The great majority of Mexican Americans remained Catholics. What, then, motivated some Mexican Americans to switch to Methodism, Presbyterianism, and other Protestant denominations? First of all, Protestantism held some compelling features. As mentioned, Protestant schools were attractive to some. For instance, a Nuevomexicano named Gabino Rendón expressed an eagerness to study the Bible in a Presbyterian school in Las Vegas, New Mexico. The school, for him, "marked the opening of the Bible to the common people and the beginning of religious liberty in our part of the world."[13] Protestantism, in this sense, opened up religious choice where before there had been only one option. Another reason people were drawn to Protestant denominations was that, in some cases, there were more opportunities for leadership. Mexican American men could be ordained as elders, evangelists, and ministers and immediately begin serving their communities while still maintaining a family life. Compared to entering the Catholic priesthood, the educational and social barriers to Protestant leadership were relatively low.[14] Theological concerns should not be discounted as an important promoter of Protestant religious switching among Mexican Americans. In their own testimonies of conversion, Mexican Americans point to the Protestant message of personal salvation and to Protestant worship styles that featured impassioned preaching and popular singing. Evangelistic camp meetings in turn-of-the-century Texas attracted thousands of Mexican American participants who enjoyed the picnic-like celebrations. Rev. Crecencio Guerrero remembered these camp meetings as multipurpose events that gathered families in recreation as well as the "preaching of God's Word ... vehemently and beautifully proclaimed."[15]

In short, Mexican Americans who switched to Protestant churches in the first hundred years after the U.S.-Mexican War had reasons to make this major change in their lives. However, it is worth considering what conversion signified in that context. First and foremost, becoming a Protestant meant leaving the Catholic Church. And to leave the Catholic Church, one had to embrace typical Protestant critiques of Catholicism: Catholic priests were distant and unresponsive to the people's needs; Catholics were not allowed to read the Bible; Catholics were idolaters who worshiped Mary and the saints; Catholics were little concerned with the saving power of Jesus's death on the cross and instead were mired in rote liturgy. Second, to switch to Protestantism was not a general act but an explicit move toward a specific denomination, such as the Methodists, the Baptists, or the Presbyterians. This often depended more on which group's missionaries were active in a particular locale rather than on tangible theological differences. New Protestants would have immediately noticed differences in worship. Church vestments were either much reduced or non-existent in Protestant churches. The minister's sermon was likely to be longer and more exhortatory than a priest's homily. Participation from the congregation was more common, from rousing singing to sharing prayer requests aloud. Time commitments to the Protestant Churches were different, with weekly Bible study, prayer meetings, and worship opportunities in addition to the Sunday service. Conversion also meant embracing a new identity, one that created a new and close-knit community even as it alienated the convert from other parts of Mexican American life. In this sense, Protestant Mexican Americans were what some have called a "double minority." Finally, it is important to remember that conversion, although often remembered as a sudden, life-changing decision, more often unfolds over time, as converts moved back and forth within their old and new religious communities and personal identities.

The decision to become Protestant, which was tantamount to the decision to stop being Catholic, often created serious tensions within Mexican American families. Protestant missionaries, echoing tropes common since the Protestant Reformation, denigrated Catholic Christianity, often explicitly stating that Catholicism was misguided and corrupt and therefore could not offer the eternal salvation that Protestants had secured. Rifts could and did occur within families when new converts, even if motivated by loving concern, informed their Catholic family members that they must also convert or face everlasting condemnation. Even when Protestants were able to maintain family relationships with Catholic relatives, the demands of Protestant church life—frequent worship, rejection of Catholic holiday celebrations, changes in social behavior—would often push Mexican American converts and their children to socialize more with their church fellowship than with their Catholic families of origin.[16] Moreover, converts often faced ostracism in their majority-Catholic communities. For instance, parish priests in New Mexico often refused to baptize newborns whose siblings were enrolled in the new Protestant schools.[17]

However, switching to Protestant denominations could also create new opportunities for Mexican Americans, though these opportunities depended on increased levels of assimilation. The most salient example of this is access to education. The use of schools as evangelistic tools throughout the Southwest underscored a Protestant commitment to education, and many Mexican American converts were first attracted to Protestant denominations precisely because of the promise of education for their children. Greater educational achievement represented more opportunity for social and economic integration into U.S. society, even if this meant embracing a U.S. identity. For example, the Mexican-born Rev. José Espino, after receiving some of his considerable education from Methodist-sponsored schools, was ordained to the ministry and served as the pastor of Methodist congregations in Texas starting in the 1930s. Espino's commitment to education intertwined with an articulate patriotism for his adopted country. He stated, "The Church. The School. The Home. These are the three great trenches of democracy."[18] Espino, and others like him, ultimately proved the effectiveness of the missionary strategy of Protestant education in both creating new converts and assimilating new citizens. The strategy sometimes inspired Catholics to open their own schools in response, creating new arenas for religious competition.

Mexican American integration in Protestant denominations

The first Protestant missions to Mexican Americans often had a paternalistic character. White, male leaders, after attracting some interest in their churches, would often lean on local Mexican Americans to carry out much of the day-to-day work of their nascent congregations. This inclusion in the work of evangelism and preaching was one of the features of Protestantism that attracted new converts in the first place, but the promise of leadership in Protestant denominations only went so far. It is true that Mexican American men could move with relative ease into positions of preaching and teaching, especially in comparison with the seminary training and social barriers to entering the Catholic priesthood. However, leadership positions at regional and denominational levels remained in the hands of Anglos. White Presbyterians in New Mexico accentuated this difference by refusing to refer to their Mexican American partners in ministry as "reverend" and basing their pay on daily work logs, which, in effect, turned them into evangelistic day laborers. Anglo leaders justified this divide by noting that Mexican Americans could rarely, if ever, complete the ordination requirements, which involved post-secondary study in Latin, Greek, Hebrew, and various other disciplines. If Mexican American evangelists spent too much time in study to try to meet these requirements, they were admonished to get back in the mission field to seek new converts.[19] The situation was similar among Methodists. From the years 1895 to 1930, there were no Spanish-speaking presiding elders (who are in charge of church districts) in the U.S., even though there had been considerable growth of Spanish-speaking congregations throughout much of the Southwest and Texas.[20]

Racial prejudice also affected how Mexican Americans could function within Protestant churches. Language differences sometimes warranted separate congregations or worship services for Mexican Americans, but at other times, Anglo animosity against Mexican Americans created divisions. For instance, a Presbyterian official reported, to his chagrin, that a church building in Ft. Collins, Colorado, which two English- and Spanish-speaking congregations shared, was no longer suitable for the arrangement. "[R]acial prejudice is such that the Spanish people [*sic.*] finally withdrew, preferring rather to meet in the basement of a home than in such an unChristian atmosphere."[21] More pervasive than open opposition to Mexican American inclusion, however, was the implicit, and sometimes explicit, assumption that Euro-American culture was naturally superior to all others. This meant that, even when missionaries and others preached about the equality and oneness of all God's people, their words did not lead to transformation. As theologian Teresa Chávez Sauceda explains, "Despite the theological opposition to the concept of racial superiority, the strong affinity perceived between Eurocentric culture and Protestant faith hampered, even neutralized, the church's ability to pose any effective opposition to the prevailing racial ideology."[22]

Soon after the establishment of Mexican American congregations and churches, Mexican American Protestant leaders began to push back, proclaiming that pay gaps between whites and Latino pastors be bridged, racial bias be eliminated, and barriers to leadership be addressed. After decades of tension and pressure, Mexican American Methodist leaders in Texas won equal pay for Anglo and Latino ministers in 1936. Newly empowered, Mexican Americans took leadership positions in the administration of Texan Methodist churches,

Figure 7.1 "Spanish Presbyterian Church," 1919, Albuquerque, New Mexico. Courtesy Second Presbyterian Church, Albuquerque, New Mexico.

and they quickly proved their effectiveness when Mexican American church membership experienced its largest growth in history.[23] During the same period, Mexican American Presbyterians were still administered as a mission field of the national Presbyterian denominations rather than as self-determining and equal units. It was not until the 1960s that Mexican American and other Latino/a Presbyterian congregations, would begin to change the paternalistic patterns in place up to that point.[24]

The civil rights movement in the United States, and the historical and cultural context that imbued the movement, helped to break down barriers in Protestant denominations that had long kept people of color, including Mexican Americans, out of leadership and full participation. Latino/a Protestant involvement in civil rights organizing also helped refocus Mexican American Protestant identity more onto their ethnic heritage rather than solely on their denominational identification. For example, historian Felipe Hinojosa, in his study of Latino/a Mennonites, notes that Mexican American Mennonites took cues from African American struggles for equality and freedom. The Mennonite Urban Racial Council (URC) formed in 1968 to advocate for racial/ethnic minorities in what was, otherwise, a very white denomination. It took some time for the URC to articulate a mission that recognized both the common struggles of African Americans, Latinos/as, and Native Americans as well as these groups' unique needs, but eventually a shared leadership structure between Black and Latino/a Mennonites emerged and changed the name of the advocacy group to the Minority Ministries Council (MMC). Interethnic solidarity in the MMC created new opportunities for Mexican Americans and their allies to gain new visibility in the denomination.[25] A similar process occurred within Methodist and Presbyterian denominations as activist Mexican Americans got involved in the Chicano/a and Farm Workers movements; their militancy in these movements inspired them to turn their attention back onto their denominations. Protestant leaders who protested their own denominations' paternalistic attitude toward Latino/a members often ended up becoming leaders in the same denominations. From that vantage point, they were able to mobilize church-based community service to meet the needs of Mexican Americans. Societal changes in the 1960s and 1970s thus helped Mexican American Protestants to gain new opportunities within Protestant denominations even if these changes stopped short of radically remaking the Protestant mainline.[26]

Ultimately, evangelical and Pentecostal Protestant groups often were nimbler when it came to including and empowering Latinos/as. Some of the same racial prejudices existed in those Protestant groups, but they often posed fewer barriers to aspiring minority leaders, perhaps because of their own more marginal social status (in comparison with the hegemonic Protestant mainline). Evangelical and Pentecostal congregations, in comparison to mainline Protestants, also had more congregational autonomy, which made local leadership a more immediate possibility. Moreover, they were often earlier to accept the contributions of women in positions of church leadership, a factor that no doubt increased their attractiveness for many. Mexican American evangelicals and Pentecostals are the subject of Chapter 8.

Mexican American Protestant integration and contemporary issues

The gains made by Mexican Americans and other Latinos/as within mainline Protestant denominations reflect these groups' persistence and commitment to full integration and equality. Mexican Americans have drawn on core values of the Protestant Reformation that the Christian Church be "reformed and always reforming" to encourage, and even demand, more openness to Mexican American voices in the life of mainline Protestant denominations. Even with this persistence, change has often been slow to occur, and Mexican Americans—along with other Latinos/as—often remain on the margins in Protestant life. They are regularly expected to assimilate completely, putting aside salient cultural differences as well as painful histories of racial prejudice. Historian Daisy Machado, drawing on metaphors of fellowship and communion, asks whether Latinos/as have "a place at the table" in Protestant churches. She incisively notes, "What the Protestant establishment has historically understood as 'pluralism' has been a United States phenomenon less about being plural than about shaping others to conform to the accepted dominant religious patterns."[27] Questions remain about mainline Latino/a Protestants. Do they enjoy the same access to theological education and leadership as their Anglo counterparts? Are their cultural traditions valued and included in the liturgical expression of these denominations? What role do racial differences still play in denominational and congregational life?

Protestant denominations, with the collaboration of their Latino/a members, have made some advances in how they imagine and support racial and ethnic diversity. Mexican Americans and other Latinos/as, however, continue to constitute only small percentages of most mainline Protestant denominations. The Pew Research Center has collected data on racial/ethnic diversity in church membership. Among mainline Protestants in 2014 (the year Pew published its research), the American Baptist Church had some of the highest percentages of Latino/a membership, with 11 percent of its membership in this category. The Presbyterian Church (USA) had 4 percent Latino/a membership. Other mainline denominations, including the Episcopal Church, the United Methodist Church, the United Church in Christ, and the Evangelical Lutheran Church in America all had fewer than 2 percent Latino/a membership.[28] Mainline Protestants, likewise, only make up 5 percent of the entire Latino/a population. (In contrast, evangelical and Pentecostal Protestant Latinos/as comprise 15 percent of this population.)[29] These numbers do not tell the total story. Another statistic, that 75 percent of Latinos/as attend congregations that are majority Latino/a, is perhaps more revealing in that it suggests that, for many Latino/a Protestants, integration in racially diverse congregations remains elusive.[30]

Mainline Protestants have long valued an educated clergy, a fact that has sometimes been used as a barrier to full inclusion of Mexican Americans. One strategy, then, to increase the number of Mexican American and other Latino/a pastors, educators, and theologians in Protestant denominations has been to ensure that they can have access to the highest levels of theological and religious education. To this end, the Fund for Theological Education (now the Forum for Theological Exploration) as well as the Pew Charitable Trusts began to fund programs in the 1980s for Latinos/as to obtain seminary and other graduate training. After some success, an advisory board of Latino/a Protestant leaders formed and proposed the formation of the Hispanic Theological Initiative (HTI) in 1996 to fund and provide mentoring to Latino/a graduate education in theology. Since then, the HTI has been an essential resource for not only Latino/a graduate students but also universities and seminaries who wish to support Latinos/as at the highest levels of educational achievement in theology and religious studies.[31] Another organization was formed in 1991 to support Latino/a church leaders, especially pastors. Called the Association for Hispanic Theological Education (AETH), the organization provides educational programming to Latino/a pastors who, even in the contemporary period, may still find it difficult to obtain seminary degrees. Through the publication of books, certification programs, and networking opportunities, AETH has strengthened Latino/a Protestant congregations.[32] AETH and HTI have greatly increased access to theological education for Mexican American and other Latino/a Protestants, and in so doing they have contributed to greater levels of inclusion of Latinos/as in mainline Protestant denominations. A third organization is the Hispanic Summer Program (HSP). Since 1989, HSP has hosted itinerant summer workshops for Latino/a ministry leaders. The ecumenical summer programs augment seminary education for Latinos/as and prepare

Figure 7.2 140th anniversary celebration of La Trinidad United Methodist Church, May 2016, San Antonio, Texas. Courtesy La Trinidad United Methodist Church.

them for church leadership in Latino/a contexts in the United States and Puerto Rico.[33]

Another sign of Mexican American integration into mainline Protestantism in recent decades is the appointment of Mexican Americans to positions of denominational leadership. Since the various denominations have different polities, or structures of internal governance, the title and rank of such leaders likewise varies. In the United Methodist Church, bishops oversee several churches in a geographical area. The first Mexican naturalized in the U.S. to be elected bishop was Elias Galvan in 1984 for the area around Phoenix, Arizona. Joel Martinez was the first Mexican American born in the United States to be made bishop, which occurred in 1992. He oversaw churches in Nebraska and Texas. In 2004 Minerva Carcaño became the first Mexican American woman to be named a bishop. She has served in Phoenix, Los Angeles, and the San Francisco area. In the Presbyterian Church (USA), the highest elected office is Moderator of the General Assembly, a two-year position that is open to both pastors and laypeople. While several Mexican Americans have led smaller Presbyterian governing bodies, to date there have been no Mexican American moderators of the entire denomination.[34] In the Episcopal Church, several Mexican bishops have served as denominational representatives in Mexico. The first native New Mexican bishop is Daniel P. Gutiérrez, who was consecrated as a bishop in 2016 to serve the Episcopal Diocese of Pennsylvania. The relatively late dates of these ascensions to leadership positions in conjunction with membership percentages suggest that Mexican Americans still have a way to go when it comes to full integration in mainline Protestant denominations.

Religion in practice

From the days of the Protestant Reformation in Europe, Protestants have generally rejected much of the statuary and representational artwork so common in Catholic churches. Arguing that these depictions of Jesus, Mary, and the saints function as sinful and distracting idols, Protestants have instead preferred more austere worship spaces with few adornments. This plainness further highlights the Protestant emphasis on Bible reading, biblical sermons, and corporate and individual Bible study. Mexican American Protestant religious practice likewise centers on the Bible. For many converts from Catholicism, frequent encounters with the Bible often come to symbolize the realignment of life and religious practice that accompanies the shift from a traditional Catholicism to a new, fervent Protestantism.

For example, Ambrosio Gonzales was an early Methodist convert in New Mexico, shortly after the U.S.-Mexican War. When U.S. missionaries placed a Bible in his hands, Gonzales found it to be transformative. "It was the first Bible of any kind I had ever seen. ... The book was a charm to me." Reading the Bible, for Gonzales and many other Mexican American Protestants, has been a key to their conversion and to their ongoing devotion to Protestant Christianity. Gonzales reported that he could not get enough of the Bible:

It was to me a new book. I read until the chickens were crowing for day. I laid down on a lounge in the same room and soon fell asleep. When I woke the sun was shining through the window into my face. The Sun of Righteousness was shining brightly in my soul. I have been a Christian and a Protestant ever since.[35]

Most Mexican American Protestants, both in the mainline denominations and in evangelical and Pentecostal groups (see Chapter 8), continue to center their worship and individual devotion in "the Word of God," which is to say, Bible study and church services that feature biblical interpretation.

Protestant theologian Luis Pedraja has surmised that this devotion to the Bible, in some ways, has replaced certain kinds of Catholic devotionalism in Hispanic Protestant life.

The primacy of the "word" in Hispanic Protestantism takes the place of the icon in Catholic popular religion. As a result, we find that testimonies, coritos [church songs], prayers, and Scriptures take the place of images, devotion to saints, and certain types of religious acts. The homes and churches of Hispanic Protestants do not have images of saints on their walls, but they do have Scripture verses. Instead of a statue of *La Virgen*, there is an adorned, Bible-shaped frame with the Ten Commandments or John 3:16 written colorfully in its center.[36]

These kinds of daily reminders and popular expressions of the Bible tie Mexican American Protestants to their religious identity as both Protestants *and* Latinos/as.

Notes

1 Mark T. Mulder, Aida I. Ramos, and Gerardo Martí, *Latino Protestants in America: Growing and Diverse* (Lanham, MD: Rowman & Littlefield, 2017), 2; Pew Research Center, "The Shifting Religious Identity of Latinos in the United States," May 7, 2014, https://www.pewforum.org/2014/05/07/the-shifting-religious-identity-of-la tinos-in-the-united-states.

2 David Stoll, *Is Latin America Turning Protestant?: The Politics of Evangelical Growth* (Berkeley, CA: University of California Press, 1990); David Martin, *Tongues of Fire: The Explosion of Protestantism in Latin America* (Oxford: B. Blackwell, 1990); Todd Hartch, *The Rebirth of Latin American Christianity* (New York: Oxford University Press, 2014).

3 See Catherine L. Albanese, *America, Religions, and Religion*, 5th ed. (Belmont, CA: Wadsworth, 2012). Albanese argues that Protestantism imposes a "oneness" on American culture that all types of Christians and other religious groups must accommodate themselves to.

4 "Conversion" means changing from one religion to another, therefore switching from Catholic to Protestant Christianity does not technically constitute a conversion. However, to match common usage among Protestants who have switched from Catholicism, this chapter treats "conversion" and "religious switching" as synonymous.

5 For instance, see Charles Alvin Brooks, *Christian Americanization: A Task for the Churches* (New York: Council of Women for Home Missions and Missionary Education Movement of the United States and Canada, 1919).

6 E. L. Cleaveland, quoted in Colin Brummitt Goodykoontz, *Home Missions on the American Frontier, with Particular Reference to the American Home Missionary Society* (New York: Octagon Books, 1971), 271–72.

7 Sherman H. Doyle, *Presbyterian Home Missions: An Account of the Home Missions of the Presbyterian Church in the U.S.A* (Philadelphia, PA: Presbyterian Board of Publication and Sabbath-School Work, 1902), 210–11.

8 Doyle, 216.

9 William Stuart Red, *The Texas Colonists and Religion, 1821–1836: A Centennial Tribute to the Texas Patriots Who Shed Their Blood That We Might Enjoy Civil and Religious Liberty* (Austin, TX: E. I. Shettles, 1924), 82–84.

10 Noah Smithwick, *The Evolution of a State, or, Recollections of Old Texas Days* (Austin, TX: University of Texas Press, 1983), 201.

11 Quoted in Paul Barton, "Inter-Ethnic Relations between Mexican American and Anglo American Methodists in the U.S. Southwest, 1836–1938," in *Protestantes/Protestants: Hispanic Christianity within Mainline Traditions*, ed. David Maldonado (Nashville, TN: Abingdon Press, 1999), 69.

12 Arnoldo De León, *The Tejano Community, 1836–1900* (Albuquerque, NM: University of New Mexico Press, 1982), 152–53.

13 Quoted in Tomás Atencio, "The Empty Cross: The First Hispano Presbyterians in Northern New Mexico and Southern Colorado," in *Protestantes/Protestants: Hispanic Christianity within Mainline Traditions*, ed. David Maldonado (Nashville, TN: Abingdon Press, 1999), 48.

14 R. Douglas Brackenridge and Francisco O. García-Treto, *Iglesia Presbiteriana: A History of Presbyterians and Mexican Americans in the Southwest* (San Antonio, TX: Trinity University Press, 1974), 27.

15 Brackenridge and García-Treto, 30.

16 Paul Barton, *Hispanic Methodists, Presbyterians, and Baptists in Texas* (Austin, TX: University of Texas Press, 2006), 49, 51–52.

17 Atencio, "The Empty Cross," 48.

18 Quoted in Barton, *Hispanic Methodists, Presbyterians, and Baptists in Texas*, 73.

19 Brackenridge and García-Treto, *Iglesia Presbiteriana*, 54–59.

20 Barton, "Inter-Ethnic Relations between Mexican American and Anglo American Methodists in the U.S. Southwest, 1836–1938," 73.

21 Brackenridge and García-Treto, *Iglesia Presbiteriana*, 168.

22 Teresa Chávez Sauceda, "Race, Religion, and La Raza: An Exploration of the Racialization of Latinos in the United States and the Role of the Protestant Church," in *Protestantes/Protestants: Hispanic Christianity within Mainline Traditions* (Nashville, TN: Abingdon Press, 1999), 186.

23 Barton, "Inter-Ethnic Relations between Mexican American and Anglo American Methodists in the U.S. Southwest, 1836–1938," 80–82.

24 Brackenridge and García-Treto, *Iglesia Presbiteriana*, 195–97.

25 Felipe Hinojosa, *Latino Mennonites: Civil Rights, Faith, and Evangelical Culture* (Baltimore, MD: Johns Hopkins University Press, 2014), 67–69, 83–86.

26 Paul Barton, "¡Ya Basta! Latino/a Protestant Activism in the Chicano/a and Farm Workers Movements," in *Latino Religions and Civic Activism in the United States*, ed. Gastón Espinosa, Virgilio Elizondo, and Jesse Miranda (New York: Oxford University Press, 2005), 138–40.

27 Daisy L. Machado, "Latinos in the Protestant Establishment: Is There a Place for Us at the Feast Table?" in *Protestantes/Protestants: Hispanic Christianity within Mainline Traditions*, ed. David Maldonado (Nashville, TN: Abingdon Press, 1999), 95.

28 Pew Research Center, "Religion in America: U.S. Religious Data, Demographics and Statistics," accessed June 24, 2019, https://www.pewforum.org/religious-landscape-study/religious-denomination.

29 Mulder, Ramos, and Martí, *Latino Protestants in America*, 6.

30 Mulder, Ramos, and Martí, 7.

31 Hispanic Theological Initiative, "The HTI Story," accessed June 25, 2019, http://hti.ptsem.edu/about/history.

32 Association for Hispanic Theological Education, "Our History," accessed June 25, 2019, https://www.aeth.org/nuestra-historia?language=english.

33 Hispanic Summer Program, "Who We Are, and What We Do," accessed February 2, 2021, https://hispanicsummerprogram.org/whoweare.

34 Vilmarie Cintrón-Olivieri, a Puerto Rican, was elected co-moderator of the denomination in 2018.

35 Eric Rivera, "The First Mexican Protestant Loved the Bible," *Christianity Today*, February 18, 2019, https://www.christianitytoday.com/history/2019/february/first-mexican-protestant-bible.html.

36 Luis G. Pedraja, "Guideposts along the Journey: Mapping North American Hispanic Theology," in *Protestantes/Protestants: Hispanic Christianity within Mainline Traditions* (Nashville, TN: Abingdon Press, 1999), 134–35.

8 Mexican American evangelicals and charismatic Christians

Protestantism in the United States is by no means limited to the older denominations discussed in the last chapter. Historically newer groups include a broad swath of Protestants known as evangelicals. Although difficult to define with precision, evangelical Christianity emerged as the product of high-spirited revival preaching and mission outreach to non-believers both in the United States and abroad. Evangelicals emphasize the importance of personal conversion rooted in Jesus's death on the cross, a pious lifestyle, emotional and participatory worship, and sharing their faith with others. While there are notable exceptions, most white evangelicals tend to be conservative on social and political issues, and since the 1980s, there has been a strong correlation between evangelicalism and support for the Republican Party. Black and Latino/a evangelicals share some of the social conservatism of their white counterparts, but they tend to be more liberal in terms of their political decisions, voting for Democratic candidates at a rate higher than that of white evangelicals.[1] Pentecostal Christianity, yet another form of Protestantism, shares many characteristics with evangelicalism in terms of lively worship and a concentration on personal conversion. Pentecostalism differs in that it focuses on spiritual gifts (or "charisms" from which comes the term "charismatic"), such as speaking in tongues, miraculous healing, and the utterance of prophecy. Pentecostal and charismatic Christians are therefore known for their exuberant worship style, which often includes time for what they experience as healing, prophesying, and other outpourings of the Holy Spirit. Since the birth of Pentecostalism in the early twentieth century, many Mexican Americans have embraced this type of Christianity for themselves and their families.

While mainline Protestants, such as the Episcopalians, Presbyterians, and Lutherans, continue to struggle to integrate Latino/a members and leadership, evangelical and charismatic churches and congregations have been more successful in appealing to Mexican Americans and incorporating them in meaningful ways. Enthusiastic and participatory worship, relatively open access to pastoral leadership, promises of healing and social well-being, and a continuous focus on evangelism have helped evangelical and charismatic variations of Protestant Christianity to attract growing numbers of Mexican Americans and other Latinos/as. Pentecostal worship styles have spilled out of Protestant

DOI: 10.4324/9780429285516-10

churches into many Catholic parishes as well. The Catholic Charismatic Renewal is popular among many Mexican American Catholics and throughout Latin America. Traditions of embodied prayer and healing as well as spiritual renewal movements within the Catholic Church have fit well with charismatic worship styles common in Pentecostal settings. In this sense, U.S.-born, charismatic Protestantism is having an influence on Catholicism both in the United States and around the world.

The previous chapter examined Protestant missions to Mexican Americans in the nineteenth and twentieth centuries and the slow inclusion of Mexican Americans in mainline Protestant denominations. This chapter explores Mexican American participation in U.S. evangelicalism and Pentecostalism. In some ways, the story of mainline missions and conversion is the same for many Mexican American evangelicals—Anglo evangelists, often working under the auspices of a particular denomination, made Mexican American converts, who then worked to expand their own leadership and involvement within their congregations. The story of Pentecostalism differs in that Mexican Americans were part of Pentecostalism's genesis in the early twentieth century and thus have always formed part of this charismatic branch of Protestant Christianity. The chapter begins with this significant history.

Mexican Americans and early Pentecostalism

The earliest stirrings of what is now known as Pentecostalism began in the southern and midwestern United States in white and Black evangelical churches that promoted personal piety and readiness for the Christian end times. Fervent preaching and "Spirit baptism," which generally included speaking in tongues, were marks of the nascent movement. Things really got off the ground with the famous Azusa Street Revival in Los Angeles, begun in 1906 and led by William Seymour, an African American evangelist. This revival, which featured daily preaching and healing services, went on for years and catalyzed the spread of Pentecostalism. Curious people and spiritual seekers came from many regions and walks of life to observe the purported miracles and spiritual gifts on display at the revival. A number of these people claimed to experience "baptism in the Spirit" and committed themselves to sharing the Pentecostal message with others. Attracting a national and international base of participation, Azusa was a highly diverse gathering. In this context, Seymour attempted to build a multiracial and multiethnic church based in common spiritual experience, a dream that would not be fully realized in the racially segregated U.S.[2] However, Seymour's vision did make it possible for Pentecostalism to spread quickly into many different ethnic communities, including among Mexicans and Mexican Americans who participated in the Azusa Street Revival.

In fact, the first reported person to manifest signs of being touched by the Holy Spirit at Azusa was a Mexican American day worker who was in the building the day before the revival got fully underway. Subsequently, hundreds

Figure 8.1 Apostolic Faith Gospel Mission, site of the Azusa Street Revival. In public
domain.

of Mexican and Mexican American Catholics in Los Angeles attended the
revival meetings, and many were converted. In 1909, Seymour himself
ordained Abundio L. López and Juan Navarro Martínez as Pentecostal ministers. López and another Mexican American, Genero Valenzuela, ran the
"Spanish Apostolic Faith Mission" in Los Angeles.[3] López and his wife believed
that the presence of the Holy Spirit in their lives was a blessing that empowered them to spread this new, experiential form of worship. They wrote, "We
testify to the power of the Holy Spirit in forgiveness, sanctification, and the
baptism with the Holy Ghost and fire. … we want to be used for the salvation
and healing of both soul and body."[4] In the following years, they and others
worked assiduously to promote Pentecostalism among Spanish-speaking and
Mexican American communities.

The spread of Pentecostalism from the Azusa Street mission to Mexican
Americans in Texas relied on several white evangelists who were converted at
Azusa and then made their way to Texas, where they ordained local Mexican
American leaders in the new movement. A notable example is Francisco Olazábal, known as "El Azteca" in his many evangelistic campaigns. A native of
Mexico, Olazábal grew up in evangelical Protestant circles—his mother was an
itinerant Methodist evangelist—and he trained in Mexican and U.S. seminaries
as a Methodist minister. In 1917, after serving several Methodist congregations
in Texas and California, he embraced the Pentecostal message after friends of
his, George and Carrie Judd Montgomery, healed his wife from an illness. The
Montgomerys had converted at Azusa, and they ushered the Olazábals out
of Methodism and into the Assemblies of God, the biggest Pentecostal

denomination to emerge from the Azusa Street Revival. As an Assemblies of God minister, Olazábal had a major impact on the growth of Pentecostalism among Mexican Americans and other Latinos/as, particularly Puerto Ricans.[5]

An early debate among Pentecostals concerning the nature of God immediately influenced divisions among Mexican American converts. Olazábal, in line with the Assemblies of God, maintained an orthodox Trinitarian doctrine of God shared by a majority of other Christians in which God is understood as three persons: Father, Son, and Holy Spirit. A faction of early Pentecostals, however, hewed closely to what is known as a "Oneness" interpretation of the Christian God wherein the Trinity is one person, Jesus, in three modes. Also called "Apostolic" Pentecostalism, this branch appealed to several Mexican Americans in southern California as well as in northern Mexico. Some of the first proponents of Apostolic Pentecostalism were Luis López, Juan Navarro, Francisco Llorente, and Romana Valenzuela. Oneness evangelists had particular success in rural areas and among immigrant farm workers.[6]

The development of Mexican American Pentecostalism

While William Seymour had visions at Azusa Street that Pentecostalism could be free of racial and ethnic distinctions—given that the Holy Spirit fell equally on all—it did not take long for typical racial hierarchies, divisions, and prejudices to impose their inequities and injustices on the new movement. As with the missions of the mainline denominations covered in Chapter 7, Anglos often monopolized the leadership of the nascent organizations of Pentecostal missions. Even so, Pentecostalism always contained within its character a fluidity and openness, perhaps because of its emphasis on receiving gifts from the Holy Spirit. For instance, one of the people responsible for spreading the Pentecostal message to many Mexican Americans in southern California was Alice Luce. She operated tent revivals in Los Angeles and eventually founded Assemblies of God-related missions in East Los Angeles, an area of the city with high concentrations of Mexican Americans. Unlike many of her male colleagues in the Pentecostal missions, Luce believed that control of Mexican American congregations should be turned over to Mexican American leaders as soon as possible. For example, Luce quickly entrusted one of her East L.A. missions, El Aposento Alto, to Francisco and Natividad Nevarez. The Nevarezes remained in charge of the church for over three decades and oversaw the conversion of many Mexican Americans in the neighborhood.[7]

However, Luce did not totally relinquish control over Assemblies of God outreach to Mexican Americans. In the 1920s, she was one of the founders of the Latin American Bible Institute (LABI), with campuses in southern California and Texas. Luce felt that proper education and preparation of Latino/a Pentecostal leaders was the best way to win and keep Mexican Americans in their proper spiritual home and protect them from the errors of Oneness theology as well as the ever-present Catholic Church. Historian Arlene Sánchez Walsh has argued that, despite Luce's commitments to Mexican American autonomy in their own congregations, "in practice, she preached supervision."[8] She lived in this tension, expecting that Mexican American graduates of LABI would go on to found their own Pentecostal missions and churches while also worrying that, without ongoing Anglo guidance, Mexican Americans would not be able to resist the temptation to defect to erroneous theologies or to backslide into old traditions. Nonetheless, LABI provided far more opportunities for Mexican American pastors and church-planters than did mainline Protestant denominations during the same period.

LABI's program of study turned all students into missionaries for the Spirit. The curriculum, much of which Luce wrote, encouraged students to embrace their role as preachers, evangelists, and warriors against spiritual evils. For many of the Mexican American students, the Catholic Church best symbolized these evils. By embracing the gifts of the Holy Spirit and constantly preaching against Catholicism and other false doctrines, LABI graduates would help to spread the Assemblies of God among Latinos/as and hasten God's final victory over sin and death. The curriculum also emphasized personal devotion and piety.[9] Proper devotion was centered in prayer and Bible reading as guided by the Spirit. "LABI became a training ground," explains Sánchez Walsh, "for Latino ministers because Luce, the missionary and teacher, helped lead the first generation to their new reality, not as Catholic converts but as Pentecostals."[10] Pentecostal study transformed Mexican Americans, who began to understand themselves as new creations in God's Holy Spirit, empowered to guide their people and others to the joys and truth of direct encounter with God.

Even as some Mexican Americans were making gains in the Assemblies of God, Mexican and Mexican American Apostolic Pentecostals also experienced growth in the first half of the twentieth century. Given Oneness's popularity among migrant farm workers, this branch of Pentecostalism often spread because of its adherents' movements, whether these were to follow crops or due to the United States' disruptive repatriation campaigns. While the repatriations often inflicted suffering and massive dislocation on Mexicans and

Figure 8.2 14th district council of the Latin American District Council of the Assemblies of God sitting and standing outside Getsemani Assembly of God in El Paso, Texas, November 18, 1942. Courtesy Flower Pentecostal Heritage Center.

Mexican Americans, they did have the unexpected outcome of spreading Pentecostalism back and forth across the border as repatriated people shared their newfound faith in Mexico and then, oftentimes, found ways to return to the United States. Others, although not officially repatriated, lived lives of transnational fluidity, crossing the border repeatedly throughout their lives. Historian Daniel Ramírez has documented the stories of many of these migratory Apostolic Pentecostals. For example, Ignacio Mariscal, a native of Durango, Mexico, converted to Pentecostalism around 1923 in El Centro, California. After his conversion, Mariscal traveled back and forth between southern California and several northern Mexican states, where he worked as kind of circuit-riding evangelist. People in Durango who converted under his leadership eventually went on to lead various Apostolic congregations in Chicago.[11] Pentecostalism's evangelistic fervor and egalitarian spirit helped it to move and multiply rapidly on both sides of the border.

Healing and community restoration

From its inception, Pentecostalism has attracted new participants, who often become converts, by promising miraculous healing for the sick. Along with *glossolalia*, the act of speaking in tongues, the other principal gift of the Holy Spirit that Pentecostals claim to experience is the power to heal others through prayer and touch, the latter referred to as "the laying on of hands." As charismatic Christianity has spread around the globe, scholars have noted that healing, in fact, is the most important factor in its growth.[12] Although Pentecostalism has not been limited only to poor regions and populations, it has been notably successful in such contexts where there may be barriers to biomedical healthcare. When going to a doctor's office or clinic is difficult or impossible, people often seek out religious and traditional alternatives. Pentecostal Christians believe in God's presence in their lives and therefore embrace God's miraculous intervention in their bodies and communities as a positive force for healing and restoration.[13]

Healing power certainly has had a role in attracting Mexican Americans to Pentecostalism. As mentioned earlier, the miraculous healing of his wife sparked Francisco Olazábal's conversion to Pentecostalism. He would go on to feature healing in his own evangelistic campaigns throughout the U.S.-Mexico border region. Olazábal understood healing as a sign of spiritual transformation in one's life. He boasted, "almost all those that have been saved through the working of miracles and healings [in his campaigns] have been completely renewed and today lead exemplary lives."[14] Physical healing continues to be an essential element for many Mexican American Pentecostals and ranks alongside speaking in tongues as one of the clearest signs of the Holy Spirit's transformative activity in people's lives. For example, in fieldwork carried out in Vineyard congregations (a popular charismatic group) in California, Arlene Sánchez Walsh discovered that significant numbers of Latino/a members reported experiences of healing, especially women.[15]

Physical healings and miracles, however, are but one aspect of the full restoration to wellness that Pentecostals expect from the Holy Spirit. Social harmony, strong families, and redemption from criminal activity also feature strongly in the Mexican American Pentecostal experience. In the difficult circumstances of some Mexican American neighborhoods, particularly in East Los Angeles, gang activity presented an outlet to young people for group identity and neighborhood protection in a dangerous world that constantly communicated Anglo prejudice and fear of people of color. Drug abuse, the drug trade, and violence, however, helped to destroy the communities and lives of the people that gangs were ostensibly in place to protect. The Pentecostal message of surrender, redemption, and the formation of a new, sanctified community found fertile ground among the gangs of East L.A. and other Mexican American urban areas.

One of the primary Pentecostal organizations that has mobilized to deal with Mexican American drugs and gangs is Victory Outreach. The organization was founded by Cruz "Sonny" Arguinzoni, a former gang member and drug addict who experienced speaking in tongues and a conversion of his life in a Pentecostal service. Preaching that the Holy Spirit would cure one from addiction and repair relationships, he started Victory Outreach in the late 1960s, and quickly decided that every new location of the growing ministry would be linked to a drug rehabilitation program. This pattern proved to be successful both in terms of church growth and in getting young people out of gangs and off drugs. Today, Victory Outreach is an international movement with congregations around the world and continues to offer rehabilitation and a new life in the Spirit.[16]

How has Victory Outreach achieved these outcomes? Several unique features of Victory Outreach's type of Pentecostalism, tailored specifically for urban contexts of racial prejudice, drug abuse, and violence, have made it successful among some urban Mexican American youth and young adults. First, the drug rehabilitation homes play a central role. Not only do these facilities help addicts to stop abusing drugs and alcohol, they also introduce Pentecostal patterns of worship and ritual to participants. In this way, regaining sobriety is tied deeply to Pentecostal conversion. Another factor of Victory Outreach's success are their evangelistic campaigns, which rely on elaborate "street dramas." These dramas, which include rap and other contemporary music, feature often violent scenes of street life in which characters come to a crisis point in their lives. In the dramas, Pentecostal ex-gang members and addicts introduce the Holy Spirit and a new life in the church to these people in crisis at just the right moment and rescue them from danger and despair. Finally, a youth ministry called God's Anointed Now Generation, or G.A.N.G., provides an alternative space for at-risk teens and young adults that attempts to provide some of the positives of gang life—strong in-group identity and a protective support system—while eschewing criminal activities and drug use. Victory Outreach, to be sure, is not the right Pentecostal community for everyone, but its ministries of community healing have addressed a vital need for some of the most marginalized elements of the Mexican American and other Latino/a communities.[17]

Mexican American Pentecostals who seek out divine healing as a gift of the Holy Spirit thus do so both to heal their bodies and to heal their communities. Religious studies scholar Luis León analyzed the overlapping meanings that emerge from this milieu of physical and social bodies. León noted that the Azusa Street Revival, under William Seymour's leadership, was "a phenomenon of the borderlands" that was steeped in the colonial mixtures and racial strife that was present in the region even before the arrival of white and Black newcomers from the United States. Los Angeles itself had been an Anglo-majority city for only twenty years at the time of Azusa, and the Mexican American presence continued to be palpable and influential. In this context, León suggested that the healing espoused and enacted by Pentecostals in Los Angeles—and in other Mexican American communities—has thrived because this corporeal and social healing "reclaims the space of the body and troubles the configuration of the nation by claiming healing spaces as sites of spiritual power, as sacred places."[18] This healing and reclamation of space is evident, for example, in the rehabilitation and transformation of urban youth culture that Victory Outreach has brought to East Los Angeles and beyond.

The Catholic Charismatic Renewal

In the 1960s, the Spirit-filled worship styles of Pentecostalism spread to English-speaking Catholics in the United States. Speaking in tongues, ecstatic worship, healing services, testimonials, and charismatic Marian devotion all form part of what has come to be known as the Catholic Charismatic Renewal. In the second half of the twentieth century, Latino/a Catholics begin to join the movement, and in 1990, the Comité Nacional de Servicio Hispano (CNSH) was founded to organize Latino/a Catholic charismatics throughout the United States. CNSH, like other Catholic charismatic groups, maintains that the Holy Spirit is active in the church today and that Catholics can and should experience the fervor of Pentecost through worship and evangelization. They not only support existing Latino/a charismatic Catholics but also actively engage in forming new communities of prayer and worship.[19] Data concerning the numbers of Latino/a Catholic charismatics vary widely. High estimates put the number at over five million, which would mean there are more Latino/a Catholic charismatics than Pentecostals in the U.S. Other estimates put the number lower, perhaps closer to one million.[20] These data do not differentiate Mexican Americans from other Latino/a Catholic charismatics, but Mexican Americans no doubt constitute one of the largest groups of participants in the movement.

In some senses, the Catholic Charismatic Renewal allows Mexican Americans to remain connected to their Catholic heritage while also embracing many of the attractive features of Pentecostal worship and community. In a study of mostly Mexican and Mexican American charismatic Catholics in Los

Angeles, the sociologist Cristina Mora-Torres found that participants often experienced their entry into the charismatic community as a kind of conversion, even though they did not officially change their membership in the Catholic Church. For some, experiencing the Holy Spirit in tongues and ecstatic worship helped them cope with life's challenges, including drug addiction and family dissolution. For example, one man reported,

> My life changed in that moment, and I traded my old life for a new one ... I've been clean now for a very long time, my job is tough and demanding but it is steady, and I feel good that my children can see me like this, not like the person I was before.[21]

Participants note that perceived personal revelations and experiences of God's love have helped transform their lives and create a sense of family in their charismatic fellowship. However, a strong Catholic element continues. Another woman explained that, prior to her entry into charismatic practice, she did not have a true understanding of God that supplemented her long-time relationship with the Virgin of Guadalupe.

> [E]ven when I wasn't in the movement and before I became close to the spirit, and when I knew nothing about the love of God, I knew the Virgen de Guadalupe, and I knew that she was with me. For everything, everything I was always going to the Virgin.[22]

The Catholic Charismatic Renewal has allowed many Mexican Americans Catholics, like this woman, to maintain their devotions to beloved saints and to the Virgin while also deepening and renewing their faith in God and the Church itself.

Mexican American evangelicals

Evangelical Protestantism in the United States is multi-faceted and can be hard to define. Generally speaking (though there are many exceptions), evangelicals are more politically conservative than mainline Protestants, they favor more literal biblical interpretation, and they focus heavily on the story of Jesus's death on the cross as a loving sacrifice that saves repentant sinners. Most evangelicals emphasize a moment of decision in a person's life to accept Jesus and his salvation. Evangelicals, though they share historical roots and some worship styles with Pentecostals, generally do not engage in charismatic practices, such as speaking in tongues or prophesying, and sometimes even condemn these kinds of activities as sinful or misled. Evangelicals also differentiate themselves from mainline Protestants in that their worship often is less rooted in denominational liturgies and creeds and relies instead on the rhetorical skills of the preacher.

Evangelicalism spread to Mexican Americans in much the same way that mainline Protestant denominations did in the nineteenth century: through the activities of Anglo-American missionaries. Indeed, the differentiation of evangelicalism from other forms of Protestantism has its origins in the revivals and evangelistic campaigns that moved westward across the North American continent with Anglos and African Americans. Revivals' emphasis on repentance and on personal salvation reinforced these themes for many U.S. Protestants, particularly in those denominations, like the Baptists and Methodists, who best utilized revivals in their ministries. (It is worth noting that it was precisely these kinds of revivals, which featured enthusiastic preaching and calls to pious living, that also led to the charismatic movement and the birth of Pentecostalism at the turn of the last century.) Since evangelical Christianity relies on moving preaching and individual salvation, it was often a hospitable home for talented Mexican American converts who could communicate immediately and effectively in their communities.

In the second half of the nineteenth century, white Southern Baptists in Texas began to evangelize Mexican Americans. By 1910, twenty-four "Mexican" churches were able to form the Convención Bautista Mexicana de Texas (Mexican Baptist Convention of Texas), a body that grew over the next decades as more Mexican American Baptist congregations were founded around the state. In 1925, the Mexican Bible Institute was founded in Texas to train Mexican American Baptists and other evangelical church leaders, and by the middle of the century, the Baptist Church was the largest Mexican American Protestant organization in Texas.[23] Similar development of a Mexican American evangelical presence advanced across the border region, especially in California. A case study of Latino/a Protestant churches in Los Angeles county in 1970 identified nearly 15,000 members of such churches, mostly in evangelical and Pentecostal congregations. The two largest bodies at that time were Baptist churches—both American Baptist and Southern Baptist—which accounted for over fifty churches and almost 4,000 members. Later studies showed that, in nine counties in southern California, by 1986 there more than 1,000 Latino/a (mostly Mexican American) churches in the region, the vast majority of them evangelical and Pentecostal.[24]

A trend in evangelical and Pentecostal Protestantism is the megachurch, a congregation that exceeds 2,000 in weekly attendance and whose worship is often professionally produced, entertaining, and geared toward attracting large audiences. While some megachurches are connected to Protestant denominations, many others are "non-denominational" but lean evangelical in their theology and worship styles. As of 2015, there were thirty-four such Latino/a megachurches across the United States, the majority of which were Pentecostal. Historian Kate Bowler explains that these churches' influence in their communities often matches their outsize congregations:

> As the largest churches drawn from the country's largest ethnic minority, supersized Latino congregations earned a public voice that resonated far beyond their church rosters. Their pastors stood at the control panel of vast television, radio, and Internet media production able to pique interest and sustain loyalties.[25]

An example is Cornerstone Church of San Diego, a megachurch led by Sergio de la Mora and his wife Georgina. De la Mora was born in Santa Barbara, California, to Mexican immigrant parents from Guadalajara, Mexico. His youth was a blend of skateboarding, working for his father in a landscaping business, entering a gang, and abusing cocaine. He converted to evangelical Christianity in his twenties and was soon called to found the Cornerstone Church in San Diego. Since then, the church has grown to over 6,000 members and has campuses around southern California, Arizona, and Mexico.[26] Like many other evangelical megachurches, Cornerstone's message, in De la Mora's hands, promises both spiritual and material well-being for church members. De la Mora's own life story becomes a testimonial for this kind of success. In an interview, he said,

> That's the new reality. I made it. And I didn't just make it for me. I did it—I'm doing it—for every young guy in the neighborhood right now, for every kid in the high school, for every guy in jail right now. For them to say, if Sergio De La Mora—who grew up in poverty, whose parents didn't even speak English, could get out of drugs and get out of gangs and become entrepreneurial and start a landscaping company, who buys houses and apartments and becomes a pastor and loves God and never forgets where he came from—it can be done. I am the new American Latino.[27]

Evangelical and Pentecostal megachurches promise to be a continuing area of growth within the Mexican American and Latino/a communities.

Religion in practice

Mexican American Pentecostals have a rich tradition of song. Of course, hymn singing, music, and chanting are commonplace in many Christian worship settings, and local song traditions often influence the musical expressions of Christian communities. Mexican Americans, familiar with *coritos*, or popular sung choruses, have combined this and other song forms with devotional lyrics. Historian Daniel Ramírez has studied Mexican and Mexican American Pentecostal singing, and he finds that Pentecostal songs and hymns reveal a great deal about the lived soundscape of this religious tradition. By casting the Pentecostal message to the sounds of popular *coritos*, in what Ramírez calls "resonant cultural frames," these songs and their singers embed Pentecostalism in "the soil of popular religiosity." Lyrics can paraphrase beloved passages from the Bible, express personal testimonials, and tell stories about the daily life of faith.[28] These heart-felt refrains lift up popular Mexican music as a purified vessel for holy words and emotions. Likewise, the guitar and other popular instruments are redeemed. Ramírez explains, "Freed of the libidinal stain of profane venues, the sanctified instruments evoked deep-seated affects embedded in the heart and memory of popular musical culture."[29]

One of the most well-known Pentecostal *coritos* is "Alabaré a mi Señor."

//Alabaré, alabaré
Alabaré a mi Señor//
Juan vió el número de los redimidos
Todos alababan al Señor
Unos cantaban, otros oraban
Pero todos alababan al Señor
//I shall praise, I shall praise
I shall praise my Lord//
John saw the number of the redeemed
They all were praising the Lord
Some were singing, others praying
But all were praising the Lord

The song recounts the vision of John in the biblical book of Revelation in which John sees God's faithful ones gathered in heaven, giving eternal praise. Ramírez suggests that the song has resonated so profoundly because it locates even the poor and the dispossessed of this world in God's divine presence, redeemed and blessed.[30] In fact, as charismatic worship styles have spread well beyond Pentecostal settings and into charismatic Catholic fellowship, "Alabaré a mi Señor" has become a standard of Latino/a Christian worship, tying together divergent Christian theological traditions in shared song.

Notes

1 For more on evangelical political attitudes, see Robert D. Putnam and David E. Campbell, *American Grace: How Religion United and Divides Us* (New York: Simon and Schuster, 2010), especially ch. 11.
2 Arlene M. Sánchez Walsh, *Pentecostals in America* (New York: Columbia University Press, 2018), xx–xxiii.
3 Gastón Espinosa, *Latino Pentecostals in America: Faith and Politics in Action* (Cambridge, MA: Harvard University Press, 2014), 35, 51–52.
4 Quoted in Espinosa, 22.
5 Espinosa, 101–3.
6 Daniel Ramírez, *Migrating Faith: Pentecostalism in the United States and Mexico in the Twentieth Century* (Chapel Hill, NC: University of North Carolina Press, 2015), 42–43, 49; Espinosa, *Latino Pentecostals in America*, 54.
7 Arlene M. Sánchez Walsh, *Latino Pentecostal Identity: Evangelical Faith, Self, and Society* (New York: Columbia University Press, 2003), 37–38.
8 Sánchez Walsh, 52.
9 Sánchez Walsh, 55, 57.
10 Sánchez Walsh, 59.
11 Ramírez, *Migrating Faith*, 91–94.
12 Candy Gunther Brown, ed., *Global Pentecostal and Charismatic Healing* (New York: Oxford University Press, 2011), 8.
13 For more on the history of healing in Pentecostalism, see Joseph W. Williams, *Spirit Cure: A History of Pentecostal Healing* (New York: Oxford University Press, 2013).
14 Sánchez Walsh, *Latino Pentecostal Identity*, 29.
15 Sánchez Walsh, 167–68.
16 Sánchez Walsh, 99–100.

17 Sánchez Walsh, 109, 141–43, 147.
18 Luis D. León, *La Llorona's Children: Religion, Life, and Death in the U.S.-Mexican Borderlands* (Berkeley, CA: University of California Press, 2004), 210–11, 249.
19 Comité Nacional de Servicio Hispano, "Quiénes Somos," Renovación Carismática Católica de los Estados Unidos y Canadá, accessed August 9, 2019, https://rcchispana.org/quienes_somos.html.
20 Timothy Matovina, *Latino Catholicism: Transformation in America's Largest Church* (Princeton, NJ: Princeton University Press, 2012), 115.
21 G. Cristina Mora-Torres, "What's So Ethnic about Ethno-Religious Identity?: Contemporary Evidence from Latino Immigrant 'Conversion Narratives,'" in *Conference Papers*, vol. 1 (American Sociological Association, Montreal, 2006), 16.
22 Mora-Torres, 23.
23 Juan Francisco Martínez, *The Story of Latino Protestants in the United States* (Grand Rapids, MI: Eerdmans, 2018), 57–59.
24 These studies are discussed in Martínez, 112–15.
25 Kate Bowler, "Looking Up: Latino Megachurches and the Politics of Social Mobility" (Unpublished paper, n.d.), 3–4.
26 Luke Travis, "Man of God, Man of Business," Fine Magazine, August 2012, http://www.finehomesandliving.com/August-2012/Man-of-God-Man-of-Business.
27 Anita K. Palmer, "Sergio De La Mora: Turning a Generation," OutreachMagazine.com, November 2, 2015, https://outreachmagazine.com/interviews/13492-sergio-de-la-mora-turning-a-generation.html.
28 Ramírez, *Migrating Faith*, 167–68.
29 Ramírez, 185.
30 Ramírez, 197.

9 Mexican American Catholics in the twentieth and twenty-first centuries

Protestantism made inroads into Mexican American communities during the late nineteenth and twentieth centuries, but overall, most Mexican Americans remained Catholic in this period, a fact which holds true today. The story of Mexican American Catholicism since the end of World War II is one of growth and struggle. Both U.S.-born Mexican Americans and Mexican immigrants in the twentieth century frequently experienced exploitation in U.S. fields and factories. The U.S. Catholic Church made various efforts to accommodate Mexican Americans, Mexican immigrants, and other Latin American newcomers, though not without internal and external opposition, often rooted in racial discrimination. This chapter profiles the work of an influential Anglo leader, Archbishop Robert Lucey of Texas, who worked to make room for Spanish-speaking Catholics in the twentieth century U.S. Church. The chapter also examines the struggles and encounters that Mexican American Catholics themselves engaged in to make their voices heard and to gain positions of leadership within the Church. Mexican American and other Latino/a Catholics organized a series of "Encuentros" that communicated their needs and positions to the rest of the Catholic Church even as these events provided opportunities for collaboration and fellowship.

Perhaps the biggest story for Mexican Americans in this period is that they, along with other Latinos/as, have become the largest ethnic minority community in the nation. This demographic sea change has had an impact on almost every aspect of life in the United States, including within the Catholic Church. Today, Latinos/as make up large percentages of the U.S. Catholic Church, a fact which is even more notable among young people. It is not an exaggeration to say that the U.S. Catholic Church will soon be a majority Latino/a organization.

Archbishop Robert E.Lucey and Mexican American Catholics

At the conclusion of World War II, Mexican American Catholics remained relatively marginalized in their dioceses. Barrio churches were active places of worship and community togetherness, but ongoing Mexican immigration, poverty, and racial discrimination—both in and out of the Church—continued

DOI: 10.4324/9780429285516-11

to stymie Mexican American integration and empowerment in Catholic parishes. Given the often top-down and hierarchical nature of the Church, it helped the Mexican American community considerably when the Archbishop of San Antonio, Robert E. Lucey, embraced a mission to address both the social and ecclesiastical inequities that plagued Mexican American Catholics.

Lucey's commitments to fighting injustice, oppression, and segregation, both in the workplace and in the Catholic Church, ran deep. A California native, Lucey embraced Catholic social doctrine, which demands justice and the right to organize for workers as well as a realignment of values for the wealthy.[1] In his first post as bishop in Amarillo, Texas, he was alarmed by the plight of Mexican American and Mexican workers. His advocacy in the Texas panhandle eventually propelled him to the post of Archbishop in San Antonio in 1941, where he continued to advocate for Mexican American Catholics. Like many reformers, Lucey believed that education was one of the best ways to confront and combat challenges. To this end, he worked to ensure that the Confraternity of Christian Doctrine, or CCD, (an educational program in Catholic teaching and tradition) was instituted throughout his archdiocese. His hope was two-pronged: he hoped that a proper Catholic education for all would protect Mexican American Catholics from Protestant proselytization and inspire Anglo Catholics to be more committed to addressing the needs of the poor and the immigrant.[2]

To address these concerns more broadly, Lucey and like-minded bishops formed the Bishops' Committee for the Spanish Speaking (BCSS) in 1945. The BCSS's mission included providing education, pastoral care, and economic assistance, primarily to Spanish-speaking migrants and citizens. The Committee's initial efforts focused on the archdioceses of San Antonio, Santa Fe, Denver, and Los Angeles, and included the creation of medical clinics, settlement houses, and catechetical programs. Eventually, the BCSS's work extended beyond the Southwest to the Midwest and New York, expanding its mission to dozens of dioceses around the nation.[3] To improve the chances that Spanish-speaking Catholics would be welcome in Catholic churches, Lucey was adamant that priests in his archdiocese learn Spanish. If all his priests were conversant in Spanish and able to preach and conduct their apostolic labors in that language, this would make it possible to assign priests of the archdiocese to any of its parishes. In this, Lucey was ahead of his time even though this measure was in line with recommendations that the Social Action Department of the National Catholic Welfare Council had issued in 1943:

> Priests should know the language of the people and use it in their ministrations. An even more important and demanding requirement is a sympathetic understanding of the people. Spanish should be learned in the seminaries, and when possible, seminarians should be sent for special training where they can imbibe the cultural atmosphere of Latin America.[4]

Lucey maintained a commitment to applying Catholic social teaching to U.S. society even when this put him at odds with fellow Catholics. His strident critiques and historical awareness went to the heart of problems faced by Mexican Americans. For instance, he wrote the following with a colleague:

> The greatest root of the trouble is that the first English-speaking people came here as conquerors and have tried ever since to rule as oppressors … instead of as brothers of the Spanish speaking in the development of a civilization that will bring both groups together. Yet the conquering attitude prevails.… Hardly anywhere in the United States is greater or more systematic injustice done to and suffered by the Spanish speaking of our dioceses.[5]

In the same document, he called on the Catholic Church to develop a program of assistance for Spanish-speaking Catholics. Such a program would help end Latinos/as "feeling that they do not belong, that they are somehow not Americans, that this country, theirs first, is not theirs now, that this region which they named with such beautiful and holy names is no longer theirs."[6] Lucey's diagnosis, though not accepted by many U.S. Catholics, had a long-lasting effect on the Church and helped to empower leaders from within Latino/a communities.

Lucey chaired the BCSS for more than twenty years. Over that time, he became convinced that the Catholic Church must speak out against labor abuses perpetrated against Latino/a agricultural workers. Lucey and other leaders in the BCSS raised a public outcry against some of the worst abuses faced by the migrant farmworkers. A key problem was that citizen workers in the fields were often pitted against Mexican guest workers (see next section) and workers who were in the U.S. illegally. The presence of foreign workers, in Lucey's estimation, made it difficult, if not impossible, for domestic farmworkers to organize in defense of their own interests.[7]

The Bracero program and the United Farmworkers

Labor shortages caused by World War II led to the creation of a guest-worker program wherein U.S. industries—primarily agribusiness—were authorized to import Mexican workers, known as "braceros," to work for a time before the laborers were sent back to their home country. The quality of the braceros' fieldwork combined with their relatively low wages made this arrangement highly profitable for U.S. agriculture so that the bracero program persisted long after the war was over. It did not come to an end until 1964, and only then after Mexican American farmworkers and a host of others, including Catholic leaders in the BCSS, successfully mobilized to end the program, citing its exploitative nature. Collaborations between Mexican American labor leaders and Catholic priests in and around the bracero program and among other farmworkers set the stage for unionization and the eventual formation of the United Farmworkers.

The bracero program presented a complex set of issues. First, the conditions in bracero labor camps were frequently abominable, including mismanaged wages, unsafe housing, insufficient medical care, and social isolation. On top of these concerns, the presence of guest workers put a damper on farmworker wages as well as the ability of farmworkers to unionize. With a steady stream of cheap, Mexican labor available, growers had little reason to meet farmworker requests for better wages and working conditions.[8] The BCSS joined labor and immigration activists in the important work of raising consciousness among Catholic laypeople about the bracero program. The Catholic Council for the Spanish Speaking, a lay and clergy group akin to the BCSS, issued a statement in 1955 calling for greater protections for farmworkers. "That since migratory farm labor is often voteless, unorganized, and poorly protected by law, [the Council] urges its members to form local citizens' committees to represent the interests of its citizens who are farm laborers." In the following year, the Council called for the termination of the bracero program altogether.[9] In short, their opposition to the bracero program was for two reasons: the unjust conditions under which braceros worked *and* a desire to strengthen domestic farmworker unionization efforts.

In California, a unique group formed in 1950 to minister to the thousands of braceros in the state. Inspired at a BCSS conference, Fathers Donald McDonnell, Ralph Duggan, Thomas McCullough, and John Garcia formed the Spanish Mission Band. Freed from all parish service by their archbishop and charged with seeing to the needs of migratory farmworkers, the members of the Mission Band organized community centers, offered Catholic education to farmworker families, and celebrated Masses in the fields themselves with braceros. During all this, they collaborated with other organizers to promote the unionization of farmworkers as the best—and most doctrinally sound—way of protecting the interests of Mexican and Mexican American workers.[10]

The priests of the Spanish Mission Band made partnerships with labor activists, most notably with budding Mexican American organizers who would go on to form the United Farmworkers (UFW), the most important union for migrant agricultural laborers. Father McCullough, in collaboration with Dolores Huerta, established the Agricultural Workers Association. This association was eventually folded into the agricultural union that became the UFW. Another Spanish Mission Band priest, Father McDonnell, worked with César Chávez. Chávez became the lead organizer for the Community Service Organization, a group that promoted labor rights, particularly in urban areas. Eventually, Huerta and Chávez would be founders and key leaders in the UFW, where their Catholicism and Catholic social teaching would continue to guide their activities (see Chapter 11).[11]

Another initiative, begun in 1953, was "Operation Migratory Labor." This operation, prompted and guided by the BCSS, created a partnership between the U.S. and Mexican Catholic hierarchies to station Mexican missionary priests among bracero and other migrant farmworkers in the United States. The Mexican Catholic Church was especially worried about Protestant proselytism as well as the threat of moral decay among Mexican citizens while they labored abroad. U.S. leaders, including Archbishop Lucey, were pleased to host the priests in order to meet the pastoral needs of thousands of underserved Catholics in the fields. Operation Migratory Labor, though it did not last long, was an important example of binational Catholic cooperation to minister to Mexicans and Mexican Americans. Under pressure from religious groups and unions, the bracero program finally ended in 1964. The legacy of Catholic social activism in support of farmworkers, however, would persist well past that date.[12]

Mexican American leadership in the U.S. Catholic Church

To be sure, Mexican Americans in the middle of the twentieth century faced challenges in their communities and places of work. And, despite the powerful if imperfect advocacy of some Catholic leaders, such as Archbishop Lucey, Mexican American Catholics often faced similar barriers to inclusion and integration within the Catholic Church. Nevertheless, the story of Mexican American Catholicism, in many ways, is one of finding a voice, clamoring for change and a place at the table, and celebrating new avenues of leadership and community support. The Second Vatican Council (1962–1965) sparked epochal changes in the Catholic Church around the world even as demographic shifts and the civil rights movement in the U.S. created new horizons for Mexican Americans. Another influence on Mexican American Catholics was liberation theology emerging from Latin America and U.S.-based Latino/a theologians. Important ecclesiastical conferences in Latin America helped to crystallize and promote liberation theology and its practices among Spanish-speaking Catholics throughout the hemisphere. Liberationist techniques of *ver-juzgar-actuar* (see-judge-act) assisted Mexican American Catholics to reframe their experience and to advocate for themselves in the U.S. Church. Mexican American theologians likewise drew on the Latino/a context to formulate liberationist perspectives in the United States.[13]

It was during this period that several Mexican American Catholic organizations were formed to make more visible the contributions as well as the needs of Latino/a Catholics. For instance, a number of south Texas priests, including Patricio Flores and Virgilio Elizondo, organized PADRES (Padres Asociados para Derechos Religiosos, Educativos, y Sociales) in 1969. The group worked to promote Mexican American pastoral and episcopal leadership as well as social change regarding education and justice for Mexican Americans. At its height, PADRES represented 350 priests, religious, and deacons throughout the country.[14] Born from the organizing of several Mexican American nuns, Las Hermanas, like PADRES, worked to strengthen "the Spanish-speaking people of God, using our unique resources as the Spanish-speaking religious women."[15] Their activism was particularly empowering for Mexican American women, whose voices had often been sidelined or silenced in the Catholic Church. Historian Lara Medina notes the importance of Las Hermanas, writing that they brought "the Chicano movement *and* Chicana feminism into the U.S. Roman Catholic Church."[16] They did this in a variety of ways, from advocating for women's ordination to promoting women's needs to high-lighting intersectional issues of race and gender among Catholic women's groups.

The changing scene both within the U.S. and internationally gave impetus to a national meeting of Latino/a Catholic leaders to discuss their needs and celebrate their unique place within the U.S. Catholic Church. This meeting, which set the stage for later gatherings, happened in 1972 and was called the Primer Encuentro Hispano de Pastoral (First Hispanic Pastoral Encounter). The first Mexican American bishop, Patricio Flores, addressed the Encuentro and noted the exclusion that Latinos/as often felt in their parishes as well as the general neutrality of the national Church when it came to advocating for Latinos/as' needs in an oppressive and discriminatory society. The 250 Encuentro participants produced a blueprint for Hispanic ministry that contained seventy-eight recommendations. While not all of these were ultimately achieved, the blueprint was successful in highlighting and promoting Latino/a Catholic needs, including more diocesan attention to their concerns, more Spanish-speaking clergy as well as married Latino deacons, more Hispanic bishops, greater levels of funding for Latino/a ministries, and the promotion of the U.S. bishops' Hispanic office to the more prominent administrative level of a secretariat. In short, the first Encuentro's general tenor was activist, with a clear focus on structural changes in the U.S Catholic Church to address decades of neglect of its Latino/a members.[17]

This first Encuentro helped set an agenda for Latino/a Catholics and set the stage for subsequent Encuentros. The second such gathering happened in 1977 and was organized by a host of Latino/a organizations and ministries within the Catholic Church. The second Encuentro enjoyed broad participation of Catholic leaders, including all eight Latino U.S. bishops and dozens of other bishops as well as 600 delegates and another 600 observers; in contrast to the first gathering, laity were in the majority in 1977. If the message of the first Encuentro was a declaration to the U.S. Catholic Church that Latinos/as were active and present, the second Encuentro communicated to the Church that Latino/a cultures, traditions, and religious devotions and customs needed to be recognized as an essential part of U.S. Catholicism. In the words of Bishop Boza Masvidal, this meant that Hispanic Catholics deserved "integration without assimilation." To this end, the Encuentro, through extensive small group consultations, articulated a bottom-up vision of Latino/a Catholic ministry that focused on economic justice, respect for various cultures, and commitment to liberation of the poor and oppressed.[18]

The third Encuentro occurred in 1985 on the heels of the U.S. Bishops' 1983 pastoral letter, *The Hispanic Presence, Challenge, and Commitment*.[19] An emphasis in this Encuentro, which would later be reflected in the U.S. Bishops National Pastoral Plan for Hispanic Ministry in 1987, was a *pastoral de conjunto*, a Latin American liberationist concept that calls for different constituencies to work together in the Church in a participatory and integrated way. However, due to budgetary cuts and administrative restructuring, some of the advances of the Encuentros had been reversed by the 1990s. Another Encuentro did not take place again until the year 2000. Encuentro 2000, in contrast to earlier gatherings, focused more on the celebration of cultural diversity than on advocacy for Latino/a Catholics.[20] Historian Timothy Matovina notes that some Catholic leaders found that Encuentro 2000 "inadvertently contributed to the waning of Hispanic ministry initiatives, as that Encuentro's accentuation of the rich cultural diversity in U.S. Catholicism buttressed a rationale for the consolidation of racial and ethnic ministry offices into multicultural ones."[21] This emphasis moved the Encuentro 2000, and Catholic Latino/a ministry in general, away from earlier reclamations for recognizing and addressing specific Hispanic concerns and toward Latino/a inclusion in more generalized multicultural programs.

The most recent Encuentro, the fifth, met in 2018 and, at the time of publication of this book, is perhaps too new to assess. The vision and theme of "V Encuentro" was "missionary discipleship." According to the event's website, participants "emphasized the necessity for a continual pastoral conversation that allows the Church, consistent with its missionary nature, to respond with more fidelity and enthusiasm to the Hispanic/Latino presence in parishes and dioceses." This missionary spirit will move the Church to "empower the Hispanic/Latino people to live their vocation more fully as joyful missionaries to the whole Church."[22] The Encuentro carried out a multi-year national consultation to gather reams of data about the state of Latino/a Catholics in the U.S. Catholic Church in the second decade of this century; it also focused specific attention on Latino/a young people and the issue of immigration. It is early to say, but this Encuentro seems to have returned somewhat to the advocacy and focus on specific Latino/a concerns and culture that marked the first Encuentros.

In addition to the Encuentros, another sign of Mexican Americans' growing influence on the U.S. Catholic Church was the emergence of Mexican American prelates and theologians. The first Mexican American priest to be ordained as a bishop was Patricio Flores in 1970. Flores was born in Texas in a migrant family, and he worked there on various ministries, including the Bishops' Committee for the Spanish Speaking and outreach to farmworkers. After first serving as the bishop of El Paso, he was elevated in 1979 to the position of Archbishop of San Antonio, where he served until his retirement in 2004.[23] Father Virgilio Elizondo, Flores's contemporary, began his career in the 1970s as one of the first and most important Mexican American Catholic theologians. With a theological education from the Sorbonne in Paris and parish experience in San Antonio's San Fernando Cathedral, Elizondo took up the concept of *mestizaje* as a foundational principle of Mexican American religious identity, one that sanctified and transcended the hierarchies and prejudices of the colonization of the Americas. His work empowered Mexican Americans by situating their racial and cultural experience of *mestizaje* within the life of Jesus in the biblical borderland of Galilee. "Our situation and struggles were anticipated by [Jesus], and in his situation and struggles the meaning and purpose of our own come to light."[24]

Figure 9.1 Most Rev. Patrick F. Flores, Archbishop of San Antonio, ca. 1979. Courtesy
Catholic Archdiocese of San Antonio Archives.

In recent years, one sign of the importance of Latino/a issues within the U.S.
Catholic Church is an institutional commitment to immigration reform and the
just treatment of immigrants. In 2003, the bishops of both the United States
and Mexico issued a joint pastoral letter entitled "Strangers No Longer Together on the Journey of Hope." Rooting their position in scripture, Church
tradition, and Catholic social teaching, the bishops called for political reform to
make migration safer and more humane. They also admonished U.S. congregations to make room for migrants: "We call on the local church to help
newcomers integrate in ways that are respectful, that celebrate their cultures,
and that are responsive to their social needs, leading to a mutual enrichment of
the local church." In addition, churches are asked to provide social service to
migrants, especially legal aid, and to make provision to care for those who have
been incarcerated as a result of immigration. In a nod to the difficult history of
the border region, the bishops reminded Catholics to afford Native peoples
"special consideration" as people whose lands are divided and militarized by

global forces.[25] This pastoral letter was hardly the last word. Hundreds of additional statements from local clergy all the way to Pope Francis have continued to bring Catholic attention to bear on the rights of immigrants, particularly at the U.S.-Mexico border.

Demographic shifts in the U.S. Catholic Church

Of course, the topic of this book is *Mexican American* religion, but recent demography concerning U.S. religious institutions rarely differentiates Mexican Americans from other Latino/a people. In such cases, it can be difficult to know what percentage of religious participants are Mexican American rather than tracing ancestry to other Latin American nations. However, it is not irrelevant to remember that over 63 percent of the nearly 57 million Latinos/as in the U.S. in 2015 identified as Mexican or Mexican American.[26] In other words, Mexican Americans continue to comprise nearly two-thirds of all Latinos/as across the nation. Of course, this can vary by region and from community to community, but in general, data about "Latinos/as" necessarily includes a solid majority of Mexican Americans.

The most salient fact, in general but also for religious institutions, is that the Latino/a population has undergone meteoric growth in the last half-century. In 1970, there were 9.6 million Latinos/as in the United States. In 2016, that figure had risen to 57.5 million, an increase of almost 600 percent. A large majority of Latinos/as were born in the U.S., with only a third being foreign-born.[27] Although Latinos/as live in all fifty states, the places where they represent the largest percentage of the population are in the northeast, Florida, and, not surprisingly, the U.S.-Mexico border states. The top five states with the highest percentage of Latinos/as in order are New Mexico, California, Texas, Arizona, and Nevada.[28] While Latinos/as in this western and southwestern region of the nation are not solely Mexican American, the majority is made up of this group.

The U.S. Catholic Church is becoming a Latino/a-majority institution, and this trend promises to continue in the foreseeable future. At least two factors are responsible for this transformation. First, the Catholic Church is losing Anglo members faster than Latino/a ones. Political scientists Robert Putnam and David Campbell reported in 2010 that around 60 percent of people who had been raised Catholic in the U.S. were no longer practicing. However, they found that this acute loss of membership was twice as high among Anglos compared to Latino/a Catholics.[29] The second factor is the growth of the Latino/a community due to high rates of immigration. In fact, the Catholic Church would have experienced steep declines as a percentage of the U.S. population if it were not for the ongoing influx of Latin American immigrants who continue to replenish Catholic membership rolls. Putnam and Campbell pull no punches in their description of this phenomenon: "Without the inflow of Latinos to shore up the number of Catholics in the United States, the American Catholic population would have experienced a catastrophic collapse."[30] This is particularly true of younger

Catholics, those 18 to 34 years of age. In this age range of U.S. Catholics, 58 percent are Latino/a. Young Latinos/as also attend Mass with far more regularity than their non-Latino/a peers.[31]

While it is a demographic inevitability that the U.S. Catholic Church will soon be a Latino/a-majority church, not all young Latinos/as are staying in the Church. Recent surveys indicate that there have been significant declines in Latino/a membership in the Catholic Church since the first decade of the twenty-first century. A study by the Pew Research Center shows a steady decline since 2010 in the percentage of Latinos/as who identify as Catholics. In 2010, 77 percent of Latinos/as said they were Catholics. Only four years later, this figure had gone down to 55 percent. The American Religious Identification Survey (ARIS) also documented a decline in Latino/a Catholicism but found it less precipitous than the Pew report. According to ARIS, from 1990 to 2008, the percentage of Latinos/as who self identify as Catholic went from 65.8 percent to 59.5 percent.[32]

There are a variety of reasons for this recent departure from the Catholic Church. First, as many Latin Americans convert to forms of Protestantism, more and more immigrants from the region had already left the Catholic Church prior to their emigration. The Pew study suggests that, of first-generation Latin American immigrants who have ceased being Catholic, roughly half switched their religious identify before entering the United States. Second, Latinos/as are not just leaving Catholicism for Protestantism (or different religions); many are entering the ranks of the religious non-affiliated, or "nones." In 2013, 18 percent of Latinos/as claimed no religious affiliation, a rapid increase from 10 percent in 2010. Finally, Pentecostal and other charismatic churches continue to be especially attractive to many Latinos/as. Around two-thirds of Latino/a Protestants identify as Pentecostal or charismatic. People in this group are often attracted to these churches because they claim to have received divine healing or gotten a direct revelation from God. These powerful experiences are playing a significant role in attracting Latinos/as away from the Catholic fold.[33]

Religion in practice

In the liturgical season of Advent, Catholics and other Christians prepare for Christmas by remembering the biblical stories related to Jesus's birth. The gospel of Luke in the New Testament recounts the journey that Joseph and Mary, who is pregnant and near the time of delivery, make to the town of Bethlehem. When they arrive, it turns out that all of the inns (*posadas* in Spanish) are full, and the holy couple have no choice but to accept make-do shelter in a stable for livestock. In this humble circumstance, Jesus is born. The story is a poignant and theologically rich start to Jesus's life since Christians believe that Jesus is the Son of God and therefore God himself in human form. To be born in this way suggests Jesus's future identification with the poor, the homeless, and with migrants on the road.

Bringing the tradition from Mexico, many Mexican American Catholics celebrate this story, called *las posadas*, in December. Members of the community dress as Mary and Joseph, or carry statues of them, and lead processions through their neighborhoods. They re-enact the biblical story, knocking on doors to seek shelter, only to be turned away again and again. Finally, they find a place to rest and are welcomed in, prayers are said, and the gathered community celebrates together with music and delicious foods, such as tamales, pan dulce, and hot chocolate. Children often break open a piñata, and a good time is had by all. *Las posadas*, like many Catholic observances, lasts for nine days—a novena. In this case, the festivities begin on December 16 and run until the night of Christmas Eve, when Jesus's birth is remembered and celebrated.

Initially, *las posadas* was primarily a neighborhood celebration. It was a festive opportunity for communities to socialize in an intimate way, visiting friends' and relatives' homes for several evenings prior to Christmas. With the growth of Mexican American parishes, however, it has become quite common today for the church building itself to be part of *las posadas*, with the church comprising the final stop—the "stable" where the baby Jesus is born—a setting which also facilitates the participation of clergy and the celebration of Mass. Some of these events have grown beyond neighborhood and parish communities and serve as a time of cultural and religious sharing with those outside of the Mexican American Catholic community.[34]

Figure 9.2 Posadas procession in Corrales, New Mexico, 1946. Courtesy Corrales Historical Society.

Las posadas, in addition to being a holiday celebration, is a meaningful and public expression of Mexican American Catholicism. It allows families, and especially children, to perform a central Christian story in a way that promotes community togetherness and good will. When linked to the local parish, it highlights the importance of Mexican American Catholic traditions. The story itself, of Joseph and Mary travelling far from home with no place to rest, can sometimes resonate with Mexican Americans, especially those still close to the experience of immigration. Theologian and priest Virgilio Elizondo wrote that *las posadas* is a "reminder and reenactment" that at least some Mexican Americans "have walked at night and through snake-infested deserts, to the U.S.A. in hope of finding work. What they found instead was rejection after rejection. But, like Joseph and Mary, they did not give up; they followed their star."[35]

Notes

1 See Robert Royal and George Weigel, eds., *A Century of Catholic Social Thought: Essays on Rerum Novarum and Nine Other Key Documents* (Washington, DC: Ethics and Public Policy Center; University Press of America, 1991), especially the essays on *Rerum Novarum* and *Quadragesimo Anno*.
2 Jay P. Dolan and Gilberto M. Hinojosa, *Mexican Americans and the Catholic Church, 1900–1965* (Notre Dame, IN: University of Notre Dame Press, 1994), 112; Timothy M. Matovina, *Latino Catholicism: Transformation in America's Largest Church* (Princeton, NJ: Princeton University Press, 2012), 72.
3 Matovina, *Latino Catholicism: Transformation in America's Largest Church*, 71–72.
4 National Catholic Welfare Council, Social Action Department, "The Spanish Speaking of the Southwest and West" (Washington, DC: National Catholic Welfare Council, 1943), 27.
5 "1945 Draft of a Pastoral Letter by R. E. Lucey and R. A. McGowan on the Condition of Hispanic Catholics in the United States," reproduced in Stephen A. Privett, *The U.S. Catholic Church and Its Hispanic Members: The Pastoral Vision of Archbishop Robert E. Lucey* (San Antonio, TX: Trinity University Press, 1988), Appendix C, 218.
6 Privett, 219.
7 Saul E. Bronder, *Social Justice and Church Authority: The Public Life of Archbishop Robert E. Lucey* (Philadelphia, PA: Temple University Press, 1982), 75–76, 79.
8 Ernesto Galarza, *Strangers in Our Fields* (Washington, DC: Joint United States-Mexico Trade Union Committee, 1956).
9 *Proceedings of the Seventh Regional Conference, Catholic Council for the Spanish Speaking*, 19–21 April 1955, cited in Rosemary E. Smith, "The Work of the Bishops' Committee for the Spanish Speaking on Behalf of the Migrant Worker" (M.A. thesis, Washington, DC, Catholic University of America, 1958), 22–23.
10 Dolan and Hinojosa, *Mexican Americans and the Catholic Church, 1900–1965*, 1:214–15.
11 Dolan and Hinojosa, 1:204, 219–20.
12 Gráinne McEvoy, "'Operation Migratory Labor': Braceros, Migrants, and the American Catholic Bishops' Committee for the Spanish Speaking," *U.S. Catholic Historian* 34, no. 3 (2016): 87, 89, 96.
13 Matovina, *Latino Catholicism: Transformation in America's Largest Church*, 75, 77.
14 Badillo, *Latinos and the New Immigrant Church*, 158–59; Richard Edward Martínez, *Padres: The National Chicano Priest Movement* (Austin, TX: University of Texas Press, 2005).

15 Lara Medina, *Las Hermanas: Chicana/Latina Religious-Political Activism in the U.S. Catholic Church* (Philadelphia, PA: Temple University Press, 2004), 13.

16 Medina, 45.

17 Matovina, 77–78.

18 Matovina, 80–82.

19 National Conference of Catholic Bishops, *The Hispanic Presence, Challenge, and Commitment: A Pastoral Letter on Hispanic Ministry, December 12, 1983* (Washington, DC: United States Catholic Conference, 1984).

20 Matovina, *Latino Catholicism: Transformation in America's Largest Church*, 83–86.

21 Matovina, 94.

22 V Encuentro, "The Call to a V Encuentro," V Encuentro, accessed October 1, 2019, https://vencuentro.org/encuentros/v-encuentro.

23 David A. Badillo, *Latinos and the New Immigrant Church* (Baltimore, MD: Johns Hopkins University Press, 2006), 157–58.

24 Virgilio P. Elizondo, *Galilean Journey: The Mexican-American Promise* (Maryknoll, NY: Orbis Books, 1983), 89; Badillo, *Latinos and the New Immigrant Church*, 156–57.

25 United States Conference of Catholic Bishops and Conferencia del Episcopado Mexicano, "Strangers No Longer Together on the Journey of Hope," 2003, http://www.usccb.org/issues-and-action/human-life-and-dignity/immigration/strangers-no-longer-together-on-the-journey-of-hope.cfm.

26 Antonio Flores, Gustavo López, and Jynnah Radford, "Facts on Latinos in America: Current Data," Pew Research Center, Hispanic Trends, September 18, 2017, https://www.pewresearch.org/hispanic/2017/09/18/2015-statistical-information-on-hispanics-in-united-states-current-data.

27 Antonio Flores, "How the U.S. Hispanic Population Is Changing," Pew Research Center, September 18, 2017, https://www.pewresearch.org/fact-tank/2017/09/18/how-the-u-s-hispanic-population-is-changing.

28 Flores, López, and Radford, "Facts on Latinos in America: Current Data."

29 Robert D. Putnam and David E. Campbell, *American Grace: How Religion United and Divides Us* (New York: Simon and Schuster, 2010), 140–41.

30 Putnam and Campbell, 299.

31 Putnam and Campbell, 300.

32 Navarro-Rivera, Juhem, Barry A. Kosmin, and Ariela Keysar, "U.S. Latino Religious Identification 1990–2008: Growth, Diversity and Transformation" (Hartford, CT: American Religious Identification Survey, Trinity College, 2008), 1.

33 Pew Research Center, "The Shifting Religious Identity of Latinos in the United States," May 7, 2014, https://www.pewforum.org/2014/05/07/the-shifting-religious-identity-of-latinos-in-the-united-states.

34 Mary MacGregor-Villarreal, "Celebrating Las Posadas in Los Angeles," *Western Folklore* 39, no. 2 (April 1980): 71–105; Roberto R. Treviño, *The Church in the Barrio: Mexican American Ethno-Catholicism in Houston* (Chapel Hill, NC: University of North Carolina Press, 2006), 49.

35 Elizondo, *Galilean Journey*, 38.

Part II

Topics in Mexican American religion

10 Curanderismo

There exists a centuries-long tradition of religious and folk healing throughout Latin America, which is often referred to as "curanderismo." The word itself is rooted in the Spanish word "curar," which means "to cure," or "to heal." The word for a healer, then is "curandera" or "curandero." Curanderas/os have served Mexican and Mexican American communities for generations, sometimes as the principal providers of healing, other times as a complement to modern biomedicine. The practices of curanderismo, moreover, are common in many Mexican American households in the form of home remedies and unique ritual and cultural practices around the experience of sickness.

A study of Mexican American curanderismo belongs in a book about Mexican American religions for at least two reasons. The first is that curanderas/os generally situate their healing within their Catholic faith. For example, and as is discussed in more detail later in this chapter, saint veneration and Catholic prayers are common features of many healing practices within curanderismo. Some contemporary curanderas/os, however, eschew the Catholic roots of the tradition in an effort to reclaim a pre-colonial, Indigenous practice. They invoke pre-Hispanic pantheons and particular Aztec gods as sources of healing and guidance. The second reason is that curanderismo itself, even when not explicitly tied to Catholicism or Mesoamerican Indigenous religions, expresses a metaphysical understanding of sickness, healing, and wellness. In this sense, curanderismo operates, if not like a stand-alone religion, as an adjunct to the religion and culture of many Mexican Americans. The study of curanderismo can, therefore, reveal a great deal about Mexican American daily religious and spiritual life.

A short history of Mexican American curanderismo

To be sure, there were many long-lived and rich healing traditions among the Indigenous people of the western hemisphere long before the cataclysmic arrival of the Europeans. For a variety of factors, it can be difficult, or even impossible, to know many accurate details about these traditions. First, most of the documentary evidence about pre-conquest Indigenous life comes to us mediated through the lens of Spanish and other European conquerors and

DOI: 10.4324/9780429285516-13

evangelists. Not only do these kinds of accounts reveal the biases of the authors, we also do not know how honest or forthcoming their Indigenous sources were with them in the first place. In a time of intense existential threat, it was not uncommon for Indigenous peoples to jealously guard their cultural knowledge. Second, the knowledge that has been passed down through the generations within Indigenous communities—another important source of information about the Indigenous past—is likewise mediated through centuries of contact, resistance, and accommodation with non-Indigenous people in the Americas. This is not to say that Indigenous people's memories about their past are inaccurate; rather, all remembrances of the past must necessarily reflect the messy influences of the passage of time. Finally, and tragically, some pre-Conquest Indigenous traditions, languages, and entire peoples were destroyed altogether by European violence and diseases.

With these caveats, there are still many ongoing and vital Indigenous healthways in the Americas, some of which have combined with Spanish ones to become what we now consider Mexican and Mexican American curanderismo. Indeed, medicinal as well as ritual knowledge about healing was a site of significant exchange between Indigenous peoples and the Europeans, at least in part because medieval European healthcare was in no way more efficacious or advanced than Native healing techniques of the same period. Of course, Native knowledge of medicinal plants in what would soon become known as the Americas was vastly superior to the that of the Europeans. The latter exported some of their own herbal pharmacopeia, but they were utterly dependent on the Indigenous people to access the medicinal plants of the western hemisphere.

Given their imperial control of central Mexico, the Mexicas' (Aztecs') customs and understandings of wellness had a major influence on the healthcare traditions that would emerge in central Mexico and spread around New Spain. According to the Mexican historian Alfredo López Austin, who has made exhaustive studies of early Nahuatl materials, the Mexica understood that several forces animated the human body. Due to Christian influence, these forces have often been equated linguistically with the notion of "soul," though in the Mexica system, the so-called soul was not a unified entity but rather a collection of forces with diverse functions. Moreover, these "souls" could and did suffer injuries that could fracture them into pieces. These pieces, or the entire soul, could depart from the body, leading to a host of symptoms that eventually came to be known as "soul loss," a category of malady that remains very common today, often referred to in Spanish as *susto* (literally "fright").[1]

Other Mexica and Mesoamerican healing practices that likely contributed to an emerging curanderismo were notions of cosmic balance and the interpretation of dreams. Details of Aztec religious worldviews are the subject of Chapter 1 of this book; it may be recalled that maintaining cosmic balance was a key principle undergirding much Mexica mythology and ritual practice. This extended to understandings of health and sickness in the human body, particularly in a perceived hot/cold dichotomy. Keeping the body in balance by the proper consumption of hot or cold foods—and sometimes medicines—

constituted part of a daily healthcare regime.[2] The interpretation of dreams also formed part of curing. The dreams in question could be those experienced during a regular night of sleep, or they could originate from trance states entered into specifically to pursue the healing of certain illnesses. Healing specialists, sometimes referred to in later literature as "shamans" or "medicine men," would interpret dreams to help lead to restoration of health, and they would sometimes enter dream states themselves alongside the patient to fight off the metaphysical causes of suffering.[3] Both these practices—maintaining balance in the body and interpreting dreams—continue to flourish in contemporary curanderismo.

Sixteenth-century Iberian healthcare did not exist outside of a Catholic worldview. For the Spanish conquistadors and friars who overtook the Aztec Empire, experiences of sickness and suffering were extrinsically tied to an all-powerful and sometimes inscrutable God. In this context, illness could often point to a known or unknown iniquity in the life of the patient that must be confessed. In the horror of Indigenous mass death due to the violence of the Conquest combined with European disease, this frequent equation of sickness with sinfulness provided a powerful justification for continued Spanish evangelization of the Natives. Their suffering and mortality acted as proofs of the Indigenous need for the Christian Gospel and immediate baptism into the faith. The priests and friars also served a medical function during evangelistic campaigns. According to a seventeenth-century Jesuit chronicler,

> In the one hand [priests] carried the holy oil, which they administered to the people along with the other sacraments for healing souls. In the other hand they carried all the medicines and aids that they could find to heal and mend bodies.[4]

European Christians had long interceded with saints as a part of healing. In Catholic theology, saints' holy lives as well as their unfettered access to God make them ideal and powerful intercessors who can influence God to act miraculously in people's lives. In medieval Europe, the cult of the saints, including many zealous devotions to images or apparitions of the Virgin Mary, often involved shrines, relics, pilgrimage, and frequent intercessory prayer. Certain saints, often due to happenstances in their lives, were associated with specific illnesses or medical conditions. For instance, St. Lucy (Santa Lucía) is the patron of eye ailments and blindness; St. Blaise (San Blas) cares for illnesses of the throat. A Jesuit who was active in northern Mexico, Juan de Esteyneffer, published an important medical text in the early 1700s that demonstrated that combinations between Native medicines and Catholic saint veneration were well underway. In his book, known as the *Florilegio Medicinal*, Esteyneffer catalogued ailments, and remedies typically included some kind of herbal or mineral medication (often using American flora) combined with instructions to intercede with the saint who best corresponded with the illness in question.[5]

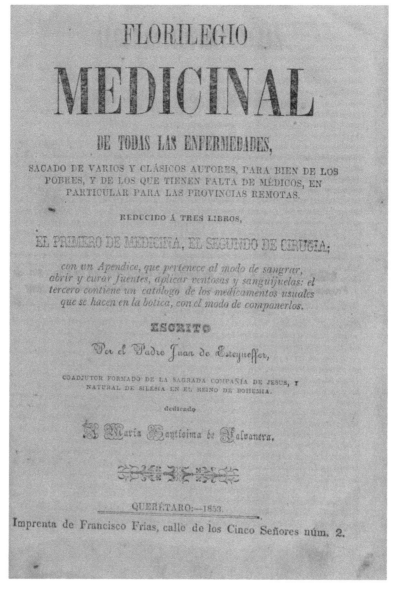

Figure 10.1 The title page of an 1853 edition of the *Florilegio Medicinal*. In public
    domain.

Another paradigmatic aspect of sixteenth-century Iberian healing was a
humoral understanding of the body, a medical system that Muslims had intro-
duced to Spain, which had roots going even farther back in the Mediterranean
world. In the humoral system, the body is thought to be ruled by four humors
made up of two opposing forces: hot/cold and dry/moist. Illnesses indicated an

imbalance in the humors such that a particular illness could be, for instance, hot and moist. Such a scenario would suggest that an appropriate treatment would introduce cold and dry elements to the body to restore balance.[6] Over time, and perhaps influenced by pre-existing Mesoamerican beliefs, the hot/cold dichotomy replaced the four humors. It remains common today in many Mexican American households for illnesses as well as certain foods to be categorized as "cold" or "hot." In such cases, a change in diet and herbal medicines are common home remedies for minor health problems.[7]

Efficaciousness is a primary driver for sick people everywhere when it comes to the types of healing they will use. In a word, people practice the medicine and treatments that work to heal them. In a colonial context of massive and recurring epidemics as well as daily health concerns, it is not surprising that Spanish and Indigenous healing beliefs and practices combined to meet the needs of the sick. Over time, the curanderos/as, "healers," developed a vital and evolving tradition. Since much of curanderismo overlapped with Catholicism, a complex relationship grew up between curanderos/as and local clergy. At times priests accused healers of heterodox beliefs and practices inimical to the faith, while at other times they acknowledged that curanderos/as' prayers and rituals were expressions of sincere Catholic devotion. With or without official Catholic support, curanderos/as were often the best, or only, option for healing in much of New Spain (and, later, Mexico).

Curanderismo spread north with the Spanish Empire into what would eventually become northern Mexico, and later the southwestern United States. Healing on this northern frontier relied heavily on community curanderos/as, especially in remote areas that sometimes went for long spells without the care of the clergy, much less medical doctors. Historian David Weber suggests that new, ostensibly scientific medicines began to enter the region in the early nineteenth century. However, these drugs and treatments, while sometimes effective, were often "therapeutically useless" or even harmful. In this context, "the familiar herbs and manners of folk doctors, or *curanderos*, were more beneficial than some of the new medicines and had the further advantage of providing psychological comfort that in itself was therapeutic"[8] As a result, curanderismo remained the healing tradition of choice for many Mexicans and Mexican Americans throughout the nineteenth century.

By the middle of the twentieth century, curanderismo, according to the anthropologist Octavio Romano, continued to be a culturally pervasive practice for Mexican Americans at many levels of social engagement. This means that, while curanderismo is often the province of specially trained healers— curanderos/as—the practice also exists within the home. The first line of care is generally the women of the household, with grandmothers, mothers, and daughters often prescribing home remedies and leading prayers. Outside of the home, curanderos/as (who may or may not work full-time as healers) handle cases that exceed the scope of the household. Romano notes that curanderos/as' place in the community has religious elements. "Common ... is the ascription of his or her power to a divine vision or visitation, and thus the practice takes on the proportions of a divine mission both in the eyes of the healer and his [or her] followers."[9]

Before the advent of modern medicine, of course, folk and religious healing traditions like curanderismo constituted the primary response to illness and injury. However, as scientific medical care has become more advanced and available, one might assume that curanderismo would be pushed to the side and possibly even forgotten. For a variety of reasons, this has generally not been the case in the Mexican American community. First, due to economic and social segregation, Mexican Americans (like other people of color in the United States) have not always had access to biomedical healthcare. As a result, the care of the curandero/a remained important. Second, according to many medical anthropologists, folk medicines often specialize in what they have called "culture-bound syndromes," which are afflictions that are limited to one cultural group. Presumably, these ailments, even when evidenced by obvious physical symptoms, are in some way caused by the cultural context of the sufferer. Since they are not recognized by scientific medicine, these syndromes must be treated by culturally appropriate healers. In studies of curanderismo, these conditions are often called "Mexican diseases" or "Mexican American folk illness," and they include several common conditions that are mostly unknown among non-Latino/a patients. These include *empacho* (a type of indigestion), *susto* (fright or soul loss resulting from a traumatic experience, often felt as irritability or depression), *caída de mollera* (fallen fontanel, or an indentation of an infant's skull), and *mal ojo* or *mal de ojo* (evil eye, often associated with children who have received too much admiration and attention).[10] Finally, being treated by a curandero/a often serves as an adjunct to seeing a medical doctor, a kind of complementary care that often feels more holistic and comforting than biomedical care alone.

In the mid- to late-twentieth century, scholarly interest in curanderismo shifted from anthropological musings on the unique and ostensibly pre-modern nature of the tradition (and its practitioners) to examinations of curanderismo's potential intersections with scientific medical care. Some of this research touched on helping doctors and other caregivers to understand their Mexican and Mexican American patients and provide them with culturally sensitive medical advice.[11] Others tried to explain, and even justify, the potential healing benefits of curanderismo, despite its general lack of scientific pedigree. For the most part, these kinds of studies found that curanderos/as provided psychological comfort to patients in ways that could have positive psychosomatic effects. Unfortunately, these attempts sometimes reinforced harmful stereotypes about Mexican Americans. For example, Ari Kiev, a psychiatry professor at Cornell University, wrote the following in 1968:

> Because of strict upbringing in a system that fosters belief in magic and folk illnesses and because of the perpetuation of certain kinds of infantile personal relationships, the Mexican grows up with much fear about his own emotions, particularly hostile and sexual ones, as well as much fear of the things that arouse his emotions.[12]

According to Kiev, the curandero/a's role in healing depends on levering these fears in symbolic ways that resonate with Mexican American culture. The healer "manipulates the patient's anxiety and guilt about the violation of cultural taboos by using a variety of culturally meaningful symbols and techniques." This results in a "cathartic, supportive experience" that leads to resolution and healing.[13]

Recent scholarship has moved away from this pathologizing approach and turned to analyses of curanderismo's role in holistic care for Mexican Americans and other Latinos/as as well as revalorization of curanderismo as part of the Mexican Americans' religious and cultural heritage. Healers themselves have begun to document their practices and beliefs. For example, in 1999, the New Mexico-based curandera Elena Avila published her autobiography, *Woman Who Glows in the Dark*. The book profiles her trajectory as a nurse who becomes more and more interested in her own Mexican American heritage related to healing. She trained with two different curanderos in Mexico and then opened a thriving practice in the Albuquerque area. Eventually, she gathered her own apprentices, leaving her mark on the practice of curanderismo throughout the Southwest.[14] Another example is an annual summer course about curanderismo held at the University of New Mexico. The course, which features local healers as well as curanderos/as from the Mexican state of Morelos, explores the history of curanderismo as well as some of its contemporary partnerships with other types of complementary and alternative medicine. The course founder, Eliseo "Cheo" Torres, explains that the class covers both the curandero/a's traditional practices as well as "the use of natural juices for healing, reiki techniques, reflexology, iridology, medicinal plants, massage therapy, and medicinal salves."[15]

Treating patients

Curanderos/as treat a broad range of complaints, from aches and pains to mental illness, although there are some specializations. For instance, hueseros/as are adept at setting bones and addressing injuries. Sobadores/as specialize in therapeutic touch, massage, and alignment. The concoction and prescription of herbal remedies is the province of the yerbero/a. Parteras practice traditional midwifery. Some curanderos/as are particularly gifted at reading Tarot cards to assist their clients.[16] A study of Mexican American curanderos/as active in Texas in the 1970s suggested that, in addition to these occasional specializations, healers confront their task on different levels. The most common of these is the material level, in which curanderos/as use herbal remedies and physical therapies to treat their patients. The spiritual level of healing includes prayers, rituals, and spirit channeling.[17] The latter, though by no means a universal feature of curanderismo, is not uncommon in many parts of the U.S.-Mexico border region. A final level is the mental level, which is akin to Mesmerism and mind cure. The curandero/a focuses his or her mental energy on the patient to eliminate the cause of illness.[18] These levels should not be understood as discrete but rather as interlacing and mutually reinforcing.

Botánicas, also known as yerberías, sell items related to healing and spiritual wellness. Products include typical Catholic devotional wares, such as candles, prayer cards, saints' medals, statues, and cleaning supplies. Many such stores also sell religious paraphernalia that falls outside of orthodox Catholicism. For example, items for sale may also include statues of Indigenous deities, the Buddha, as well as folk saints, such as Jesús Malverde or Santa Muerte. Spiritual soaps and cleaning products allow users to clean both their physical and spiritual environments. Botánicas also sell a wide selection of herbal remedies, tinctures, minerals, and other *materia medica* used in Latino/a home remedies and in curanderismo.[19] It is common that a curandera or curandero is the proprietor, or at least an employee, of neighborhood botánicas. Many botánicas therefore have a room for consultations, where the curandero/a on staff can see patients and prescribe treatments.

In his study of a curandera and her botánica in Los Angeles, religious studies scholar Luis León found that the curandera sees her role as meeting people in their various needs. This sometimes means prescribing remedies, treatments, and massage therapy for specific illnesses, but it also includes helping people to fix the broken and hurting aspects of their lives. León discovered that men especially "sought help from [the curandera] to ease the stresses of separation from their families who remained in Mexico." Women likewise went "with similar problems centering on family separation, employment, love, money, and health." Some mothers came with their sons who had become involved in gang activities. One such mother explained that, "her son was full of bad energies and needed to be cleaned so that he could be put back on the right path." León eventually concluded that both the curandera and her patients found the botánica to be a place where religion, culture, and community

Figure 10.2 Yerbería Esotérica San Miguel, Tucson, Arizona. Photo courtesy Ken McAllister and Rachel Srubas.

norms could work together to bring healing and solutions to problems. "In her heart and soul [the curandera] believes that what she is doing is helping people: she appeals to conviction, and that conscience enables her poetics of material salvation and power to forcefully unfold and take place."[20]

Instead of working out of a botánica, the curandera Elena Avila operated a practice in her home in suburban Albuquerque. There, she treated a wide variety of patients, many of whom were suffering from traumatic memories. Avila employed several traditional and novel rituals to help her clients to find a path to healing. For instance, in her practice room she maintained an altar that featured candles, images of Mesoamerican deities, Jesus, the Virgin of Guadalupe, family photos, and depictions of other Catholic saints, such as St. Anthony and St. Jude. Relying less on herbal remedies than some curanderos/as, Avila focused her sessions on a type of extended talk therapy that she referred to as a *plática* (literally, "chat"). "A *plática* is a deep heart-to-heart talk that continues in installments for as long as it needs to."[21] After talking through a patient's problems, sometimes over the course of many sessions, Avila's prescriptions often included a *limpia* (described below) as well as other tailor-made rituals that helped the patient re-narrate traumatic memories in healthy and empowering ways. Sometimes, Avila linked these rituals to a restored connection to Mexican Americans' Indigenous past. For instance, in some cases, she led patients in a "ceremony of the five directions" reminiscent of an Aztec cosmovision of the cardinal points. "The whole purpose" explained Avila, "of setting up the directions and placing objects in them is to tell the client's story."[22] In so doing, patients confront their traumas, reconnect with their heritage, and discover wholeness.

Curanderismo and religio-cultural identity

Mexican Americans who embrace and practice curanderismo must often negotiate how this relates to their self-understanding and identity within their community. Despite the fact that this healing tradition has a long and historical tie to Catholicism, its relationship to the Catholic Church has often been tense. For instance, the Spanish Inquisition in seventeenth- and eighteenth-century New Mexico tried several curanderos/as as proponents of witchcraft, and thus devilish enemies of the faith. These cases were often complicated by the general admission that curanderos/as' herbal remedies were good and necessary, but the conceptual basis for some of their cures was deeply rooted in "superstition."[23] This tension persists today for some. Returning to the botánica in Los Angeles, León discovered that clients were uncomfortable about linking their use of curanderismo with their Catholicism. Some swore that the botánica, and what happened inside of it, was not Catholic, while others remembered that the resident curandera considered herself to be a faithful Catholic, complicating the issue. But they worried that they should perhaps be satisfied with prayer to God even though they found the curandera more effective.[24] León suggested that a doctrinal difference concerning the power of saints could be an important sticking point between official Catholicism and curanderismo. In a word, curanderos/as and their patients generally believe that saints themselves have an innate power to help people, while Catholic doctrine restricts their power to intercession with God on behalf of others. However, according to León, this does not set curanderismo apart from the people's religion; curanderismo is rather "a logical extension" of Mexican Americans' popular Catholicism.[25]

Besides its intersection with Catholicism, curanderismo also provides a salutary venue for examining Mexican American ethnic identity. Some contemporary curanderos/as consider their healing practices to be a reclamation of long-hidden Mesoamerican Indigenous traditions. For instance, Patrisia Gonzales is a Mexican American Studies professor as well as an herbalist and public health promoter. In her book about Indigenous birthing and healing rituals, she includes Mexican Americans—whom she refers to frequently as "Chicano" or "Xicano"—within lists of other Indigenous peoples, such as the Nahua, Mam, Mohawk, and Ojibwe. She argues, therefore, that curanderismo has its foundation primarily in Indigenous knowledge.[26] Another contemporary curandera active in New Mexico has begun to replace the names of Jesus and Mary in her prayers and healing rituals with the names of Aztec deities, such as the male and female gods of duality, respectively Ometecuhtli and Omecíhuatl. She explains that this helps her and her patients to confront and address the pain of centuries of colonialism and acculturation.[27] Elena Avila has referred to this process of reclamation as sifting "through the bones of my own ancestors to unearth my own tradition."[28] Curanderismo, in this light, recognizes that Mexican American healing, while often experienced in Catholic idioms, also remains connected to the Indigenous side of Mexican American mestizo identity.

In recent years, people outside of the Mexican American community, including non-Latinos/as, have begun to practice curanderismo, albeit in small numbers. What has made this possible is curanderismo's partial entry into what is often referred to as complementary and alternative medicine, or CAM. Many contemporary curanderos/as combine their traditional practices with other CAM therapies from around the globe, including acupuncture, Reiki, various kinds of therapeutic touch and massage, yoga, and ayurvedic medicine. People, Mexican American or not, who are interested in these approaches to healing can thus experience curanderismo alongside other CAM-type services and modalities.[29] Moreover, some non-Latinos/as have begun to study curanderismo with the intention of becoming curanderos/as themselves. It is not difficult to find online training programs in curanderismo that are open to the general public without regard for ethnic or cultural heritage.[30] An assumption undergirding these developments in curanderismo is that it need not be restricted to Mexican Americans or other Latinos/as but rather is a universalizable spiritual and healing tradition open to all. In this sense, as with other aspects of Mexican American religious life, curanderismo is having a growing influence outside of its community of origin.

Religion in practice

One of the most common practices related to curanderismo is the *limpia* ("cleansing" in English). The *limpia* treats a variety of illnesses in that it addresses negative energies or intrusions into the body that must be dispelled, it aligns one's energy or spirit to restore balance, and it provides an invitation for pieces of one's fractured soul to re-enter the body after cases of *susto* or *espanto* (literally "fright" or "terror," but often referred to in English as "soul loss.") Moreover, patients typically report that the experience of a *limpia* is itself soothing and comforting, creating feelings of well-being and protection. An egg *limpia* can both draw sickness out of the body and help to detect illness. For example, a Texan curandera in the mid-twentieth century reported, "I diagnose the case by cleaning the patient's body with an egg. When I crack the shell and drop the raw egg into a glass of water, I can tell whether the affliction is fright [*susto*] or another illness." She explained, "Some of the disease enters the egg and you can see it is fright by the way it curls in the water ... To treat the patient, I must remove the fright from his body." She goes on to explain that her treatment involves a nine-day sequence of *limpias*, prayers, and herbal remedies.[31]

To perform a *limpia*, the curandero/a typically sweeps or rubs a bundle of herbs, feathers, or a raw egg all over a person's body, starting at the crown of the head and moving downward toward the feet. During the procedure, the curandero/a prays for the healing of the patient either with a set prayer—such as the Lord's Prayer or the Hail Mary—or with unique petitions tailored to the patient's case. One curandera shares which herbs she uses in her *limpias* and why:

> I personally grow the herbs that I use in my *limpias* and rituals: *ruda* (rue), *romero* (rosemary), *pirul* (pepper tree) and *albacar* [*sic*] (sweet basil) are very popular. I could use other plants in my *limpias*, but I use *ruda* and *romero* because these plants grow where I live. I sweep bundles of herbs, and sometimes flowers, over a client's body to help remove sadness and energies that do not belong to him. To receive a *limpia* with a bunch of herbs or fresh flowers is pure pleasure.[32]

During or after this procedure, especially if the diagnosed problem is *susto*, or soul loss, the healer will often admonish the person's soul to be restored to the body, thus recreating wholeness and wellness.[33]

Notes

1 Alfredo López Austin, *The Human Body and Ideology: Concepts of the Ancient Nahuas*, trans. Thelma Ortiz de Montellano and Bernard Ortiz de Montellano (Salt Lake City, UT: University of Utah Press, 1988), 204–7.

2 Bernard R. Ortiz de Montellano, *Aztec Medicine, Health, and Nutrition* (New Brunswick, NJ: Rutgers University Press, 1990), 213–21.

3 These practices persist among Nahuatl-speaking communities today. See Timothy J. Knab, *The Dialogue of Earth and Sky: Dreams, Souls, Curing, and the Modern Aztec Underworld* (Tucson, AZ: University of Arizona Press, 2004), especially Chapter 5.

4 Andrés Pérez de Ribas, *History of the Triumphs of Our Holy Faith amongst the Most Barbarous and Fierce Peoples of the New World*, ed. Daniel T. Reff (Tucson, AZ: University of Arizona Press, 1999), 538.

5 Juan de Esteyneffer, *Florilegio Medicinal*, ed. Ma. del Carmen. Anzures y Bolaños (Mexico City: Academia Nacional de Medicina, 1712); Margarita Artschwager Kay, "The Florilegio Medicinal: Source of Southwest Ethnomedicine," *Ethnohistory* 24, no. 3 (1977): 251–59.

6 Luis García-Ballester, *Medicine in a Multicultural Society: Christian, Jewish and Muslim Practitioners in the Spanish Kingdoms, 1222–1610* (Burlington, VT: Ashgate, 2001).

7 Gregory Juckett, "Caring for Latino Patients," *American Family Physician* 87, no. 1 (2013): 50–51.

8 David J. Weber, *The Mexican Frontier, 1821–1846: The American Southwest under Mexico* (Albuquerque, NM: University of New Mexico Press, 1982), 236.

9 Octavio Ignacio Romano V, "Charismatic Medicine, Folk-Healing, and Folk-Sainthood," *American Anthropologist* 67, no. 5 (1965): 1156.

10 For example, see Robert T. Trotter and Juan Antonio Chavira, *Curanderismo: Mexican American Folk Healing*, 2nd ed., (Athens, GA: University of Georgia Press, 1997), 90–92.

11 For example, see W. D. Smithers, "Nature's Pharmacy and the Curanderos," *Sul Ross State College Bulletin* XLI, no. 3 (1961): 5–39; Arthur J. Rubel, "Concepts of Disease in Mexican-American Culture," *American Anthropologist* 62, no. 5 (1960): 795–814; Sara M. Campos Carrasco, "Mexican American Folk Medicine: A Descriptive Study of the Different Curanderismo Techniques Practiced by Curanderos or Curanderas and Used by Patients in the Laredo, Texas Area," M.A. thesis, Texas Woman's University, 1984.

12 Ari Kiev, *Curanderismo: Mexican-American Folk Psychiatry* (New York: Free Press, 1968), 167.

13 Kiev, 152.

14 Elena Avila and Joy Parker, *Woman Who Glows in the Dark: A Curandera Reveals Traditional Aztec Secrets of Physical and Spiritual Health* (New York: J.P. Tarcher/Putnam, 1999).

15 Eliseo Torres and Timothy L. Sawyer, *Curandero: A Life in Mexican Folk Healing* (Albuquerque, NM: University of New Mexico Press, 2004), 150. See also University of New Mexico Curanderismo Class, "Curanderismo," *UNM Curanderismo Class*, accessed January 31, 2020, http://curanderismo.unm.edu; Brett Hendrickson, *Border Medicine: A Transcultural History of Mexican American Curanderismo* (New York: New York University Press, 2014), 141–57.

16 Trotter and Chavira, *Curanderismo: Mexican American Folk Healing*, 52–58.

17 So-called fidencistas are channelers of the Niño Fidencio, a famous northern Mexican curandero who, according to believers, continues to provide healing from the spirit world. For more on fidencistas and fidencismo, see Hendrickson, *Border Medicine*, 86–105.

18 For longer descriptions of these three levels, see Trotter and Chavira, *Curanderismo: Mexican American Folk Healing*, chapters 5, 6, and 7.

19 See Joseph M. Murphy, *Botánicas: Sacred Spaces of Healing and Devotion in Urban America* (Jackson, MS: University Press of Mississippi, 2015); Carolyn Morrow Long, "Candle Shops, Botánicas, Yerberías, and Web Sites," in *Spiritual Merchants: Religion, Magic, and Commerce* (Knoxville, TN: University of Tennessee Press, 2001), 159–85.

20 Luis D. León, "'Soy Una Curandera y Soy Una Católica': The Poetics of a Mexican Healing Tradition," in *Horizons of the Sacred: Mexican Traditions in U.S. Catholicism*,

ed. Timothy M. Matovina and Gary Riebe-Estrella (Ithaca, NY: Cornell University Press, 2002), 106–7, 117.

21 Avila and Parker, *Woman Who Glows in the Dark: A Curandera Reveals Traditional Aztec Secrets of Physical and Spiritual Health*, 143.

22 Avila and Parker, 159.

23 Malcolm Ebright and Rick Hendricks, *The Witches of Abiquiu: The Governor, the Priest, the Genízaro Indians, and the Devil* (Albuquerque, NM: University of New Mexico Press, 2006), 108–17.

24 León, "'Soy Una Curandera y Soy Una Católica': The Poetics of a Mexican Healing Tradition," 109.

25 León, 114.

26 Patrisia Gonzales, *Red Medicine: Traditional Indigenous Rites of Birthing and Healing* (Tucson, AZ: University of Arizona Press, 2012), 3.

27 Hendrickson, *Border Medicine*, 151.

28 Avila and Parker, *Woman Who Glows in the Dark: A Curandera Reveals Traditional Aztec Secrets of Physical and Spiritual Health*, 38.

29 Hendrickson, *Border Medicine*, 134–38.

30 For example, see Paloma Cervantes, "Ancient Ways for a Modern Life," Institute of Shamanism and Curanderismo, accessed February 18, 2020, https://www.instituteofshamanismandcuranderismo.com.

31 William Madsen, *Mexican-Americans of South Texas* (New York: Holt, Rinehart, and Winston, 1964), 79.

32 Avila and Parker, *Woman Who Glows in the Dark: A Curandera Reveals Traditional Aztec Secrets of Physical and Spiritual Health*, 70.

33 Torres and Sawyer, *Curandero: A Life in Mexican Folk Healing*, 40.

11 Religion and Mexican American civil rights

The struggle for civil rights for minority groups in the United States has long been linked with religion. Indeed, some of the most prominent leaders of the civil rights movement of the mid-twentieth century—people like Martin Luther King, Jr., Malcolm X, Fannie Lou Hamer, and Abraham Joshua Heschel—relied on their religious traditions to animate their activism. "Religious belief, culture, and practice gave ordinary people ground down by racism and exploitation the spiritual sustenance to stand up and, in some cases, to lay their lives on the line," explains historian Paul Harvey.[1] This is likewise true for Mexican Americans who have fought for civil rights in the United States. To be sure, César Chávez, one of the leaders of the United Farm Workers union and someone deeply influenced by his Catholic faith, stands out as an important figurehead in the civil rights movement, but there are many others.

This chapter examines the role religion has played in the Mexican American movement for civil rights. Religion, in this sense, is not merely Catholicism, Protestantism, or some other religious background, but also the power to embrace ultimately meaningful stories about who Mexican Americans are and what place they ought to occupy in U.S. political, social, economic, and religious life. This broader view of religion in the civil rights movement prompts the examination not only of explicitly religious groups and actors but also parts of the movement associated with meaning-making and the fight for justice, equity, and other ethical values. Of course, many of those active in pursuing civil rights for Mexican Americans self-identified as religious people. These included portions of the U.S. Catholic Church hierarchy, Católicos por la Raza, and a variety of Protestants. Civil rights and other groups that were not primarily religious in nature but nonetheless drew on religious language and symbols include the United Farm Workers, MEChA, and La Alianza, just to name a few.

The ideological formation and reclamation of an ancestral homeland known as Aztlán likewise resonates with religious meaning. Aztlán's connection to Aztec historical narratives helped to connect the movement for civil rights to Mexican Americans' mestizo and Indigenous heritage, even as it endeavored to correct the injustices inflicted by centuries of European colonialism. This chapter explores how people in the movement drew on new narratives of

DOI: 10.4324/9780429285516-14

ethnic, national, and religious identity to propel the struggle for civil rights and, in some cases, self-determination.

The roots of the Chicano movement

Mexican Americans have worked for their dignity, property, and rights in the United States ever since the conclusion of the U.S.-Mexican War in 1848. For example, Mexicans in Los Angeles in 1856 organized schools in neighborhood homes to maintain the Spanish language in the face of English-only public schools. As Anglo land speculators defrauded Nuevomexicanos of their lands, las "Gorras Blancas" ("White Hats") formed as a guerrilla force in the 1890s. They rode out at night to tear down fences and generally resist white incursions onto ancestral familial land.[2]

The modern Mexican American civil rights movement, according to historian Cynthia Orozco, originated in the early twentieth century among Mexican Americans in south Texas. After years of segregation, racialization and racial violence, lack of educational opportunities, and political disempowerment, the community was ripe for organization. But, it was not until the rise of a small middle class that a movement was able to form for the protection and advancement of Mexicans and Mexican Americans in Texas.[3] In the late 1920s, various labor and community organizations came together to form the League of United Latin American Citizens (LULAC) to advocate for Mexican American civil and political rights. LULAC's first constitution, written in 1929, called for a clear separation between politics and religion, making religion a private matter. Orozco argues that this did not represent a lack of religiosity among LULAC's founders but rather an acknowledgement of the sometimes violent situation in Mexico between the Mexican government and the Catholic Church.[4] Later Mexican American civil rights activists would often criticize LULAC for its assimilationism, but it represents—and remains—a moderate yet constant voice for Latino/a civil rights. Its position on religion reflects this desire to integrate Latinos/as through accommodation.

A more radical group active in the early part of the twentieth century was El Congreso del Pueblo de Habla Española (the Spanish-Speaking People's Congress). Founded in 1938 in Los Angeles by Luisa Moreno and Josefina Fierro de Bright, the Congreso made common cause with labor movement activism, a partnership generally eschewed by LULAC. Briefly attracting the attention of prominent Hollywood stars like Rita Hayworth and Anthony Quinn, the Congreso's aims echoed LULAC's—educational and occupational equity and rights—but also included appeals for pan-Latino/a unity, including the non-citizen Mexican community in the United States. The Congreso, unlike LULAC, was short-lived as an organization, but its radical positions presaged later developments.[5]

By the turbulent years of the 1960s, which included the famous marches, bus boycotts, sit-ins, and other activism for African American civil rights, Mexican Americans would also join the movement in their own ways. It soon became clear that LULAC's advocacy for incremental integration was not moving quickly enough for many younger Mexican Americans, now often calling themselves Chicanos and Chicanas as a marker of ethnic pride. As young people radicalized, leaders, such as Rodolfo "Corky" Gonzales, helped various groups to coalesce into a Chicano Movement. Among other explicit goals, Gonzales and other leaders called for access to education (including bilingual education), economic development in Mexican American neighborhoods, restitution for land that was stolen from Mexicans in the wake of the U.S.-Mexican War, and better housing stock.[6] Another part of the movement, led by José Angel Gutiérrez, worked to form the Raza Unida Party. This third party was intended to provide a political home for Chianos/as and their issues.[7]

Chicana women, despite the often patriarchal nature of the movement, took active roles in promoting their own rights in their communities and beyond. Historian Vicki L. Ruiz has documented the many ways that women participated in labor and other kinds of activism from picket lines to college campuses. In addition to organizing, protesting, and other forms of direct action, women's literary outpourings provided both an outlet for expression and an interpretive node for the movement. These writings combined pleas for greater Chicano/a self-determination, challenges to machista paternalism, and painful acknowledgments of racial discrimination within feminism.[8] Ruiz notes that the Catholic Church was an important institution for organizing Chicanas. Since the local parish was almost always a central feature of Mexican American neighborhoods, women often organized their efforts in cooperation with the church calendar of holidays and processions. They also held leadership roles in Catholic-related community organizations. For example, several Tejana women were presidents and leading organizers in San Antonio's Communities Organized for Public Service (COPS), a group that worked with Mexican American parishes to improve neighborhood governance and infrastructure. In California, Chicana Catholics formed ecclesiastical base communities, following the patterns of Latin American liberation theology. These communities worked to build up local businesses and cooperative initiatives for neighborhood empowerment.[9]

The Chicano Movement, although occasionally based in Mexican American Catholic parishes and neighborhoods, also made the Catholic Church a focus of its activism. Católicos por la Raza (or, Católicos, for short) formed in 1969 in Los Angeles from a group of other student-led Chicano rights groups. Organizers in Católicos insisted that their Catholicism was a key part of their identity, one that they explicitly tied to care for the poor. In this, they linked themselves theologically to Latin American liberation theology; this liberationism maintained that God, as evidenced over and over in the Bible and in the self-giving incarnation of Jesus, had a "preferential option for the poor."[10] Historian Mario García has shown how members of Católicos por la Raza carried out research on the Archdiocese of Los Angeles to uncover the extent of its wealth and to highlight how little effort was being spent on ministry to the large numbers of Mexican Americans in the Archdiocese. The activists likewise noted how little representation Mexican Americans had among the clergy, especially at the upper echelons.[11]

To pursue a solution to these inequities, Católicos drew up a list of demands that included funding for Chicano education programs, a Church-provided housing program in Mexican American neighborhoods, free or low-cost healthcare for the poor in Catholic hospitals, education programs for clergy to learn about Chicano issues, freedom of speech for nuns, and an explicit public commitment by the Catholic Church to support the Chicano movement in its various iterations. On December 18, 1969, members of the group went to the Los Angeles residence of Cardinal James Francis McIntyre to deliver their list of demands. When they were rebuffed, they stormed into the cardinal's office, where he was forced to hear their concerns. When nothing came of this impromptu meeting, the Católicos hatched a plan to demonstrate at the cardinal's Christmas Midnight Mass at St. Basil's Catholic Church. In the process of disrupting the Mass, fights broke out, and police who had been made aware of the planned protest dispersed the crowd with riot gear and mace. Cardinal McIntyre retired early in the following year and was replaced by Cardinal Timothy Manning. Manning took a more conciliatory approach, including meeting some of the activists' initial demands, especially in the areas of cultural accommodation and general support for the movement.[12]

Two other Catholic groups (see also Chapter 9) were PADRES and Las Hermanas. Padres Asociados por los Derechos Religiosos, Educativos, y Sociales (Fathers Associated for Religious, Educational, and Social Rights), or PADRES, organized in 1969 as a group of like-minded priests active in building up the Mexican American community. One of the founders was Father Juan Romero, a New Mexico native serving in California. Early in his ministry, he became involved with César Chávez and outreach to farmworkers, participating actively in protests and pickets. Later, after helping organize PADRES and taking a leadership role within it, Romero promoted liberationist ecclesiastical base communities, a grassroots method for studying the Bible and addressing community issues. He and other members of PADRES helped Mexican American Catholics in Los Angeles and San Antonio win new rights for their communities. Other Mexican American priests involved in PADRES worked to empower the Latino/a community in diverse ways, including fighting for legal protection of immigrants, expanding public health programs, and promoting Mexican American culture.[13]

Several Mexican American women religious, following on the early successes of PADRES but also recognizing that women faced several unique and additional challenges, organized Las Hermanas in 1971 as a progressive Catholic advocacy group for Mexican American women and other Latina Catholics. Las Hermanas, in addition to supporting civil and ecclesiastical rights for Latino/a Catholics, also worked for greater equality and opportunity for women in the Catholic Church as well as for theological reforms that recognized women's ordination. While Las Hermanas and PADRES did often work together on initiatives, particularly in the Encuentros, many of the priests were unable to fully embrace some of the more inclusive and radical proposals put forward by their women colleagues in ministry, highlighting what historian Lara Medina has called the "sanctified patriarchy" present in the Catholic Church.[14] Las Hermanas, perhaps due to their decades of practice working on the edges of the Catholic Church, had made them nimble and responsive. "Clearly, the organization succeed[ed]," notes Medina, "at addressing bicultural and bilingual realities by respecting language preferences, class, and cultural diversity in its activities."[15] Las Hermanas, in its inclusive yet challenging approach, reflected some of the most progressive religious elements in the Mexican American struggle for civil rights.

Aztlán: A Chicano homeland

An aspect of the Mexican American civil rights movement redolent with religious significance was the reclamation of an ancestral homeland in the U.S.-Mexico border region. According to colonial-era chroniclers and contemporary historians, the Aztec people of central Mexico claimed to have migrated from a northern land known as "Aztlán"—indeed, "Aztec" means "people of Aztlán." While archaeologists have not been able to verify the precise location of this original homeland, there are preconquest pictorial manuscripts that indicate that the Aztecs did come from somewhere north of modern-day Mexico City.[16] As a gesture signaling that they belonged in the land, leaders of the Chicano movement embraced the idea that the southwestern United States was, mythological or not, their birthright and homeland since even before the European conquest.

Aztlán emerged as a symbolic touchstone early in the movement. In 1969, Corky Gonzales and others hosted the First National Chicano Youth Liberation Conference in Denver. "El Plan Espiritual de Aztlán," which was issued from this conference, was a clarion call for Mexican American nationalism, activism, and empowerment. The preamble of the plan, signaling the centrality of the land in terms of national identity, states:

> With our heart in our hands and our hands in the soil, we declare the independence of our mestizo nation. We are a bronze people with a bronze culture. Before the world, before all of North America, before all our brothers in the bronze continent, we are a nation, we are a union of free peoples, we are *Aztlán*. [17]

"El Plan Espiritual" reinterpreted the experience of being Mexican American as one of pride, with a long and storied history and a profound connection to the land. This Chicano nationalism helped reverse decades, and even centuries, of discrimination and internalized racism. Historian F. Arturo Rosales explained the forceful function of Aztlán: "[A] catharsis emerged that put an emphasis on the acceptance of being brown or mestizo and not being ashamed of it." "Aztlán," continued Rosales, "gave the mestizo-Indian aesthetic, which

Chicanos had been conditioned to see in negative terms, a heretofore unknown dignity."[18]

Religious studies scholars have long noted that myths, contrary to popular usage of the term, are not fictions but rather repositories of communal meaning-making. It is in this sense that the Chicano movement self-consciously adopted Aztlán as a powerful metaphor of Mexican American nationalism. The Chicano poet, Alurista—who was the author of "El Plan Espiritual de Aztlán"—understood well the force of myth. He wrote that, "Myth has historically been the fabric with which civilizations, that is to say, large social formations, were bound together in a covenant." But this did not mean that the myth of Aztlán was limited to abstractions. For Alurista and others, Aztlán was "a mission and a state of mind, a way of facing contemporary reality and social conditions."[19] Key to that mission was regaining the land and its produce that had been alienated from the people in multiple waves of colonialism, exploitation, and marginalization.

The Chicano nationalism implicit in claiming Aztlán as the rightful land of Mexican Americans demonstrates how myth can fuel collective action. Militant student groups coalesced into the Movimiento Estudiantil Chicano de Aztlán (MEChA) in 1969. They called for the creation of curricula and academic programs that recognized and honored the contributions of Mexicans and Mexican Americans. They also militated against the Vietnam War as an imperialist conflict that disproportionately sent young brown men to fight and die.[20] MEChA activists were sometimes joined by the Brown Berets, a revolutionary nationalist group akin to the Black Panthers, the Young Lords, and the American Indian Movement. Laying claim to Aztlán as a physical homeland, the Brown Berets' demands echoed those of other Chicano groups but in a militant, and sometimes violent, register.[21] (It is interesting to note that, in 2019, a national MEChA conference voted to begin to change the organization's name, dropping "Chicano" and "Aztlán." The latter term was singled out for not recognizing the identity and land rights of the many non-Aztec Indigenous groups in Mexico.[22])

The United Farm Workers and Mexican American religion

As discussed in Chapter 9, a group of activist priests in California called the "Spanish Mission Band" collaborated with Mexican American labor leaders and community organizers to carry out their ministry to agricultural workers. One of the priests, Fr. Thomas McCullough, worked with Dolores Huerta to form the Agricultural Workers Association. Another Mission Band priest, Fr. Donald McDonnell, recruited César Chávez as a community organizer for a group that eventually merged with the AFL-CIO. Huerta and Chávez would go on to found the United Farm Workers (UFW), arguably the most influential majority-Mexican American labor organization in U.S. history.[23]

During the 1960s and 1970s, the UFW was one of the most visible organizations working for the rights of Mexican American workers, especially migrant farm laborers. Not only was the union successful in drawing attention to the plight of farmworkers, it also drew deeply on the Catholicism of its leaders and members. At the forefront of UFW demonstrations and marches, a banner of the Virgin of Guadalupe led the workers. Moreover, the head of the UFW, César Chávez, characterized these marches as more than mere labor actions; they were "pilgrimages" and an opportunity for the workers to do "penance" as a spiritual discipline for justice.[24] Chávez, during his time at the UFW's helm, carried out various fasts, akin to hunger strikes. Again, these tactics were not only a way to fight for the union. "My fast is informed by my religious faith and by my deep roots in the church," Chávez explained. "It is not intended as a pressure on anyone but only as an expression of my own deep feelings and my own need to be in penance and to be in prayer."[25]

Dolores Huerta, a fellow leader in the UFW, noted that Chávez's fasts and religious language often confused the public. The key, she said, was his ethnic and religious heritage. "I know it is hard for people who are not Mexican to understand, but this is part of Mexican culture—the penance, the whole idea of suffering for something, of self-inflicted punishment." Huerta continued, "César has often mentioned in speeches that we will not win through violence, we will win through fasting and prayer."[26] These disciplines taught Chávez and others about the inherent human dignity of each person, no matter how despised by the dominant society. This dignity led to action. Chávez implored:

> Rebel against the injustice of your grower. Revolt against the injustice of your labor contractor. God is witness that what you ask for is just. God is witness to the abuses that have been committed against you. God is witness and judge and will judge in the near future. All the abuses are against the dignity of man, who is made by God in his own image.[27]

This insistence on the humanity of the Mexican American worker, rooted in religious visions of the person, echoed similar declarations across the U.S. civil rights movement.

Protestants in the Movement

Like their Catholic counterparts, Protestant Mexican Americans, from Presbyterians to Pentecostals, have also participated in labor and civil rights movements. Likewise, the ethos and mandates of their faith have influenced their actions. And, just as Catholic Mexican Americans pressured their church hierarchy to join and support them in the struggle for rights, Protestants also attempted to redirect their denominations' and congregations' emphases toward justice and inclusion for all people. Of course, these efforts were not always successful, and not all Mexican American Protestants were engaged in the civil rights movement. However, those who did enter into the movement, in various ways, often found a new appreciation for how their ethnicity and their religious convictions were mutually related.

Figure 11.1 Supporters of the UFW march through the streets carrying signs, crucifixes, and banners with Our Lady of Guadalupe on them to the Mass that ended Cesar Chavez's 24-day "Fast for Justice", Phoenix, Arizona. Walter P. Reuter Library/Archives of Labor and Urban Affairs, Wayne State University.

One arena in which mainline Protestants contributed to the struggle for rights was in the fight to organize farm workers. Historian Paul Barton has chronicled how several Mexican American Methodist, Baptist, and Presbyterian pastors and laypeople from California to Texas joined or led efforts to address the needs of agricultural laborers. For example, a group of Methodist pastors in Texas worked closely with the multi-denominational National Farm Workers Ministry, including board members Reverends Joél Martínez and Leo Nieto. Presbyterians in California, New Mexico, and Texas also spearheaded various initiatives to protect migrant workers. Reverend Jorge Lara-Braud not only promoted Christian action for workers, he also successfully lobbied the Presbyterian Church (U.S.) to increase funding for Spanish-speaking ministries throughout the nation. Another Presbyterian minister, Reverend Lydia Hernández, worked in migrant ministry and also maintained ties with César Chávez and the UFW.[28] To be sure, not all Mexican American mainline Protestants were supportive of these efforts—some criticized them as being unpatriotic or not sufficiently focused on evangelism. Nonetheless, many of the activist clergy eventually went on to long and distinguished ministerial careers, some entering denominational leadership.[29]

Mexican American Mennonites, according to historian Felipe Hinojosa, challenged their largely white and rural denomination to embrace the need for social action around civil rights for people of color. As with much of the

Chicano rights movement, Mennonite involvement grew out of young people's activism in the 1970s. The Mennonite Church had formed a Minority Ministries Council (MMC) to address the needs of its Black and Latino/a congregations. At an MMC youth gathering in 1972, Black, Chicano, and Puerto Rican Mennonite youth came together to forge interethnic solidarity, to work out what it meant to be part of a pacifist denomination in a time of struggle and social upheaval, and to embrace the growing focus on the plight of migrant farm workers.[30] However, many white Mennonites owned and operated farms and, like others in agriculture, relied on migrant and seasonal workers. Members of the MMC were forced to walk a fine line between advocating for farm workers and maintaining denominational support. Under threat of losing their funding, the MCC was forced to accept that their denomination would not take a stance on supporting farm workers.[31]

Mexican American evangelical and Pentecostal congregations sometimes also got involved in the civil rights movement, especially if their local leaders and pastors led them in this direction. Others got involved as part of evangelistic campaigns to bracero workers. César Chávez reported that he drew inspiration from Mexican American Pentecostals, who, though often gathered in small congregations, sang with spirit and joy. He adopted this singing for UFW meetings, and he made alliances with Pentecostals, who became active in organizing for the union.[32] Perhaps the most famous and flamboyant Pentecostal to be involved in the Chicano Movement was Reies López Tijerina. Tijerina, a complicated and bombastic figure, was a Pentecostal evangelist in the 1940s and 1950s who eventually came to lead a movement in New Mexico to reclaim land that Anglos took illegally from Mexicans in the wake of the U.S.-Mexico War. Tijerina's leadership of the movement to reclaim Spanish land grants, according to religious studies scholar Rudy Busto, grew from his theology; his actions mimic prophetic images from the Bible that sacralize the land and its inhabitants.[33] His fervid rhetoric helped attract followers, who came together as the Alianza Federal de Mercedes, or Federal Alliance of Land Grants. Tijerina led members of the Alianza in a violent 1967 raid on a New Mexico courthouse, for which he was imprisoned. Between the raid and his incarceration, Tijerina briefly worked alongside other national leaders in the civil rights movement.[34]

Religion in practice

Pilgrimage is a communal religious activity in which people, sometimes massive numbers of people, journey from one place to another. The pilgrimage itself is motivated by some devotional purpose, but it also often incorporates festive elements. Christian pilgrimages have existed for centuries and have been significant forms of devotion throughout Latin America as well as among Mexican Americans. Pilgrimages, as communal expressions of religion, exercise a unique kind of power as a highly public and united ritual act.

In the arena of the civil rights movement, the United Farm Workers (UFW) drew on the rich symbolic heritage of pilgrimage to strengthen their activism.

In 1966, the UFW planned a 300-mile pilgrimage march through California, which culminated in their arrival in Sacramento on Easter Sunday, 1966. The event was christened "Pilgrimage, Penance, and Revolution," and it helped galvanize the movement, focus media attention, and gain a wide circle of support. Luis León, one of César Chávez's biographers, wrote of the march:

> The procession was headed from the start by pilgrims bearing a banner emblazoned with an image that fused Mexico's Virgin of Guadalupe with the totem of Chavez's crusade—a black eagle against a crimson background. For spectators, this image tore the veil separating the sacred from the profane, by melding the primary emblem of Mexican Catholicism of *La Causa*. The entry of the pilgrims into California's capital city heralded Chavez's arrival on the national stage as a prophetic agent.[35]

To be sure, the goals of the pilgrimage were multiple, including exerting political pressure, building spiritual fortitude in the movement, and educating the public. In this sense, it matched Chávez's own faith-based ideology, which was, as León writes, "at once catholic, that is, universal, and Catholic, that is defined by the rituals of the Church and expressed in a Mexican idiom, emphasizing the rites of contrition and service to humanity."[36]

In some ways, this catholic and Catholic approach was open-armed and welcoming. For instance, Chávez insisted that Filipino farmworkers be allowed to join the pilgrimage alongside the Chicano workers. According to Jacques Levy, another of Chávez's biographers, Chávez said, "Both [Chicanos and Filipinos] have some identical roots, the same religion and the same Spanish influence."[37] They were natural allies because of their similar background in Spanish colonialism and Catholic religion. Along the road, the pilgrims picked up support from farm workers, Mexican Americans, and "church people."[38] Some even joined the pilgrimage as it went.

Religious studies scholars have long argued that pilgrimages can upend social structures by throwing people from various walks of life together for a shared purpose, but, by this same circumstance, they can also highlight and reinforce stratification and division. This happened in the 1966 UFW pilgrimage around questions of gender. In his memories of the planning of the action, Chávez recalled that,

> We timed the twenty-five-day march so we'd arrive in Sacramento on Easter Sunday and decided to take the men and leave the women on the picket lines. Dolores [Huerta] had to stay back. Of course, none of the women liked it, but they stayed.[39]

Even in this religiously symbolic and game-changing moment in the history of the farmworker movement, women were required to remain behind and "man" the pickets while the men carried the banners of the Virgin toward the streets of the capital.

Notes

1 Paul Harvey, "Civil Rights Movements and Religion in America," in *Oxford Research Encyclopedia of Religion* (New York: Oxford University Press, 2016), https://oxfordre.com/religion/view/10.1093/acrefore/9780199340378.001.0001/acrefore-9780199340378-e-492.
2 F. Arturo Rosales, ed., *Testimonio: A Documentary History of the Mexican American Struggle for Civil Rights* (Houston, TX: Arte Público Press, 2000), 26–30.
3 Cynthia E. Orozco, *No Mexicans, Women, or Dogs Allowed: The Rise of the Mexican American Civil Rights Movement* (Austin, TX: University of Texas Press, 2009), 26–39.
4 Orozco, 168.
5 F. Arturo Rosales, *Chicano! The History of the Mexican American Civil Rights Movement* (Houston, TX: Arte Público Press, 1996), 123–24.
6 Rosales, 180.
7 Armando Navarro, *La Raza Unida Party: A Chicano Challenge to the U.S. Two-Party Dictatorship* (Philadelphia, PA: Temple University Press, 2000).
8 See Vicki L. Ruiz, *From Out of the Shadows: Mexican Women in Twentieth-Century America* (New York: Oxford University Press, 1998), especially chapter 5.
9 Vicki L. Ruiz, "Claiming Public Space at Work, Church, and Neighborhood," in *Las Obreras: Chicana Politics of Work and Family*, ed. Vicki L. Ruiz (Los Angeles, CA: UCLA Chicano Studies Research Center, 2000), 24–29.
10 A seminal text is Gustavo Gutiérrez, *A Theology of Liberation: History, Politics, and Salvation*, 15th Anniversary ed. (Maryknoll, NY: Orbis Books, 1988). In the United States, Virgilio Elizondo, a leading liberationist theologian, argued that the Mexican American experience echoed Jesus's own life. See, for example, Virgilio P. Elizondo, *Galilean Journey: The Mexican-American Promise* (Maryknoll, NY: Orbis Books, 1983).
11 Gastón Espinosa and Mario T. García, *Mexican American Religions: Spirituality, Activism, and Culture* (Durham, NC: Duke University Press, 2008), 134–35.
12 Espinosa and García, 139–45.
13 Mario T. García, "PADRES: Latino Community Priests and Social Action," in *Latino Religions and Civic Activism in the United States*, ed. Gastón Espinosa, Virgilio Elizondo, and Jesse Miranda (New York: Oxford University Press, 2005), 77–95.
14 Lara Medina, *Las Hermanas: Chicana/Latina Religious-Political Activism in the U.S. Catholic Church* (Philadelphia, PA: Temple University Press, 2004), 102–4.
15 Medina, 149–50.
16 Manuel Aguilar-Moreno, *Handbook to Life in the Aztec World* (New York: Oxford University Press, 2006), 28–29; Davíd Carrasco, *Religions of Mesoamerica*, 2nd ed. (Long Grove, IL: Waveland Press, 2014), 35–37.
17 Rudolfo A. Anaya and Francisco A. Lomelí, eds., "Plan Espiritual de Aztlán," in *Aztlán: Essays on the Chicano Homeland* (Albuquerque, NM: University of New Mexico Press, 1989), 1.
18 Rosales, *Chicano!*, 253.
19 Alurista, "Myth, Identity and Struggle in Three Chicano Novels: Aztlán … Anaya, Méndez, and Acosta," in *Aztlán: Essays on the Chicano Homeland*, ed. Rudolfo A. Anaya and Francisco Lomeli (Albuquerque, NM: University of New Mexico Press, 1989), 221–22.
20 Zaragosa Vargas, *Crucible of Struggle: A History of Mexican Americans from Colonial Times to the Present Era* (New York: Oxford University Press, 2011), 323; Rosales, *Chicano!*, 200.
21 Vargas, *Crucible of Struggle*, 321.
22 Amanda Alcántara, "Student Group MEChA Holds Vote to Change Name, Prompting Strong Reactions," *Latino USA*, April 3, 2019, https://www.latinousa.org/2019/04/03/mechanamechange.

23 Jay P. Dolan and Gilberto M. Hinojosa, *Mexican Americans and the Catholic Church, 1900–1965* (Notre Dame, IN: University of Notre Dame Press, 1994), 204, 219–20; United Farm Workers, "The Rise of the UFW," *United Farm Workers*, accessed March 16, 2020, https://ufw.org/the-rise-of-the-ufw.

24 Mario T. García, *The Gospel of César Chávez: My Faith in Action* (Lanham, MD: Sheed and Ward, 2007), 95–100.

25 Quoted in Luis D. León, "César Chávez and Mexican American Civil Religion," in *Latino Religions and Civic Activism in the United States*, ed. Gastón Espinosa, Virgilio Elizondo, and Jesse Miranda (New York: Oxford University Press, 2005), 59.

26 León, 59–60.

27 García, *The Gospel of César Chávez: My Faith in Action*, 40.

28 Paul Barton, "¡Ya Basta! Latino/a Protestant Activism in the Chicano/a and Farm Workers Movements," in *Latino Religions and Civic Activism in the United States*, ed. Gastón Espinosa, Virgilio Elizondo, and Jesse Miranda (New York: Oxford University Press, 2005), 128–31.

29 Barton, 136, 138.

30 Felipe Hinojosa, *Latino Mennonites: Civil Rights, Faith, and Evangelical Culture* (Baltimore, MD: Johns Hopkins University Press, 2014), 99–115.

31 Hinojosa, 141–43.

32 Gastón Espinosa, *Latino Pentecostals in America: Faith and Politics in Action* (Cambridge, MA: Harvard University Press, 2014), 335–38; Lloyd Barba, "More Spirit in That Little Madera Church: Cesar Chavez and Religious Soundscapes, 1954–1962," *California History* 94, no. 1 (2017): 26–42.

33 Rudy V. Busto, *King Tiger: The Religious Vision of Reies López Tijerina* (Albuquerque, NM: University of New Mexico Press, 2005), 168–69.

34 Lorena Oropeza, *The King of Adobe: Reies López Tijerina, Lost Prophet of the Chicano Movement* (Chapel Hill, NC: University of North Carolina Press, 2019), 114–15, 219–21.

35 Luis D. León, *The Political Spirituality of Cesar Chavez: Crossing Religious Borders* (Oakland, CA: University of California Press, 2015), 2.

36 León, 5–6.

37 Jacques E. Levy, Fred Ross, and Jacqueline M. Levy, *Cesar Chavez: Autobiography of La Causa* (Minneapolis, MN: University of Minnesota Press, 2007), 208.

38 Levy, Ross, and Levy, 211.

39 Levy, Ross, and Levy, 207.

12 Transnational religious devotions

Mexican American religions in transit

Like all religions, Mexican American religions are in a constant state of change, innovation, and recreation. Religions evolve as a response to their changing circumstances and contexts. An essential feature of Mexican American religions is not only their setting within the United States but also in proximity—and historical relation—to Mexico. With the exception of those who trace their ancestry to Canada, no other immigrant group in the United States comes from a country that shares a border with the U.S. And, as earlier chapters have discussed, the current territory of the U.S. *contains* a large portion of what was formerly Mexico. It is fair to say that this creates a unique situation for Mexican Americans, even those whose families have lived in the United States for many generations. In a globalized world, many people can participate in transnational flows—the ongoing movement of people, ideas, resources, culture, and religion across borders. For Mexicans and Mexican Americans, these kinds of transnational flows have been happening for a long time, which has had and continues to have significant influence on religious practice. Religious developments in one nation almost certainly will soon have an impact on the other in a mutually constitutive process.

In addition to the proclivity of religion to move back and forth across borders, some religions incorporate movement and travel into their ritual practice. Catholic Christianity, for instance, has long featured pilgrimages to holy sites. Pilgrims make periodic journeys to venerate saints, pray, fulfill devotional promises, and spend time with one another. This chapter examines Mexican American pilgrimages within the geographic United States and also in transnational cases. Many of the largest pilgrimage sites in North America attract mostly Mexican and Mexican American pilgrims.

Given the history of labor migration between the United States and Mexico, it is perhaps not surprising that Mexican and Mexican American religions have developed ways to sacralize the often dangerous journey across the international border. Devotees believe that several saints watch over and bless movement through the U.S.-Mexico border region. Pentecostal Christians have also found ways to sanctify cross-border movement. They, too, seek to hold sacred the reality of many Mexican and Mexican American families: having family members in both countries. This chapter, in short, explores the ongoing movement of religious people between Mexico and the United States.

DOI: 10.4324/9780429285516-15

The Virgin of Guadalupe, Queen of the Americas

One of the central figures, if not *the* central figure, of Mexican and Mexican American Catholicism is Our Lady of Guadalupe, a famous sixteenth-century apparition of the Virgin Mary. According to seventeenth-century accounts, a Nahua man and Christian convert named Juan Diego was walking near Tepeyac hill in 1531 outside of Tenochtitlán, or Mexico City, which had been conquered only a decade before by the Spanish. A young woman appeared to Juan Diego and spoke to him in Nahuatl, his native language and explained to him that she was the Virgin Mary. She greeted him and told him to bring a message to Juan de Zumárraga, the first bishop of Mexico, that she desired a church to be built on the site where she had appeared. The faithful Juan Diego did as the Virgin asked, but Zumárraga was not receptive. Mary appeared to Juan Diego several other times over the following days and miraculously healed his ailing uncle. During this time, the bishop rebuffed Juan Diego and demanded a sign before he would believe the apparition story. On December 12, 1531, Juan Diego returned to Tepeyac, where he again encountered the Virgin, who was surrounded by beautiful flowers blooming out of season. He gathered them in his *tilma*, or cloak, and brought them to Zumárraga. After pouring the blooms out onto the floor, a miraculous image of the Virgin remained imprinted on the *tilma*. The bishop finally accepted Juan Diego's story, and the Virgin soon became known as Our Lady of Guadalupe.[1]

Mentions of devotion to Guadalupe at Tepeyac enter the historical record in a 1556 deposition and crop up in a few other sixteenth-century records.[2] However, the first major narrative accounts of devotion to Guadalupe occurred in 1648 and 1649, Miguel Sánchez's *Imagen de la Virgen* and Luis Laso de la Vega's *Huei tlamahuiçoltica*, respectively. These texts, the first in Spanish and the second in Nahuatl, give evidence that a strong local devotion had developed in the area of Mexico City among various populations. Over the next two centuries, Guadalupe grew in popularity such that she emerged as a symbol of the Mexican nation itself before and after independence. Her Indigenous features and the fact that she spoke to the Native man, Juan Diego, while simultaneously being one of the central figures in the Christian religion made her a symbol of national unity between Mexico's European and Indigenous heritages.

In the modern era, this symbolic unity so appealed to Pope John Paul II that, in a 1999 visit to Mexico, he named the Virgin of Guadalupe the "Queen of All America." He suggested that Guadalupe's salience in Mexico and other parts of Latin America should apply to the whole hemisphere. "In America, the *mestiza* face of the Virgin of Guadalupe was from the start a symbol of the inculturation of the Gospel, of which she has been the lodestar and the guide." The pope continued, "Through her powerful intercession, the Gospel will penetrate the hearts of the men and women of America and permeate their cultures, transforming them from within."[3]

Even before this papal recognition of her hemispheric importance, Guadalupe had been beloved of many Mexican American Catholics in the United

States. For instance, San Fernando Cathedral in San Antonio has been dedicated in part to the Virgin of Guadalupe since the founding of the parish in
1731. Confraternities celebrated Guadalupe in the streets of the city even as
Mexican and Mexican American families venerated her around home altars and
in private devotions.[4] During the civil rights movement, her image was
emblazoned on the banners of farm workers during their pickets and marches
(see Chapter 11). She also has been a powerful signifier in the Chicana feminist
movement. Guadalupe, in these contexts, can symbolize connection with the
Aztec past, matriarchal power, and an affirmation of women's sexuality. Religious studies scholar Socorro Castañeda-Liles explains, "Chicanas have extrac-
ted [Guadalupe's] inner strengths and made them visible."[5]

The Virgin Mary, in a sense, is a transitional figure *par excellence.* While she
exists on one level as the historical person of Mary, the mother of Jesus of
Nazareth, she also dwells across space and time as the Mother of God, appear-
ing over and over again to believers in diverse global contexts, including at
Tepeyac as the Virgin of Guadalupe. Guadalupe has accompanied her faithful
beyond the historical borders of New Spain, even to the Chicago suburbs.
Anthropologist Elaine Peña has documented a place known as Second Tepeyac
in Des Plaines, Illinois, a sanctioned replica of the original site of Guadalupe's
apparition to Juan Diego. Lay volunteers and Catholic officials worked together
over a ten-year period to build the Second Tepeyac and inaugurate the space
in 2001. It includes a copy of the image found in Juan Diego's cloak, various
statues that recount the story of the Virgin's appearance, a hill—the Cerrito—
for pilgrims to climb, and a large space for gathering and worship.[6] Every
December, just as in Mexico City, devotees re-enact the apparition over a
twelve-day period of prayer. The Mexican American leaders at the site do not
merely wish, however, to recreate Mexico's Tepeyac; they hope to appeal to
and increase Guadalupe's international devotional base. To do so, "they culti-
vate a meeting place for all Catholics from the five continents who reside in the
Chicago area," explains Peña, and they "work toward that goal by officially
naming the annual December gathering La Fiesta Guadalupana de los 5 Continent's Continente's del Mundo (The Guadalupan Festival of the Five Continents of the World)."[7] In so doing, they acknowledge that immigrants to the
Chicago area come from all over the planet, and they expand Guadalupe's
status as Queen of the Americas to the globe.

For some, faithfulness to the Virgin of Guadalupe includes pilgrimage. Jour-
neying to Tepeyac in Mexico, or the Second Tepeyac in Illinois, constitutes an
act of devotion, a time of communal togetherness with fellow pilgrims, and an
opportunity to make and fulfill promises to Guadalupe. Mexican and Mexican
American women who regularly carry out walking pilgrimages to Tepeyac,
according to Peña, perform Catholic devotion in an embodied way that is rich
with meaning and memory. Remembering the features of the road and the
sites of prior prayers and interactions with fellow pilgrims gives the pilgrimage a
recursive character in which each new walk overlaps and intertwines with all
previous experience. Moreover, with "every step, Guadalupanas' actions give

substance and shape to the holy; they not only possess but also circulate it, thereby reaffirming their relationship with the Virgin and with their environment."[8] When the pilgrims eventually arrive after their journey to the basilica in Tepeyac, they sing and recite prayers that invoke Guadalupe as a personal and national protector. In Illinois, Mexican immigrants, Mexican Americans, and an international community of devotees make similar prayers and remembrances that thus tie together Guadalupe's faithful across international borders. This becomes a prime example of how the Catholic Church can simultaneously function as a deeply local and national church as well as a global network of pious devotion and practice.

Devotion to the Virgin of Guadalupe has spilled out of the Mexican American and Latino/a Catholic communities into the greater U.S. Catholic Church. Dozens of parishes in every region of the country are now named for Guadalupe and Juan Diego, and the famous image of Guadalupe greets Catholics in sanctuaries even as she also appears on billboards and murals outside of church buildings. Multivalent in its deployment, Guadalupe's story is invoked as a beacon of immigrant rights as well as a new icon of the movement to end legalized abortion.[9] As Latinos/as continue to grow as a percentage of the U.S. population, there is every reason to think that the sixteenth-century, Nahuatl-speaking, Marian apparition to the Indigenous convert Juan Diego will only become more popular as a symbol of Catholic faith.

Pilgrimage to the Santuario de Chimayó

Without question, the largest Catholic pilgrimage in the Americas is to the Basilica of Our Lady of Guadalupe in Mexico City. Within the United States, this designation goes to a small adobe church in the northern New Mexican village of Chimayó. The Santuario de Chimayó is famous for its ostensibly miraculous dirt. In a side chapel off the nave of the church, there is a small hole in the floor, known as the *pocito*, from which pilgrims and other visitors gather the sandy soil of the region. Believers apply the dirt to ailing parts of their bodies, rubbing it on achy joints and troubled heads. Although the practice is discouraged by church officials today, the dirt was also once mixed with water as a kind of medicinal tea. Today, over 300,000 people visit the Santuario every year, some as faithful pilgrims, others as curious tourists.

A number of origin stories circulate about the Santuario and its holy earth. The most prominent of these, featured in interpretive materials around the Santuario's grounds, focuses on the life of Bernardo Abeyta, a landowner and community leader in Chimayó in the waning years of the Spanish empire. In this version of events, Abeyta was on his property, possibly doing penance, when he noticed a glowing light coming from the ground. When he went to investigate, he discovered that the light was coming from a large crucifix buried in the earth. Abeyta was moved by the miraculous discovery, and he took the crucifix to the nearest church at the time, some eight miles away in the town of Santa Cruz. There, he and the priest installed the crucifix on the church's

Figure 12.1 The Santuario de Chimayó. Author's photo.

altar. The next day, the crucifix was discovered to be missing from the church, and Abeyta again found it buried in his field, where it had been the day before. He returned it to the church only to have the crucifix remove itself once again to his property. Realizing that God intended the crucifix to remain in this spot, Abeyta built the Santuario around the hole in the earth, the *pocito*, and hung the crucifix on the main altar screen. Abeyta named the crucifix "el Señor de Esquipulas," the Lord of Esquipulas, after a similar and famous crucifix in Guatemala, on the other side of New Spain.[10]

Another origin story connects the healing dirt of the Santuario to the Tewa Pueblo people upon whose ancestral land the church and the entire village of Chimayó is now situated. According to early anthropological accounts concerning the region, Chimayó lies where a Pueblo settlement was once located, and where the Santuario sits there was a pool called Tsimajopokwi. Mud from this pool was thought to have healing properties.[11] Historian Ramón Gutiérrez has suggested that the *pocito* represents a *sipapu*, the word used by Hopi people for the hole at the bottom of a kiva that connects this world with the under-world.[12] To gather dirt from the *pocito*, in this scenario, is to recognize Tewa claims to the land and to its meaning. This understanding of the Santuario's origins—as a kind of overlay on top of an earlier Indigenous site of earthy healing—acknowledges the mutual influencing that occurred between Spanish Catholic colonizers and Native peoples.

The earliest documentary records concerning the Santuario suggest that people were already making pilgrimage to the area to seek out healing even before the church was built, which was accomplished from 1813 to 1816.[13] During the nineteenth century, many people from northern New Mexican villages and Pueblos made frequent journeys to the Santuario to collect holy dirt as a medicine for healing, to pray, and to meet together with far-flung family members. Early in the Santuario's life, the Abeyta family's devotion to the Lord of Esquipulas was eclipsed by a popular devotion to the Santo Niño de Atocha, an advocation of the Christ Child. The Santo Niño, Holy Child, is dressed as a pilgrim, and his devotees believe that he visits the needy at night, with particular care for children, the imprisoned, and the sick. A side chapel of the Santuario, adjacent to the room that contains the *pocito*, houses a venerated image of the Santo Niño, and many pilgrims have long associated the power of the healing earth with the Holy Child.[14]

The pilgrimage to the Santuario gained focus after World War II when a group of New Mexican veterans, who had suffered in the Bataan Death March, organized a walking pilgrimage with their family and friends. During their tribulations in the war, they had relied on their devotion to the Santuario and its healing earth to give them strength, and the pilgrimage both expressed their gratitude and allowed them to seek healing from the effects of war.[15] Since then, the pilgrimage, which takes place during the Christian Holy Week and climaxes on Good Friday, has grown dramatically. Today, approximately 30,000 pilgrims walk to the Santuario on Good Friday alone from various points around New Mexico and southern Colorado. Over the course of the year, the site receives around 300,000 pilgrims, tourists, and other visitors.[16]

The Santuario de Chimayó, with its holy dirt and Holy Week pilgrimage, is poised to become a site of international devotion. For years now, media sources, encouraged by the Santuario's clergy administrators, have referred to the place as "the Lourdes of America," after the hugely popular shrine in France known for its miraculous, healing water. In the last decade, the Santuario's ecclesiastical overseers, under the auspices of the Archdiocese of Santa Fe, have carried out renovations and built new buildings, additional gift shops, and parking areas to accommodate the growing crowds of tourists and pilgrims. Behind the Santuario itself now lies an extensive "Madonna Gardens," where several statues of Mary from around the world as well as other devotional figures are located. Prominent is a large statue of Our Lady of La Vang, a Vietnamese image of the Virgin that was gifted to the Santuario by a group of Vietnamese American devotees who travel regularly to Chimayó as part of their own Catholic observance. While not all local New Mexican Catholics, who claim an ancestral connection to the Santuario, the Santo Niño de Atocha, and the holy dirt, are pleased with these new developments, it seems likely that the Santuario will continue to grow in popularity, spilling out of its local context onto an international stage of pilgrimage and devotion.[17]

Border-crossing devotion to saints

Some religious practice around the U.S.-Mexico border focuses, not surprisingly, on the often harrowing experience of crossing the international boundary. Ever since the border began to be monitored—and militarized—people who need to cross from Mexico to the U.S. have called on the assistance of saints to guard and help them in the transit. These same saints are enjoined to help people with their endeavors and transactions, whatever they may be, as border-crossers pursue their livelihoods in a context where real and metaphorical walls constantly threaten free passage. Some of these saints have themselves traversed the official canonization process of the Catholic Church, while many others are sainted only by the acclaim of the faithful. In both cases, devotees rely on saints not only for intercession with God but to exercise the saints' own inherent power to protect and bring prosperity. Several scholars have suggested that the border region has been an especially rich site for the veneration of so-called folk saints, or subjects of popular devotion who were never recognized in the Vatican's canonical courts. Figures like Santa Teresita de Urrea, Don Pedrito Jaramillo, and El Niño Fidencio were renowned borderlands healers in life and now intercede in death on behalf of the sick and suffering. Others, like Juan Soldado, Jesús Malverde, and even Pancho Villa, had less savory lives, but perhaps because of that fact they are now able to address and bless the vagaries of life near the border.[18]

Not all the saints who aid border crossers are "folk" saints. Any saint of the Church can be called upon to intercede on a supplicant's behalf, but some are known to care particularly for migrants. For instance, both the Virgin of Guadalupe and St. Jude, the patron of lost causes, receive the prayers and devotion of many border crossers. A recently canonized Mexican saint, Toribio Romo of the state of Jalisco, has become one of the most popular saints for Mexican immigrants to the United States. In life, Toribio Romo was a young Catholic priest who, with twenty-four others, was assassinated in 1928 by federal Mexican troops as part of the Cristero War. Anti-clerical laws in Mexico had led to the repression of Catholic clergy and restriction of public worship. In the Catholic heartland of west-central Mexico, both clergy and laypeople alike resisted these laws, which unleashed a bloody conflict. Fr. Toribio was one of the victims of the unrest. Even prior to Romo's official canonization, a popular devotion had begun to form around him as a strong protector of immigrants. While the connection between Romo and immigration is not immediately obvious, it is important to note that Jalisco and the surrounding states have been some of the biggest senders of immigrants to the U.S.[19] The Texan historian David Dorado Romo, who is Santo Toribio's relative, notes that the saint is an obvious presence in Jalisco as well as in the personal effects of detained migrants. He writes, "Santo Toribio is a superstar among saints. No certified holy man has lent his name and image to as many restaurants, grocery stores, pharmacies, travel agencies, and employment centers." But that is not all. "Border Patrol agents frequently arrest undocumented border crossers carrying scapulars and key chains with the image of this ubiquitous blue-eyed miracle worker."[20]

These kinds of items are by no means limited, however, to officially canonized saints like Toribio Romo. Several so-called folk saints are actively venerated in the border region and beyond, and any of them can be called on to aid border-crossers. Two examples include Juan Soldado and Jesús Malverde. Unlike the officially sainted Fr. Toribio Romo, neither of these men was a paragon of virtue in life, but their suspect and dramatic lives only seem to augment their power to help their supplicants. Juan Soldado, as his name suggests, was a Mexican soldier stationed in Tijuana who was accused of raping an eight-year-old girl and summarily executed. Neighbors soon began to doubt that Juan was the actual guilty party but rather unjustly railroaded through a trial to a tragic end. A devotion soon grew up around him that emphasized protection for those who rarely benefited from the world's reigning structures of economy and justice, which include the militarized border between Mexico and the United States. Juan Soldado's life and death in Tijuana, at the border, make him a popular saint for those trying to cross safely.[21] Jesús Malverde, unlike Juan Soldado, begins his story on the wrong side of the law as a kind of Mexican Robin Hood. While the historical details of his life are sketchy, Malverde's devotees are confident that the saint, perhaps because of his criminal past, is ready to do what it takes to answer their appeals. Known in the media as the "narcosaint" because of his popularity among drug traffickers, Malverde's faithful followers include many outside the drug trade who ask him to watch over their endeavors around the border. Historian Carolina da Cunha Rocha

Figure 12.2 Amulet of Jesús Malverde, worn for protection when crossing the U.S.-Mexico border. Author's photo.

explains his appeal: "If God and the other Catholic saints are far away, in heaven, Malverde the saint is near, he knows each one of his countrymen and governs their daily fortunes."[22] The same could be said of Juan Soldado and other unofficial saints of the border region.

Another transnational saint of sorts that has gained tremendous popularity in recent years is no mere human but Death herself. Avid and growing devotion to Santa Muerte, as she is known, can be found on both sides of the U.S.-Mexico border. Religious studies scholar Andrew Chesnut explains that "her reputation as a prompt and efficacious miracle worker … has propelled the meteoric growth of her cult since 2001."[23] Anthropologist Claudio Lomnitz has described death as Mexico's "tutelary sign," where images of death are commonplace and deeply tied to national identity.[24] The personification of Death in Santa Muerte captures this national fascination and holds it in a powerful tension with both the contrasting image of the Virgin of Guadalupe and the myriad difficulties faced by the down and out. Santa Muerte's efficaciousness has made her attractive to those with a wide variety of urgent needs, including economic betterment, physical safety and protection, healing, and the strengthening of relationships. She also, like other non-official saints, helps people to transact dangerous situations on both sides of the law. Like Jesús Malverde, Santa Muerte has become a guide and protector for narcotraffickers as well as for those in prison. Her persona as the Grim Reaper holding the scales of justice provides hope and confidence for those who feel alienated, condemned, or forgotten by the legal system.[25] Devotions to folk saints, especially to Santa Muerte, are often controversial with church officials.

Transnational Pentecostalism

Since the explosive Pentecostal revival on Azusa Street in Los Angeles in the first decade of the twentieth century, Pentecostalism has expanded across the planet. Some of the first people to attend the revival and to embrace the new movement were Mexicans residing in California. Mexican and Mexican American converts helped to spread Pentecostalism on both sides of the U.S.-Mexico border in the first decades of the twentieth century.[26] In this same time period, an Assemblies of God-related educational institute was founded to serve the needs of Latino/a evangelists, the Latin American Bible Institute (LABI). With campuses in Texas and southern California, LABI was well-situated and made quick advances. In 1937, a denominational leader praised LABI and its students: "The Latin American people make splendid Christians…. Graduates of these schools are now making effective ministers not only in the U.S.A., among their own people, but also among the Spanish-speaking people in Mexico, Nicaragua, Cuba, and Spain."[27]

According to scholar of religion and historian Lloyd Barba, Mexican and Mexican American Oneness Pentecostals (a branch of Pentecostalism that departed from traditional Christian Trinitarianism) in California drew implicitly on the frameworks of a transnational life. The religious activities, assumptions, and aesthetics of Oneness Pentecostals reflected the experiences of people whose lives were lived by a "hidden transcript," which helped them to resist the insults and degradations that often accompanied migrant life. For instance, Spanish-language hymns both praised God and communicated migrant paths, and religious rites, such as river baptisms, took place on growers' lands, promising rebirth and blessing on the sites of back-breaking labor.[28] Historian Daniel Ramírez's study of transnational Pentecostalism touches on the Iglesia Apostólica, a Oneness group active in both Mexico and California. In the 1940s, the church's publications show that Mexican and Mexican American Pentecostals were in frequent contact across the border in the form of correspondence, joint retreats, a shared hymnody, and intertwined pastoral leadership. By the 1950s, a transnational team of Apostólico missionaries had formed and was having success spreading their message to various sites in Central America.[29]

In recent years, migratory flows of Pentecostals between the United States and Mexico have been complicated by the growing militarization of the border, a nativist resurgence in the U.S., and difficult economic realities in Mexico. Some Pentecostals in central Mexico have responded to this complex environment by actively promoting staying in Mexico. Many residents of the village of El Alberto in the state of Hidalgo converted to Pentecostalism early in the twentieth century after migrants from the town returned from the U.S. carrying the charismatic movement back home. Today, Pentecostal residents have organized an immigration-themed touristic experience called the Caminata Nocturna, "Night Walk," in which visitors can get a taste of what it is like to cross the international border at night while being chased by border patrol, smugglers, and other dangers. One of the objectives of the Caminata—in addition to providing employment opportunities for townspeople—is to make people aware of the very real dangers of emigrating. Inside their churches, the Pentecostal residents of El Alberto are dealing with border-crossing in explicitly religious terms. Anthropologist Leah Sarat explains that Pentecostals who do choose to make the journey are sent off with prayers for the Holy Spirit's protection. One pastor prayed, "Lord blind the eyes of the *migra* [border agents], so that our companions can pass safely! Make them invisible, Lord; we know you have the power to make them invisible."[30] Sarat describes how prayers for supernatural safety as well as the organization of the Caminata Nocturna are both expressions of Pentecostal agency. "Pentecostalism provides an alternate system of authority that counters the social divisions and spatial schemes of nation-states."[31] In this sense, the people's faith in the Spirit transcends transnational realities.

Religion in practice

This chapter has examined movement in Mexican American religion—in pilgrimage and in transnational religious devotions. Moving across space and mutual flows of religious practice to and from Mexico and the United States contribute to the ever-evolving vitality of Mexican American religion. At the actual border between the two countries, religious practices and places help border-crossers orient themselves. In her study of Nuevo Laredo, Tamaulipas, and Laredo, Texas, anthropologist Elaine Peña argues that the international bridge over the Río Grande and the nearby Catholic Church (on the Mexican side), the Parroquia Santo Niño, comprise an intertwined infrastructure for the practice of religion.[32]

The parish on the U.S. side of the border, San Agustín Cathedral, was constructed in the eighteenth century to serve the people of Laredo. It was only after the city was rent asunder by the Treaty of Guadalupe-Hidalgo that a new parish church, the Parroquia Santo Niño, was built in 1851 to serve Nuevo Laredo. Today, with its location only minutes from the international bridge, the Parroquia serves as an adjunct space to the border itself. Since Nuevo Laredo is a terminus for the cross-Mexico train known colloquially as the *bestia* ("beast"), the city is the destination of many Central American and southern Mexican migrants on their way to the United States. Prior to the dangerous cross, many migrants stop in the Parroquia for a time of prayer. But it is used just as much by day-travelers who are crossing the bridge to shop or work in the U.S. before returning home to the Mexican side. Father Martínez Ramírez, the parish priest at the Parroquia Santo Niño, explains:

> There are people who come to la Parroquia specifically to pray to God for help before crossing the bridge, or better said, crossing the river. But there are also people who come into la Parroquia, during their prayer time, before going to work in Laredo [Texas, USA] or stop in on their way home to thank God for having a job.

The church is also a place of respite from, supplication against, and even repudiation of decades of drug cartel-related violence. "Here, the doors are open to everyone," says Martínez Ramírez. "It is a place where people come to find peace, to pray for peace and for the violence to end. Violence may exist but it will not hold us back, even in the slightest way."[33]

The border church both moves and it contains. Like the international bridge with its thousands of pedestrians crossing back and forth, the church is a place where people are constantly streaming in and out. People bring in their prayers and concerns, they kneel and light candles, and they hope for safety for themselves, their loved ones, and their cities. In all this human movement, the church also contains. It holds these prayers even as it holds the stories and memories of the residents of Nuevo Laredo and Laredo. The Parroquia Santo Niño and the San Agustín Cathedral are "living repositories for border residents who have celebrated baptisms, confirmations, or their marriage vows on site."[34] Moving from church to bridge, and moving through a life of faith, are all elements of the place.

Notes

1 This retelling of the apparition synthesizes the *Nican mopohua*, a Nahuatl-language account published in 1649 as a part of a longer narrative about the Virgin of Guadalupe known as the *Huei tlamahuiçoltica*. See Luis Laso de la Vega et al., *The Story of*

Guadalupe: Luis Laso de La Vega's Huei Tlamahuiçoltica of 1649 (Stanford, CA: Stanford University Press, 1998).

2 Timothy Matovina, *Theologies of Guadalupe: From the Era of Conquest to Pope Francis* (New York: Oxford University Press, 2019), 21–22.

3 John Paull II, *Ecclesia in America* (Vatican City: The Holy See, 1999), secs. 11 and 70.

4 Timothy Matovina, "Companion in Exile: Guadalupan Devotion at San Fernando Cathedral, San Antonio, Texas, 1900–1940," in *Horizons of the Sacred: Mexican Traditions in U.S. Catholicism*, ed. Timothy Matovina and Gary Riebe-Estrella (Ithaca, NY: Cornell University Press, 2002), 18, 38.

5 Socorro Castañeda-Liles, "Our Lady of Guadalupe and the Politics of Cultural Interpretation," in *Mexican American Religions: Spirituality, Activism, and Culture* (Durham, NC: Duke University Press, 2008), 175. See also Jeanette Rodriguez, *Our Lady of Guadalupe: Faith and Empowerment among Mexican-American Women* (Austin, TX: University of Texas Press, 1994).

6 Elaine Peña, *Performing Piety: Making Space Sacred with the Virgin of Guadalupe* (Berkeley, CA: University of California Press, 2011), 33–35.

7 Peña, 39.

8 Peña, 54.

9 For instance, see Tom Hoopes, "Our Lady of Guadalupe and U.S. Immigration," *The Gregorian Institute at Benedictine College*, December 12, 2016, https://www.the gregorian.org/2016/our-lady-of-guadalupe-and-u-s-immigration; Frank Pavone, "Our Lady of Guadalupe and the Pro-Life Movement," *Priests for Life*, accessed April 14, 2020, https://www.priestsforlife.org/articles/2791-our-lady-of-guadalup e-and-the-pro-life-movement.

10 Stephen F. De Borhegyi and E. Boyd, *El Santuario de Chimayo*, reprint ed. (Santa Fe, NM: Ancient City Press, 1982), 32; Julio González, *The Santuario de Chimayo in New Mexico: The Shrine of Our Lord of Esquipulas and the Holy Child* (Chimayó, NM: Sons of the Holy Family, 2013), 11.

11 John Peabody Harrington, "The Ethneogeography of the Tewa Indians. Twenty-Ninth Annual Report of the Bureau of American Ethnology to the Secretary of the Smithsonian Institution." (Washington, DC: Bureau of American Ethnology, 1916), 341–42.

12 Ramón A. Gutiérrez, "El Santuario de Chimayo: A Syncretic Shrine in New Mexico," in *Feasts and Celebrations in North American Ethnic Communities*, ed. Ramón A. Gutiérrez and Geneviève Fabre (Albuquerque, NM: University of New Mexico Press, 1995), 74.

13 See Fray Sebastián Álvarez's letter to the Lord Provisor and Capitular Vicar of the Diocese of Durango, November 13, 1813, document 2, Churches in New Mexico Collection, folder 17, New Mexico State Records Center and Archives, Santa Fe.

14 Juan Javier Pescador, *Crossing Borders with the Santo Niño de Atocha* (Albuquerque, NM: University of New Mexico Press, 2009), 81, 86–91.

15 New Mexico National Guard Museum, "New Mexico National Guard's Involvement in the Bataan Death March," 2014, http://www.bataanmuseum.com/bataa nhistory; Michael P. Carroll, *American Catholics in the Protestant Imagination: Rethinking the Academic Study of Religion* (Baltimore, MD: Johns Hopkins University Press, 2007), 124.

16 Interview with site administrator Joanne Dupont Sandoval, July 2, 2014. See also Irene S. Levine, "A Little Church in New Mexico with Some Big Healing Power," *Washington Post*, 2014, http://www.washingtonpost.com/lifestyle/travel/a-little-church-in-new-mexico-with-some-big-healing-power/2014/04/10/6989ca34-b9bf-11e3-9a05-c739f29ccb08_story.html.

17 Brett Hendrickson, *The Healing Power of the Santuario de Chimayó: America's Miraculous Church* (New York: New York University Press, 2017), 187–94.

18　For an overview of these "folk" saints, see James S. Griffith, *Folk Saints of the Borderlands: Victims, Bandits & Healers* (Tucson, AZ: Rio Nuevo Publishers, 2003).

19　César Gallo Medina, "Magnetismo espiritual: Toribio Romo, sus reliquias y la expansión territorial del culto," *Espaço e Cultura*, no. 37 (January 2015): 205–7.

20　David Dorado Romo, "My Tío, the Saint," *Texas Monthly*, November 1, 2010, 153.

21　See Paul J. Vanderwood, *Juan Soldado: Rapist, Murderer, Martyr, Saint* (Durham, NC: Duke University Press, 2004), especially chapter 8.

22　Carolina da Cunha Rocha, "Blessed Are You among Bandits: The Cross-Border Cult of Jesús Malverde (19th–21st Centuries)," *Frontera Norte* 31 (2019): 8.

23　R. Andrew Chesnut, *Devoted to Death: Santa Muerte, the Skeleton Saint* (New York: Oxford University, 2012), 8.

24　Claudio Lomnitz, *Death and the Idea of Mexico* (New York: Zone Books: MIT Press, 2005).

25　Chesnut, *Devoted to Death*, 177–78.

26　Daniel Ramírez, *Migrating Faith: Pentecostalism in the United States and Mexico in the Twentieth Century* (Chapel Hill, NC: University of North Carolina Press, 2015), 50, 76.

27　Quoted in Arlene M. Sánchez Walsh, *Latino Pentecostal Identity: Evangelical Faith, Self, and Society*, Religion and American Culture (New York: Columbia University Press, 2003), 54.

28　Lloyd Barba, "Farmworker Frames: Apostólico Counter Narratives in California's Valleys," *Journal of the American Academy of Religion* 86, no. 3 (2018): 718.

29　Ramírez, *Migrating Faith*, 144–47, 158–59.

30　Leah Sarat, *Fire in the Canyon: Religion, Migration, and the Mexican Dream* (New York: New York University Press, 2013), 128.

31　Sarat, 197.

32　Elaine A. Peña, "Time to Pray: Devotional Rhythms and Space Sacralization at the Mexico-US Border," *Material Religion* 13, no. 4 (2017): 473.

33　Peña, 471–73.

34　Peña, 466.

13 Mexican American Jews, Muslims, Buddhists, Mormons, and "nones"

Any general account of Mexican American religions will focus primarily on Christianity, and particularly on Catholicism, but not all religious Mexican Americans are Christians, and not all are religious. These populations remain relatively small, but they nevertheless form an important part of the story of Mexican American religions. While Mexican Americans participate in a wide variety of religions, in this chapter, four groups will be profiled: Mexican American Jews, Muslims, Buddhists, and the so-called "nones." Stretching back to Iberian history, people of Mexican descent have a long association with both Judaism and Islam. The chapter will summarize this history, give profiles of Mexican American Jewish and Muslim communities, and discuss some of the unique issues that they face. Latino/a practice of Buddhism has a shorter history, but the percentage of U.S. Buddhists who self-identify as Latino/a is surprisingly high. Finally, especially among younger generations, a growing number of Mexican Americans claim no religious affiliation at all, or, in some cases, identify as atheist. Given the stereotype that Mexican Americans are all Catholic, or at least Christian, having no religion can be challenging.

Mexican American religious minorities: Demographic data

Demographic information concerning Mexican American religious minorities can be hard to come by. To start, most data are collected for "Latinos/as" or "Hispanics" in general and do not always break down by Latin American country of ancestral origin. The imprecision of the terms "Latino/a" and "Hispanic" and respondents' self-identification (or not) with one of these ethnic labels can lead to inaccurate results. Pinpointing which of the respondents are Mexican American is not always possible. Moreover, people may not fully identify with a particular religion even though their behavior would suggest that they practice it regularly. Or, they may practice more than one religion simultaneously. Finally, the "nones," or those that claim no religious affiliation, share little that unites this group. A great many "nones" hold some belief in God or a supernatural power, while others self-identify decidedly as atheists.

Bearing these challenges in mind, it is nevertheless helpful to know approximately how many Mexican Americans are practicing religions other

DOI: 10.4324/9780429285516-16

than Christianity or no religion. First of all, a very small percentage of Latinos/as belong to any religion other than Christianity. Second, the number of Latinos/as who identify with no religion is growing. In 2003, the Hispanic Churches in American Public Life project carried out a large survey and found that only 1 percent of Latinos/as reported being part of a non-Christian religion while 6 percent said that they had "no religious preference/other."[1] By 2015, the Pew Research Center discovered that the percentage of Latinos/as who identified with a non-Christian religion remained low at 2 percent, while the number of religiously non-affiliated had risen sharply to around 20 percent.[2] Since together all adherents of Judaism, Buddhism, Hinduism, and Islam of any racial or ethnic background make up approximately 5 percent of the United States' population, the number of Latinos/as who practice these religions is quite small indeed. Within these religions, Latinos/as are a minority within a minority. Counting only those who identify solely as "Latino/a" (and excluding, therefore, any Latinos/as who reported having a mixed racial/ethnic heritage), Latinos/as comprise 4 percent of Jews, 4 percent of Muslims, and 12 percent of Buddhists in the U.S.[3] Survey data regarding Latino/a Muslims show that, of all Latino/a Muslims, 31 percent identify as Mexican or Mexican American.[4]

Despite these small percentages, Latino/a religious diversity as well as non-affiliation is growing, and the story of Mexican American religions is incomplete without taking these groups' experiences and histories into account. For these religious minority groups within the larger Mexican American community, questions of religion's relationship to ethnicity are highlighted in ways that probe the boundaries of Mexican American identity.

Mexican American Jews

For the most part, Latino/a Jews in the United States, including Mexican American Jews, are parts of families that have experienced several waves of international migration. The first move was to Latin America from eastern Europe and other locales outside of the Americas; the second migration was to the U.S. from Latin American nations. While some Jews in Latin America can trace their ancestry to Sephardic Jewish populations in the Iberian Peninsula—many of whom came to the Americas in an attempt to distance themselves from the Spanish Inquisition—a majority of Latin American Jews today are Ashkenazi Jews from central and eastern Europe, similar to the majority of the Jewish population in the United States. The largest and best-known population of Jews in Latin America is in Argentina, but there are also sizable communities in Mexico, Brazil, Venezuela, and the Caribbean. When U.S. immigration laws were eased in 1965, more and more Latin Americans were able to immigrate to the United States, including Jewish Latin Americans. Surveys put the number of Latino/a Jews in the United States today somewhere between 86,000 and 150,000 people.[5]

Compared with the United States, there are very few Jews in Mexico. Most of those that live there are concentrated in Mexico City and can trace their history to the 1920s, when anti-immigrant legislation in the United States forced many Jewish emigres to find other destinations, including Mexico. Subethnic divisions exist in the Mexican Jewish community based on country or region of origin, particularly between Ashkenazi Jews from Europe and Jews from the former Ottoman Empire. As a result, as of 2019, there were twenty-three synagogues in Mexico City serving the various national-origin communities. To unite these various groups and to strengthen their social and political clout, the Comité Central de la Comunidad Judía de México (the Central Committee of the Mexican Jewish Community) was founded in the 1930s. The Comité Central as well as the Centro Deportivo Israelita—an athletic and social club akin to Jewish Community Centers in many U.S. cities—continue to be important centers of Mexican Jewish life today.[6]

Mexican Jews who immigrate to the United States find that the experience of being Jewish in the U.S. differs in several ways from being Jewish in Mexico. First, the Jewish community in Mexico is a tiny minority of the population, a fact which has promoted tight-knit ethnic enclaves.[7] In contrast, while Jews make up only a small percentage of the U.S. population, they still represent the largest Jewish population in the world outside of Israel and have a long history of relative integration and dispersion throughout the nation. A Mexican Jew living in Miami reported that, "In Mexico—since there are so many class differences and physical differences—you can be 100 percent of the time with Jews." She lamented that this was not the case in the U.S. and that she had lost a "sense of community."[8] The flipside can also be true in that some Latino/a Jews are content to be in a more ethnically and religiously mixed context. A Mexican Jew in New York noted that this contributed to his desire to immigrate. "I left, in part, because the community and the society were, in general, too close minded. It was difficult to have contact with people outside of the Jewish community [in Mexico]."[9]

Another important difference that Mexican American and other Latino/a Jews report between their experiences in Latin America and the United States has to do with how they are identified and how they are expected to identify themselves. Like many immigrants, they sometimes find it difficult or unnatural to be lumped into a panethnic group known as "Latinos/as." This sometimes contrasts with a strong national identity—for example, as Mexican—or as ethnically Jewish. Questions of racial identity also come into play as many Latino/a Jews are able to choose whether or not to identify as white. While this can create opportunities in the United States' racialized society, it can also create distance with other Latinos/as. Sociologist Laura Limonic explains: "Latino Jews possess an array of ethnic options; in other words, they can be Latino and white, or Latino and Jewish, options that are not available to the majority of the Latinos living in the United States."[10] Given the relatively recent immigration of many Latin American Jews to the U.S., it remains to be seen how these differences will be expressed in the second and third generations.

Sizable Latino/a Jewish population centers exist in New York, Miami, and in California, but San Diego is perhaps the location with the most cohesive

Mexican American Jewish community. As is the case for most Latino/a Jews in the United States, the hub of the community is not the synagogue or religious observance but rather Jewish community centers that gather people around shared cultural identity, recreational activities, opportunities for youth, and service.[11] An excellent example is the KEN Jewish Community in San Diego. The organization was founded in the early 1980s to meet the needs of Mexican Jewish immigrants from Mexico City and Tijuana, who had come to the U.S. to address "economic and security concerns." Today, the KEN, according to the group's website,

> is the place where Latin Jewish families find friends for life who share their beliefs, values and traditions. Through a wide range of educational, leadership, social, performing arts, and sports programs and activities, its members strengthen their Jewish identity, build a connection with Israel, and maintain their Latin culture.[12]

An example is the Bat Mitzvah Group at the KEN, a program for girls to prepare them for adolescence. "During one year they participate in a dynamic and practical course that teaches Jewish Values, Traditions, and Zionism."[13] With scheduled activities for all ages in both English and Spanish, the KEN assists Mexican American Jews in southern California to balance and express the various parts of their ethnic and religious identity.

Mexican American Muslims

Islam is growing among Latinos/as, including among Mexican Americans. Latinos/as who come to embrace Islam often speak of this transformation as a "reversion" rather than a "conversion" to draw an explicit link to the long Muslim history of the Iberian Peninsula. In 711 C.E., Muslims crossed the strait of Gibraltar and took possession of much of what is now Spain and Portugal. The Muslim rulers of the region generally did not enforce conversion to Islam but instead promoted *convivencia*, a situation wherein Jews, Christians, and Muslims could live together in relative peace. Scholars debate the practical success of *convivencia*, but, in any case, Muslim rulers and large Muslim populations existed in Spain for more than seven hundred years. It was only in the final part of the fifteenth century that Christian monarchs and their armies were able to topple Muslim rule and expel many Muslims (and Jews) from the peninsula. While a direct connection to this Muslim Iberian past is difficult to reconstruct, Latinos/as today who become Muslim nonetheless articulate this link as a reversion to earlier Iberian norms.[14]

Dawah is the Muslim practice of spreading the religion, and it often includes personal interaction, education about Islam, and the sharing of literature, such as brochures about Islam as well as the Muslim scripture, the Qur'an. Since the current majority of Mexican American and other Latino/a Muslims are reverts to Islam, most of them have direct experience as the recipients of dawah; after their reversion, many then practice dawah to share Islam with their friends, relatives, and neighbors. Religious studies scholar Harold Morales notes that the "Islamic mandate to propagate the religion's teachings to non-Muslims has encouraged many Latino Muslim groups to organize around the production of English and Spanish books, flyers, and websites directed at Latino audiences."[15] One such organization that has served many Mexican Americans is the Los Angeles Latino Muslim Association (LALMA). Founded around the turn of the twenty-first century, LALMA, which operates in mosques throughout the Los Angeles area, meets weekly as a group to study the Qur'an, the Arabic language, and Sufi thought. They also perform dawah for the Latino/a community and beyond, meeting with Catholic Church groups, the Los Angeles Police Department, and at neighborhood festivals.[16]

Juan Galvan is a third-generation Mexican American from Texas who reverted to Islam as a young man. In addition to being a vocal advocate for and interpreter of Latino/a Islam, he has interviewed dozens of reverts to try to better understand people's motivations for conversion and what they gain from being part of the U.S. Muslim community. When he asked his respondents to name reasons for their reversion, most indicated that they had studied the religion and found it inherently attractive in its emphasis on the unity of all people and the oneness of God. Others explicitly pointed out a dissatisfaction with Catholicism. One revert, Teqwa, said, "I think it's mostly about disillusionment with the Catholic Church … Simplicity and unity are lacking in the Christian Church."[17] Others cite positive interactions with Muslim workmates or friends that led to an interest in the religion. Others, particularly women, came to Islam as part of their marriage to Muslim men. For example, when Theresa Vargas met and fell in love with a man whose Islam, in her eyes, made him kind, reliable, and patient, she embraced his religion. Her own belief in Allah has flourished, and she now considers her marriage and conversion to be part of God's plan. "Allah (SWT) had my whole life planned out since the day I was born … I give thanks to Allah (SWT) for choosing me to come into Islam."[18]

Harold Morales analyzed reversion narratives to parse their basic features. He found that many Latino/a Muslims prefer to speak of a "reversion" not merely because of the historical Iberian connection to Islam but also as an ontological declaration. One "reverts" to one's true identity. One feature of this logic, suggests Morales, is that it addresses "accusations that Latino and Muslim identities are incompatible. Further, reversion stories promote pluralism in American by helping debunk Latino-therefore-Christian and Muslim-therefore-Arab misrepresentations." While these are positive features of the logic of reversion narratives, the same logic can also imply that Latinos/as, because of their racial-ethnic heritage, are Muslim as part of their essential being even if they have not yet reverted. This essentializing way of thinking, argues Morales, mimics the erroneous assumption that all Latinos/as are Catholic by their very nature.[19]

Mexican American and other Latino/a Muslims face several challenges because of their religion and ethnic identity, but by the same token, they challenge popular assumptions about race, religion, and ethnicity. On the one hand, Mexican American Muslims share some characteristics with Mexican American Jews. They are religious minorities that often find it necessary to interpret their own experience both to non-Latino/a co-religionists and to other Mexican Americans. On the other hand, since most Mexican American Muslims have reverted to Islam (rather than being born into it), they must also grapple with the tensions that can arise in their families as a result. Reverts sometimes find themselves having to defend their continued identity as Mexican Americans as compatible with their new religious identity.[20] Moreover, U.S. Muslims, Latino/a or otherwise, confront anti-Muslim bigotry, suspicion, and even violence.[21] In balance, Latino/a reverts to Islam call into question the fixed nature of identity. Morales argues that a fluid and dynamic approach to identity makes more sense and is more just. After all, "Categories like 'Latino,' 'Muslim,' and even so-called minorities become themselves untenable universals relative to the particularities or diversity that exists within these broader umbrella identities."[22]

Mexican American Buddhists

While there are not many Mexican American Buddhists, there is reason to believe that the number of Latinos/as who identify as Buddhist is growing. In 2014, the Pew Research Center reported that 12 percent of U.S. Buddhists were Latino/a, up from 7 percent in 2007.[23] To date, there has been very little documentation of this community, much less academic study. However, the statistics reported by Pew would indicate that Latino/a Buddhists deserve more attention. Since practicing Buddhism does not require renunciation of other religions, it may be possible that some Latinos/as who report themselves as Buddhist may also identify as simultaneous adherents of other religions. One reporter discovered in 2016 that, "for many Latinos that enter into the world of meditation, Buddhism is nothing more than an enjoyable and healthy practice," which coincides with a common desire for "mental health through meditation and other Buddhist practices" without having to give up "their own religion."[24] For example, the renowned Mexican American novelist Sandra Cisneros has described herself as a Buddhist, but she also maintains a deep love for the Virgin of Guadalupe. "I tell people that I am a 'Buddhalupist,'" Cisneros explained. "I have to invent it and take parts of the Catholic religion that work for me, like the Virgin of Guadalupe, and toss out the parts that I [sic] don't."[25]

Others are turning definitively to Buddhism and joining Buddhist organizations. Soka Gakkai International, a Japanese-origin Buddhist organization that promotes lay leadership and participation, has had considerable success in promoting multiracial and multiethnic communities. The organization has hosted a regular Spanish-language meeting in the U.S. since 2001. This has allowed Latinos/as to forge Buddhist community even as they learn about the teachings of Nichiren, a thirteenth-century Japanese sage whose teachings form the basis of Soka Gakkai's Buddhist practice. The community-based format of Soka

Gakkai as well as other forms of Buddhism that feature temple services have been popular with Latinos/as who are seeking out religious community rather than solitary mediation or study. As one Latina practitioner said of her experience as a Buddhist convert,

> It's the community, it's the family service, it's the reading I get to do and talk to people about—I was looking for that. I knew I needed more than reading on my own. I knew you could only go so far in your spiritual growth with that.[26]

However, there are also growing opportunities for Latino/a Buddhists to enter into more meditative branches of Buddhism. For instance, the San Francisco Zen Center offers weekly lessons in Zen in Spanish and maintains a library of Spanish-language Buddhist materials for the community.[27] Sanathavihari Bhante Bhikku is a Mexican American monk at the Sarathchandra Buddhist Center in Los Angeles. He emphasizes that technology is a popular way to reach Mexican American, Latino/a, and Latin American audiences. Bhante explains, "Technology just works for everyone. The person who wants to spread that kind of teaching and the person who's looking for different kinds of teachings." To this end, Bhante has put together a YouTube channel called "Monje en la Modernidad" ("Monk in Modernity") where he posts instruction in meditation.[28]

Mexican American Mormons

The Church of Jesus Christ of Latter-day Saints is a variation of Christianity that emerged in the early nineteenth century in western New York. Adherents are often referred to as "Mormons" in reference to the Book of Mormon, one of the Church's signature scriptures. They are also called Latter-day Saints, which is often abbreviated as "LDS." Since its founding, the LDS Church has spread through the United States and around the world. Headquartered since the 1840s in Utah, the Mormons have had a distinctive presence and impact in the western United States, putting them in close contact with Mexicans and Mexican Americans for a long time. This adjacency did not immediately lead to Mexican American conversions, but over time and through Mormon missionary efforts, a number have joined the Church. In 2009, the Pew Research Center reported that 7 percent of U.S. LDS members were Latino/a (the survey did not further break down this population into specific communities, such as Mexican Americans). That number has likely risen since that date.[29]

While the Church of Jesus Christ of Latter-day Saints has made efforts to include and incorporate Latino/a members, Mormon understandings of race and ethnicity in the Americas have sometimes been an obstacle for Mexican Americans and other people of color. Joseph Smith, the first prophet and president of the Church, claimed to have discovered golden plates buried in the ground near his home in upstate New York. Smith translated these plates, which contained the Book of Mormon. The Book of Mormon tells the story of Israelite migration to the Americas, a visit by Jesus to the inhabitants of this continent, and a saga of conflict and warfare among tribes. Ultimately, the righteous—the Nephites—are defeated by a group known as the Lamanites, a dark-skinned group who had rejected the gospel of Jesus. Mormons understand Lamanites to be the ancestors of Indigenous people, including the majority of today's mestizo Mexican Americans. According to Mormon belief, God chose Smith to restore the true church and to bring long-awaited salvation to the Lamanites. While Mormons have long recognized a place for so-called Lamanites in the LDS fold, the contentious and overtly racial nature of LDS sacred history has not always made for a smooth incorporation of people of color.

Further complicating this narrative is an overt linking of skin color and salvation in the Book of Mormon. Ignacio García is a Mexican American history professor at Brigham Young University in Utah and a bishop in the LDS Church. In his many writings about Latino/a Mormons, he has noted that the Book of Mormon "affirms that the 'colored' righteous will someday become 'fair and delightsome.'"[30] García argues that, "Privileging white skin over colored not only led to conquest and oppression in the secular world but also to a diminished role for people of color within the Church." As a result, he notes that many Mormons of color feel like "stepchildren" in the family of faith.[31] Nonetheless, García points out that Latinos/as and other people of color are the fastest growing demographic in Mormonism.

> The white population around the world is not converting—so the LDS Church, like other churches, is counting on immigrants to fill the pews. I don't think there is anyone in the church hierarchy who can see anything but a church of color in the next 25 years.[32]

What attracts Mexican Americans and other Latinos/as to the Church of Jesus Christ of Latter-day Saints? Several scholars have found that many Latinos/as find value in Mormonism. Sujey Vega, a scholar of women and gender studies, has found that Mexican American Mormons in Arizona have a long-standing community, including the first Spanish-speaking branch in the Church. Vega explains that there is a sense of ethnic belonging in Mormonism, alongside feelings of conflict. She notes that positives for many Mexican American Mormons include "direct relationships with the scriptures" and "a gendered support network for women." This network takes shape in the Relief Society, an LDS women's organization that offers charitable support, education, and other forms of compassionate service to members.[33] Historian Jorge Iber likewise finds that access to the scriptures as well as to positions of leadership have been features of Mormonism that are attractive to Latinos/as. Since the LDS Church has no professional clergy, barriers to leadership are lower than in the Catholic Church and even in many Protestant denominations. "Latinos, in my view, have found a wonderful home in the LDS Church. The Mormons value God, country, and family, just as most Latinos do," Iber suggests, and he adds that the LDS Church often also provides helpful social and business contacts.[34] Finally, ongoing Mormon missionary efforts to Latino/a communities continue to contribute to conversions.

The religiously non-affiliated

A growing number of people in the United States, when surveyed, report no religious affiliation—this group, such as it is, is often referred to as the "nones." It is perhaps misleading to think of the nones as a unified category of people as there is considerable variation with respect to religion within this population. Elizabeth Drescher, a religious studies scholar who has written about nones, says that there are various types of religiously non-affiliated people. Atheists explicitly do not believe in God, gods, or any other transcendent force, while agnostics range from those who hold that proving God's existence is impossible to those who are merely unsure. Others in the none group include ethical humanists, those who claim to be "spiritual but not religious," and avowed secularists. Many nones are not opposed to religion but are not personally interested; they may even believe in God or some other kind of supernatural being but nevertheless find no interest in affiliating with a religious organization or tradition.[35] With all this internal diversity, it is important to remember that, despite the umbrella term of "nones," this group should not be treated as a monolith.

In demographic terms, there is no doubt that the nones represent a significant and growing segment of the U.S. population. In 2016, 22 percent of people in the U.S. reported no religious affiliation, up from a mere 7 percent in 1972.[36] Among the 22 percent, some are apostates, or people who have chosen explicitly to leave a religious tradition. However, as the number of nones grows, there is also a growing group of people who were socialized by their parents to have no religious affiliation. Indeed, the nones tend to be young— 44 percent are under the age of 35.[37] Sociologists and other scholars have developed several theories to explain the increase of non-affiliation. One explanation is that religion has been declining for a long time as a result of the Enlightenment and scientific revolution. The idea here is that religion becomes less and less relevant to people as they embrace a rationalistic worldview. Moreover, religious pluralism in modern times also contributes to the decline of religious authority. A second theory suggests that religion is not so much declining as changing from an institutional format to an individual, spiritual orientation. A third approach notes that polarization can lead to disaffiliation. When religious groups set themselves in opposition to social norms or practices, some people can become alienated from religion and consider it close-minded or even dangerous. For instance, there is some evidence that the rise of the religious right in the United States in the late-twentieth century has contributed to young people's disillusionment with religion.[38]

In general, scholars and the media have paid very little attention to Latino/a nones, much less to Mexican American people who are religiously non-affiliated. On the one hand, this is surprising given demographic realities. According to political scientist Juhem Navarro-Rivera, nones comprise the largest "religious" group among Latinos/as after Catholics and Protestants. Citing a 2008, survey, he points out that the number of Latino/a nones surpasses the number of Latino/a adherents of all non-Christian religions put together. Latino/a nones, for instance, outnumber Latino/a Muslims six to one. On the other hand, enduring stereotypes about Latinos/as likely obscure the rising numbers of the non-religious. Navarro-Rivera suggests that, "the media are more interested in stereotyping Latinos as a God-fearing, Virgin-worshipping, religiously conservative group." He notes that this not only ignores a substantial Latino/a population but also gives short shrift to a long history of secularism in Latin America. For example, the Mexican government's stance on religion, especially under liberal regimes, has often been pointedly secular and even anticlerical. This would indicate that, while Mexico remains an overwhelmingly Christian nation, secular elements have certainly been present and active there for some time.[39] To be sure, more study is required of Mexican Americans who do not identify as religious.

Religion in practice

When the holy month of Ramadan concludes, Muslims around the world gather together to observe Eid al-Fitr, the festival that celebrates ending the fast. (Devout Muslims fast during Ramadan from all food, water, and sexual activity during daylight hours.) In addition to offering prayers and giving to the poor, on Eid Muslims gather, wearing new or fine clothes. Gifts are often given, especially to children, as a sign of Allah's abundance. Likewise, the Eid meal is extravagant and a fitting end to a month of fasting. It is a joyful time, one that Muslims look forward to celebrating.

Houston, Texas, is a city with a large Latino/a presence—44 percent of the population. To share Islam with this community the Centro Islámico formed in 2016. The Centro Islámico celebrated Houston's first Eid al-Fitr in Spanish that year, attracting over 300 worshipers. Juan Pablo Osorio was in attendance. He said, "To be there and to see such a diversity of people from several different continents—Africans, Asians, Middle Easterners, Europeans and Latinos—was humbling, and to hear the message was very touching." The diversity of the community is one of the core values of Islam. Jaime Mujahid Fletcher, the Colombian leader of Centro Islámico, explains,

> We wanted it to be a place where when people come they feel instantly comfortable, and I think we've been successful because no one has ever come and felt alienated or isolated or felt that it's just a Latino thing.[40]

Latino/a Muslims in Houston and elsewhere are proud that their faith unites them with fellow Muslims around the world.

Feasting after Ramadan has brought Muslims and Mexican Americans together in southern California as a sign of mutual support and encouragement against discrimination that both groups sometimes experience. In Orange

County, activists Rida Hamida and Ben Vazquez teamed up to promote unity through the sharing of food. Their campaign, spearheaded in 2017, was called "Taco Trucks at Every Mosque." Hamida explained, "This is perfect timing. The purpose of [Ramadan] is to give charity, to grow our character and our inner lives, and to nourish our soul through service. What better way to do that than by learning from one another?" Gathering with Mexican American neighbors to break the fast with a feast of tacos attracted hundreds of participants and opened lines of communication and solidarity. "We have a saying—*la cultura cura*—the culture cures," said Vazquez. "There's nothing better than two sides coming together to cure evil thoughts about each other."[41]

Notes

1 Gastón Espinosa, Virgilio Elizondo, and Jesse Miranda, *Hispanic Churches in American Public Life: Summary of Findings* (Notre Dame, IN: Institute for Latino Studies, University of Notre Dame, 2003), 14.
2 Pew Research Center, "Latinos, Religious Landscape Study," *Pew Research Center, Religion & Public Life.*
3 Pew Research Center, "Racial and Ethnic Composition, Religious Landscape Study," *Pew Research Center, Religion and Public Life*, accessed May 13, 2020, https://www.pewforum.org/religious-landscape-study.
4 Gastón Espinosa, Harold Morales, and Juan Galvan, "Latino Muslims in the United States: Reversion, Politics, and Islamidad," *Journal of Race, Ethnicity, and Religion* 8, no. 1 (2017): 15.
5 Laura Limonic, *Kugel and Frijoles: Latino Jews in the United States* (Detroit, MI: Wayne State University Press, 2019), 2, n. 1.
6 Limonic, 37–38.
7 Evelyn Dean-Olmsted, "Shamis, Halebis and Shajatos: Labels and Dynamics of Syrian Jewishness in Mexico City," *Language and Communication* 31 (2011): 130–40.
8 Limonic, *Kugel and Frijoles*, 49.
9 Limonic, 59.
10 Limonic, 91.
11 Latino Decisions, "Focus Groups with Latino Jews in Five American Cities" (American Jewish Committee and the Arthur and Rochelle Belfer Institute for Latino and Latin American Affairs, December 11, 2015), 10.
12 KEN Jewish Community, "About Us," *KEN Jewish Community*, n.d., http://kenjc.org/new/about-us.
13 KEN Jewish Community, "Bat Mitzvah Group," *KEN Jewish Community*, n.d., http://kenjc.org/new/bat-mitzvah.
14 Harold D. Morales, *Latino and Muslim in America: Race, Religion, and the Making of a New Minority* (New York: Oxford University Press, 2018), 18–24.
15 Morales, 10.
16 Juan Galvan, "Latino Muslims Leading Others to Enlightenment," *Islamic Horizons*, August 2002; Morales, *Latino and Muslim in America*, 64–69.
17 Galvan, Juan, ed., *Latino Muslims: Our Journeys to Islam* (San Antonio, TX: Self-published, 2017), 13.
18 Galvan, Juan, 203. "SWT" stands for *Subhanahu Wa Ta'ala* and means "The Most Glorified and Most Exalted is He (Allah)." Muslims often use this expression whenever the name of Allah is pronounced or written.
19 Morales, *Latino and Muslim in America*, 103–4.
20 Morales, 204.

21 For one account of the toll this bigotry takes on the Muslim community in the U.S., see Lori Peek, *Behind the Backlash: Muslim Americans after 9/11* (Philadelphia, PA: Temple University Press, 2011).

22 Morales, *Latino and Muslim in America*, 205.

23 Pew Research Center, "Racial and Ethnic Composition, Religious Landscape Study."

24 Laura Gamba, "Perdió el pelo y el nombre para encontrar su espiritualidad," *El Nuevo Herald*, August 23, 2016, https://www.elnuevoherald.com/noticias/sur-de-la-florida/article97421802.html. My translation.

25 Jorge Chino, "The Buddhalupist: The Spiritual Life of Sandra Cisneros," *El Andar*, 1999, http://www.elandar.com/back/winter99/stories/story_cisneros.html.

26 Caitlin Yoshiko Kandil, "Buddhist Groups Increasingly Taking Root in Latinx Communities," *Lion's Roar*, November 21, 2018, https://www.lionsroar.com/buddhist-groups-increasingly-taking-root-in-latinx-communities; Diana L. Eck, *A New Religious America: How a "Christian Country" Has Now Become the World's Most Religiously Diverse Nation*, 1st ed. (San Francisco, CA: HarperSanFrancisco, 2001), 160.

27 San Francisco Zen Center, "Bienvenidos a City Center," *San Francisco Zen Center*, accessed June 3, 2020, https://www.sfzc.org/practice-centers/city-center/bienvenidos-city-center.

28 Kandil, "Buddhist Groups Increasingly Taking Root in Latinx Communities"; Sanathavihari Bhante Bhikku, "Monje En La Modernidad," *YouTube*, accessed June 3, 2020, https://www.youtube.com/channel/UCgX_kcAhHCuaDTdjejB1LZQ.

29 Pew Research Center, "A Portrait of Mormons in the U.S.," *Pew Research Center's Religion & Public Life Project*, accessed June 4, 2020, https://www.pewforum.org/2009/07/24/a-portrait-of-mormons-in-the-us.

30 Ignacio M. García, "Thoughts on Latino Mormons, Their Afterlife, and the Need for a New Historical Paradigm for Saints of Color," *Dialogue: A Journal of Mormon Thought* 50, no. 4 (2017): 12. In the Book of Mormon, see 2 Nephi 5:21–23.

31 García, 14.

32 Raul A. Reyes, "The Future of the Mormon Church? It's Latino," *NBC News*, August 22, 2016, https://www.nbcnews.com/news/latino/future-mormon-church-it-s-latino-n570621.

33 Brenden W. Rensink, "Q&A with Sujey Vega about LDS Latinos and Ethnic Religious Belonging in Arizona," *Borderlands History*, March 28, 2016, https://borderlandshistory.org/2016/03/28/qa-with-sujey-vega-about-lds-latinos-and-ethnic-religious-belonging-in-arizona.

34 Kate Shellnutt, "On a Mission: Mormons Reach out to Hispanics," *Houston Chronicle*, May 6, 2010, https://www.chron.com/life/houston-belief/article/On-a-mission-Mormons-reach-out-to-Hispanics-1694354.php.

35 Elizabeth Drescher, *Choosing Our Religion: The Spiritual Lives of America's Nones* (New York: Oxford University Press, 2016), 28–29.

36 Joel Thiessen and Sarah Wilkins-Laflamme, *None of the Above: Nonreligious Identity in the US and Canada* (New York: New York University Press, 2020), 7.

37 Thiessen and Wilkins-Laflamme, 15.

38 Robert D. Putnam and David E. Campbell, *American Grace: How Religion Divides and United Us* (New York: Simon and Schuster, 2010), 91–133.

39 Juhem Navarro-Rivera, "Media Stereotypes and the Invisible Latino 'Nones,'" *Free Inquiry*, December 2010, 15, 46.

40 Carissa Lamkahouan, "Latinos Mark 'Eid in America's First Spanish Muslim Center," *AboutIslam*, July 8, 2016, https://aboutislam.net/muslim-issues/n-america/latinos-mark-eid-americas-first-spanish-muslim-center.

41 Anh Do, "Muslim and Latino Groups Unite during Ramadan, Breaking Fast with Tacos at Mosques," *Los Angeles Times*, June 4, 2017, https://www.latimes.com/local/lanow/la-me-ln-tacos-ramadan-20170604-story.html.

Conclusion

The Aztecs, in poetic reference to the complexity, beauty, and profundity of life, spoke of *flor y canto*, flower and song. *Flor y canto* has spiritual and religious overtones, articulating the cosmic and the sublime into language. Mexican American religions are their own kind of *flor y canto*, embodying people's connections to their history, to each other, and to the objects of their worship and devotion. Understanding Mexican American religions helps us understand the Mexican American experience as well as the complex interplay between ethnicity and religion in the United States.

This book, beginning with Indigenous traditions, addressed the cataclysm of Spanish colonialism and the resulting spread of Iberian Catholicism throughout New Spain. As Catholic missions spread throughout the Spanish empire, they also moved northward into territory that would, centuries later, become the Mexican north and the U.S. west and southwest. After Mexican independence in 1821, these northern Catholics often found themselves far from centers of ecclesiastical and political oversight. By 1848, Mexico was forced to cede much of its northern territory to the expanding United States. Mexican inhabitants of these lands became Mexican Americans and minorities in their own Catholic Church. Not long after, Protestant missionaries to the newly-acquired lands began to proselytize Mexican Americans, a slow process that often highlighted racial inequities between white missionaries and Mexican American converts. By the twentieth century, the U.S. had received large numbers of Mexican immigrants, many who grew the congregations of Catholic parishes, while others found new religious community in the nascent Pentecostal movement. Over the last hundred years, Mexican Americans have become one of the largest population groups in the U.S., and through struggle and perseverance they have found leadership roles in their diverse religious organizations, including within non-Christian religions, such as Judaism, Islam, and Buddhism. This leadership is perhaps most notable in the Catholic Church, still the largest single religious home for Mexican Americans. In the twenty-first century, the U.S. Catholic Church will become a majority Latino/a church, with Mexican Americans representing the largest portion.

Embedded within this sweeping history are the daily details of religious practice. This book has looked at several examples of the practical ways that

DOI: 10.4324/9780429285516-17

Mexican Americans have experienced their religion in the things they do, the people they care about, and the goals they pursue. A transformative example is Mexican American participation and leadership in the civil rights movement, in which religious symbols and narratives played a major part. Religious world-views and long traditions of devotion have undergirded Mexican American healing traditions, particularly in the collection of practices known as cur-anderismo. Likewise, Mexican Americans have practiced their faith in pilgrim-age as well as in multi-faceted devotions to beloved figures, such as the Virgin of Guadalupe and the Santo Niño de Atocha. The richness of Mexican American religions touches all aspects of life.

Mexican Americans and pan-Latino/a identity

As this book has shown, there is clearly a unique Mexican American religious story to tell. However, as that story arrives at the present day, Mexican Amer-icans are often grouped with other people with Latin American heritage in the U.S. It is useful to note that thinking of "Hispanic" or "Latino/a" people as an ethnic, and even a racial, category that includes all people descended from Spanish-speaking or Latin American ancestors is a relatively recent phenomenon. It was not until the 1970s that the U.S. government instituted use of the term "Hispanic" in its census and other data-gathering materials; "Latino" did not appear in the census until 2000.[1] Then, and now, many so-called Latinos/as first identify with a national origin, such as "Mexican American," "Puerto Rican," or "Colombian American." However, the pan-ethnic labels of "Latino/a" and "Hispanic" are pervasive and communicate common assumptions that people with Latin American descent must share certain cultural, historical, and linguistic characteristics.

A scholar of ethnic identity and representation, Suzanne Oboler, has noted that the use of terms like "Hispanic" and "Latino/a" can function in very dif-ferent ways. For example, lumping all people of Latin American descent into an artificial ethnic category—something she calls a "bureaucratic invention"— often serves as a tool for insidious racial profiling. She argues that "[t]he increasing visibility of Latinos has compelled US society to transcend the black-white binary, superimposing a new native/foreigner binary on the traditional understanding." This classification system rests on an oppressive logic of privi-leging whiteness over and against every other racial group. In this sense, "Latinos" join all other people of color as less-than in comparison to white people.[2] Moreover, labels like "Latino/a" erase real distinctions between diverse people. However, pan-ethnic terms can also have positive effects and even be used as tools of self-determination and political agency. Latino/a clas-sification can be a source of pride and build solidarity among groups that do, in fact, often share at least some historical and cultural experience. To use a reli-gious example, Mexican American Catholics share a similar history of Spanish colonialism and evangelization with other Latino/a Catholics, even if particular practices and devotions may vary widely. The shared experiences may help

Latinos/as secure greater inclusion in the leadership structures and daily rhythms of the Catholic Church and the local parish even while diverse groups, such as Mexican Americans or Cuban Americans, may yet maintain unique identities.

Future trends

Although it can be risky to make predictions, some trends in Mexican American religions seem clear, while others are strong possibilities. For example, Mexican American and other Latino/a participation in the U.S. Catholic Church promises to continue to grow as a percentage of the whole. Within the U.S. Catholic Church, the plurality of members already are Latino/a, and they will very likely become the majority before the middle of the century. According to Hosffman Ospino, a professor of Hispanic ministry and religious education at Boston College, Latinos/as are "redefining" the U.S. Catholic Church, not only in terms of demographic ascendency but also in the devotional character of the Church. Latin American connections and history will continue to nudge U.S. Catholicism toward connections with fellow Catholics throughout the Americas. Moreover, the geographic center of U.S. Catholicism, because of its Latino/a membership, is shifting from the Northeast and Midwest to the South and West. Ospino believes that Latinos/as "find themselves in a unique position to build the foundations of U.S. Catholicism for decades."[3] While Ospino's vision of the future is based in real demographic shifts, it should be noted that Catholicism is not a predetermined religious affiliation for Mexican Americans and other Latinos/as.

Protestant denominations, especially charismatic and Pentecostal groups like the Assemblies of God and the Church of God (Cleveland, Tennessee), have attracted Latinos/as, but no single denomination—in contrast to the Catholic Church—is likely to become majority Latino/a. The story rather seems to be one of stability. The overall percentage of Latino/as who claim to be Protestants of any type—approximately 25 percent—has remained virtually the same over the past decade.[4] Mexican Americans have formed part of Pentecostalism since its birth in the early twentieth century and will continue to play a role in charismatic churches in the United States, especially in regions of the country with large Mexican American populations. Mainline and liberal Protestants, such as Presbyterians, Methodists, and Lutherans, despite years of mission efforts, have seen little in the way of Latino/a growth.

Although not a religious group, those who claim no religious affiliation—the "nones"—are a growing group among Latinos/as, up from 15 percent in 2009 to 23 percent in 2019. In this, however, Latinos/as show little difference with the rest of the U.S. population.[5] It is unclear whether the number of "nones" in the U.S. will continue to rise, or if it will eventually reach a plateau. But given that Latino/a nones have grown at the same rate as the rest of the nation, it seems quite likely that Latinos/as will continue to keep pace with the nonaffiliated of all ethnic backgrounds.

Another trend that is worth noting is that Mexican American heritage, including religious heritage, may continue to be folded into a pan-Latino/a identity. Churches, including the Catholic Church, generally have framed their outreach and inclusion of Mexican Americans as part of an undifferentiated Latino/a population. In this, they are following common practice of governmental and commercial organizations, which likewise have been more likely to consider Latinos/as as the most salient and targetable population rather than specific national heritage groups, such as Mexican Americans. However, Mexican Americans represent over 60 percent of all Latinos/as combined, and the United States' southern border is with Mexico, therefore there is little reason to think that being a "Mexican American" will lose meaning anytime soon. Indeed, perhaps as Latinos/as continue to grow as a percentage of the population, public understanding of what it means to be a Mexican American versus, for example, a Cuban American, will develop further.

Finally, it is extremely likely that Mexican American religions will have a growing impact on the religious culture of the United States in general. (Indeed, more scholarship is needed to explore just how important Mexican Americans have been in shaping broader trends in U.S. religious history and practice.) Perhaps the most prominent example is the flourishing popularity of the Virgin of Guadalupe, whose devotion has spread far beyond the Mexican and Mexican American communities. The story of her apparition, her Indigenous connections, and the continental outpouring of love and regard for her have made Guadalupe a source of comfort and challenge for millions. Another way in which Mexican American religious people have had an impact on U.S. religion and culture more generally is through their participation in the U.S. civil rights movement. Figures such as César Chávez, Dolores Huerta, Reies López Tijerina, and a host of others with less name recognition have drawn on their religious traditions to fight for justice and fairness and, in so doing, have inspired people both in and out of the Mexican American community. A final example to mention, among many others, is in the area of traditional healing and medicine. Mexican American religious and traditional medicine has integrated in many ways with other complementary, spiritual, and alternative medicines in the United States. The *botánicas* that dot U.S. cities have a wide-ranging and multiethnic clientele. In short, Mexican American religions are a vital component of the overall U.S. religious and cultural context.

The United States, a country that often prides itself on being a nation of immigrants, has yet to come to terms with its Latin American heritage. Latinos/as are the largest minority group and already constitute a majority in some areas, with Mexican Americans representing well over half of this group. Millions and millions of acres of U.S. land were once part of Mexico and remain deeply shaped by centuries of Spanish colonialism. But the matter is not merely one of demographic or geographic critical mass. The history of the United States, including the history of its religions, must take stock of the nation's profound Mexican connection. To ignore this connection is to practice a violent erasure.

Mexican American people and their religious practices, beliefs, and traditions are at the center of who we are.

Notes

1 Suzanne Oboler, "Citizenship and Belonging: The Construction of US Latino Identity Today," *Iberoamericana* 7, no. 25 (2007): 118.
2 Oboler, 119.
3 Hosffman Ospino, "10 Ways Hispanics Are Redefining American Catholicism in the 21st Century," *America Magazine*, October 30, 2017, https://www.americamagazine. org/faith/2017/10/30/10-ways-hispanics-are-redefining-american-catholicism-21st-century.
4 Pew Research Center, "In U.S., Decline of Christianity Continues at Rapid Pace," *Pew Research Center*, October 17, 2019, https://www.pewforum.org/2019/10/17/ in-u-s-decline-of-christianity-continues-at-rapid-pace.
5 "In U.S., Decline of Christianity Continues at Rapid Pace."

Bibliography

Adams, E. Charles. *The Origin and Development of the Pueblo Katsina Cult.* Tucson, AZ: University of Arizona Press, 1991.

Aguilar-Moreno, Manuel. *Handbook to Life in the Aztec World.* New York: Oxford University Press, 2006.

Albanese, Catherine L. *America, Religions, and Religion.* 5th ed. Belmont, CA: Wadsworth, 2012.

Alcántara, Amanda. "Student Group MEChA Holds Vote to Change Name, Prompting Strong Reactions." *Latino USA*, April 3, 2019. https://www.latinousa.org/2019/04/03/mechanamechange.

Almaráz, Jr., Félix D. "San Antonio's Old Franciscan Missions: Material Decline and Secular Avarice in the Transition from Hispanic to Mexican Control." *The Americas* 44, no. 1 (1987): 1–22.

Alurista. "Myth, Identity, and Struggle in Three Chicano Novels: Aztlán … Anaya, Méndez, and Acosta." In *Aztlán: Essays on the Chicano Homeland*, edited by Rudolfo A. Anaya and Francisco Lomeli, 219–229. Albuquerque, NM: University of New Mexico Press, 1989.

Anaya, Rudolfo A., and Francisco A. Lomelí, eds. "Plan Espiritual de Aztlán." In *Aztlán: Essays on the Chicano Homeland*, 1–5. Albuquerque, NM: University of New Mexico Press, 1989.

Anna, Timothy E. *Forging Mexico: 1821–1835.* Lincoln, NE: University of Nebraska Press, 1998.

Applegate, Richard B. "The Datura Cult Among the Chumash." *The Journal of California Anthropology* 2, no. 1 (1975): 7–17.

Association for Hispanic Theological Education. "Our History." *AETH.org*. Accessed June 25, 2019. https://www.aeth.org/nuestra-historia?language=english.

Atencio, Tomás. "The Empty Cross: The First Hispano Presbyterians in Northern New Mexico and Southern Colorado." In *Protestantes/Protestants: Hispanic Christianity within Mainline Traditions*, edited by David Maldonado, 38–59. Nashville, TN: Abingdon Press, 1999.

Avila, Elena, and Joy Parker. *Woman Who Glows in the Dark: A Curandera Reveals Traditional Aztec Secrets of Physical and Spiritual Health.* New York: J.P. Tarcher/Putnam, 1999.

Badillo, David A. *Latinos and the New Immigrant Church.* Baltimore, MD: Johns Hopkins University Press, 2006.

Barba, Lloyd. "Farmworker Frames: Apostólico Counter Narratives in California's Valleys." *Journal of the American Academy of Religion* 86, no. 3 (2018): 691–723.

Barba, Lloyd. "More Spirit in That Little Madera Church: Cesar Chavez and Religious Soundscapes, 1954–1962." *California History* 94, no. 1 (2017): 26–42.

Barton, Paul. *Hispanic Methodists, Presbyterians, and Baptists in Texas.* Austin, TX: University of Texas Press, 2006.

Barton, Paul. "Inter-Ethnic Relations between Mexican American and Anglo American Methodists in the U.S. Southwest, 1836–1938." In *Protestantes/Protestants: Hispanic Christianity within Mainline Traditions*, edited by David Maldonado, 60–84. Nashville, TN: Abingdon Press, 1999.

Barton, Paul. "¡Ya Basta! Latino/a Protestant Activism in the Chicano/a and Farm Workers Movements." In *Latino Religions and Civic Activism in the United States*, edited by Gastón Espinosa, Virgilio Elizondo, and Jesse Miranda, 127–143. New York: Oxford University Press, 2005.

Bean, Lowell John, and Sylvia Brakke Vane. "California Religious Systems and Their Transformations." In *California Indian Shamanism*, edited by Lowell John Bean, 33–51. Menlo Park, CA: Ballena Press, 1992.

Beecher, Lyman. *A Plea for the West.* Cincinnati, OH: Truman & Smith, 1835.

Bennett, Herman L. *Africans in Colonial Mexico: Absolutism, Christianity, and Afro-Creole Consciousness, 1570–1640.* Bloomington, IN: Indiana University Press, 2003.

Billington, Ray A. "Anti-Catholic Propaganda and the Home Missionary Movement, 1800–1860." *The Mississippi Valley Historical Review* 22, no. 3 (1935): 361–384.

Bowler, Kate. "Looking Up: Latino Megachurches and the Politics of Social Mobility." Unpublished paper, n.d.

Brack, Gene M. *Mexico Views Manifest Destiny, 1821–1846: An Essay on the Origins of the Mexican War.* Albuquerque, NM: University of New Mexico Press, 1975.

Brackenridge, R. Douglas, and Francisco O. García-Treto. *Iglesia Presbiteriana: A History of Presbyterians and Mexican Americans in the Southwest.* San Antonio, TX: Trinity University Press, 1974.

Bremer, Thomas S. *Blessed with Tourists: The Borderlands of Religion and Tourism in San Antonio.* Chapel Hill, NC: University of North Carolina Press, 2004.

Bronder, Saul E. *Social Justice and Church Authority: The Public Life of Archbishop Robert E. Lucey.* Philadelphia, PA: Temple University Press, 1982.

Brooks, Charles Alvin. *Christian Americanization: A Task for the Churches.* New York: Council of Women for Home Missions and Missionary Education Movement of the United States and Canada, 1919.

Brown, Candy Gunther, ed. *Global Pentecostal and Charismatic Healing.* New York: Oxford University Press, 2011.

Burns, Jeffrey M. "The Mexican Catholic Community in California." In *Mexican Americans and the Catholic Church, 1900–1965*, edited by Jay P. Dolan and Gilberto M. Hinojosa, 127–233. Notre Dame, IN: University of Notre Dame Press, 1994.

Busto, Rudy V. *King Tiger: The Religious Vision of Reies López Tijerina.* Albuquerque, NM: University of New Mexico Press, 2005.

Byrne, Julie. *The Other Catholics: Remaking America's Largest Religion.* New York: Columbia University Press, 2018.

Campbell, Frances Margaret. "American Catholicism in Northern New Mexico: A Kaleidoscope of Development, 1840–1885." PhD dissertation. Graduate Theological Union, 1986.

Carrasco, Davíd. *Quetzalcoatl and the Irony of Empire: Myths and Prophecies in the Aztec Tradition.* Chicago, IL: University of Chicago Press, 1982.

Carrasco, Davíd. *Religions of Mesoamerica.* 2nd ed. Long Grove, IL: Waveland Press, 2014.

Carrasco, Sara M. Campos. "Mexican American Folk Medicine: A Descriptive Study of the Different Curanderismo Techniques Practiced by Curanderos or Curanderas and Used by Patients in the Laredo, Texas Area." M.A. Thesis, Texas Woman's University, 1984.

Carroll, Michael P. *American Catholics in the Protestant Imagination: Rethinking the Academic Study of Religion*. Baltimore, MD: Johns Hopkins University Press, 2007.

Castañeda, Carlos. *Our Catholic Heritage in Texas*. Reprint. ed. 7 vols. New York: Arno, 1976.

Castañeda-Liles, Socorro. "Our Lady of Guadalupe and the Politics of Cultural Interpretation." In *Mexican American Religions: Spirituality, Activism, and Culture*, 153–179. Durham, NC: Duke University Press, 2008.

Castillo, Ana. *Goddess of the Américas = La Diosa de Las Américas: Writings on the Virgin of Guadalupe*. New York: Riverhead Books, 1996.

Cervantes, Paloma. "Ancient Ways for a Modern Life." *Institute of Shamanism and Curanderismo*. Accessed February 18, 2020. https://www.instituteofshamanismandcura nderismo.com.

Chávez, Fray Angélico. *But Time and Chance: The Story of Padre Martínez of Taos, 1793–1867*. Santa Fe, NM: Sunstone Press, 1981.

Chávez, Fray Angélico, and Thomas E. Chávez. *Wake for a Fat Vicar: Father Juan Felipe Ortiz, Archbishop Lamy, and the New Mexican Catholic Church in the Middle of the Nineteenth Century*. Albuquerque, NM: LPD Press, 2004.

Chávez Sauceda, Teresa. "Race, Religion, and La Raza: An Exploration of the Racialization of Latinos in the United States and the Role of the Protestant Church." In *Protestantes/Protestants: Hispanic Christianity within Mainline Traditions*, 177–193. Nashville, TN: Abingdon Press, 1999.

Chesnut, R. Andrew. *Devoted to Death: Santa Muerte, the Skeleton Saint*. New York: Oxford University Press, 2012.

Chino, Jorge. "The Buddhalupist: The Spiritual Life of Sandra Cisneros." *El Andar*, 1999. http://www.elandar.com/back/winter99/stories/story_cisneros.html.

Chipman, Donald E., and Harriet Denise Joseph. *Spanish Texas, 1519–1821*. Revised ed. Austin, TX: University of Texas Press, 2010.

Comité Nacional de Servicio Hispano. "Quiénes Somos." *Renovación Carismática Católica de los Estatos Unidos y Canadá*. Accessed August 9, 2019. https://rcchispana.org/quienes_somos.html.

"Constitución de 1824." *Texas Law: Tarlton Law Library*. Accessed September 7, 2018. https://tarltonapps.law.utexas.edu/constitutions/mexican1824spanish/t1s1.

Conway, Christopher B., ed. *The U.S.-Mexican War: A Binational Reader*. Translated by Gustavo Pellón. Indianapolis, IN: Hackett, 2010.

Cook, Noble David. *Born to Die: Disease and New World Conquest, 1492–1650*. New York: Cambridge University Press, 1998.

Costeloe, Michael P. *Church and State in Independent Mexico: A Study of the Patronage Debate, 1821–1857*. London: Royal Historical Society, 1978.

da Cunha Rocha, Carolina. "Blessed Are You among Bandits: The Cross-Border Cult of Jesús Malverde (19th–21st Centuries)." *Frontera Norte* 31 (2019): 1–20.

Darley, Alex M. *The Passionists of the Southwest, or the Holy Brotherhood: A Revelation of the "Penitentes"*. Reprint ed. Glorieta, NM: Rio Grande Press, 1968.

Davalos, Karen Mary. "'The Real Way of Praying': The Via Crucis, Mexicano Sacred Space, and the Architecture of Domination." In *Horizons of the Sacred: Mexican Traditions in U.S. Catholicism*, edited by Timothy Matovina and Gary Riebe-Estrella, 41–68. Ithaca, NY: Cornell University Press, 2002.

Dean-Olmsted, Evelyn. "Shamis, Halebis, and Shajatos: Labels and Dynamics of Syrian Jewishness in Mexico City." *Language and Communication* 31 (2011): 130–140.

De Borhegyi, Stephen F., and E. Boyd. *El Santuario de Chimayo*. Reprint ed. Santa Fe, NM: Ancient City Press, 1982.

De la Cruz, Juana Inés, Electa Arenal, and Amanda Powell. *The Answer / La Respuesta, Including a Selection of Poems*. New York: Feminist Press at the City University of New York, 1994.

De las Casas, Bartolomé, and Stafford Poole. *In Defense of the Indians: The Defense of the Most Reverend Lord, Don Fray Bartolomé de Las Casas, of the Order of Preachers, Late Bishop of Chiapas, against the Persecutors and Slanderers of the Peoples of the New World Discovered across the Seas*. DeKalb, IL: Northern Illinois University Press, 1992.

De la Teja, Jesús F., and John Wheat. "Béxar: Profile of a Tejano Community, 1820–1832." In *Tejano Origins in Eighteenth Century San Antonio*, edited by Gerald E. Poyo and Gilberto M. Hinojosa, 1–24. Austin, TX: University of Texas Press, 1991.

De León, Arnoldo. *The Tejano Community, 1836–1900*. Albuquerque, NM: University of New Mexico Press, 1982.

Díaz, Mónica. *Indigenous Writings from the Convent: Negotiating Ethnic Autonomy in Colonial Mexico*. Tucson, AZ: University of Arizona Press, 2010.

Do, Anh. "Muslim and Latino Groups Unite during Ramadan, Breaking Fast with Tacos at Mosques." *Los Angeles Times*, June 4, 2017. https://www.latimes.com/local/lanow/la-me-ln-tacos-ramadan-20170604-story.html.

Dolan, Jay P., and Gilberto M. Hinojosa. *Mexican Americans and the Catholic Church, 1900–1965*. Notre Dame, IN: University of Notre Dame Press, 1994.

Domenech, Emmanuel. *Missionary Adventures in Texas and Mexico: A Personal Narrative of Six Years' Sojourn in Those Regions*. London: Longman, Brown, Green, Longmans, and Roberts, 1858.

Don, Patricia Lopes. "Franciscans, Indian Sorcerers, and the Inquisition in New Spain, 1536–1543." *Journal of World History* 17, no. 1 (2006): 27–49.

Donahue, William H. "The Missionary Activities of Fray Antonio Margil de Jesús in Texas, 1716–1722." *The Americas* 14, no. 1 (1957): 45–55.

Donohue, John Augustine. *After Kino: Jesuit Missions in Northwestern New Spain, 1711–1767*. Sources and Studies for the History of the Americas, VI. St. Louis, MO: St. Louis University, 1969.

Doyle, Sherman H. *Presbyterian Home Missions: An Account of the Home Missions of the Presbyterian Church in the U.S.A.* Philadelphia, PA: Presbyterian Board of Publication and Sabbath-School Work, 1902.

Drescher, Elizabeth. *Choosing Our Religion: The Spiritual Lives of America's Nones*. New York: Oxford University Press, 2016.

Duverger, Christian. *La conversión de los indios de La Nueva España*. Collección 500 Años 18. Quito, Ecuador: Abya-Yala, 1990.

Ebright, Malcolm, and Rick Hendricks. *The Witches of Abiquiu: The Governor, the Priest, the Genízaro Indians, and the Devil*. Albuquerque, NM: University of New Mexico Press, 2006.

Eck, Diana L. *A New Religious America: How a "Christian Country" Has Now Become the World's Most Religiously Diverse Nation*. 1st ed. San Francisco, CA: HarperSanFrancisco, 2001.

Eggan, Fred. "The Hopi Cosmology or World-View." In *Kachinas in the Pueblo World*, edited by Polly Schaafsma, 7–16. Salt Lake City, UT: University of Utah Press, 2000.

Elizondo, Virgilio P. *Galilean Journey: The Mexican-American Promise*. Maryknoll, NY: Orbis Books, 1983.

Ennis, Sharon R., Merarys Ríos-Vargas, and Nora G. Albert. "The Hispanic Population: 2010." *U.S. Census Bureau*, 2010. https://www.census.gov/prod/cen2010/briefs/c2010br-04.pdf.

Espinosa, Gastón. *Latino Pentecostals in America: Faith and Politics in Action*. Cambridge, MA: Harvard University Press, 2014.

Espinosa, Gastón, and Mario T. García. *Mexican American Religions: Spirituality, Activism, and Culture*. Durham, NC: Duke University Press, 2008.

Espinosa, Gastón, Virgilio Elizondo, and Jesse Miranda. *Hispanic Churches in American Public Life: Summary of Findings*. Notre Dame, IN: Institute for Latino Studies, University of Notre Dame, 2003.

Espinosa, Gastón, Harold Morales, and Juan Galvan. "Latino Muslims in the United States: Reversion, Politics, and Islamidad." *Journal of Race, Ethnicity, and Religion* 8, no. 1 (2017): 1–48.

Esteyneffer, Juan de. *Florilegio Medicinal*. Edited by Ma. del Carmen. Anzures y Bolaños. Mexico City: Academia Nacional de Medicina, 1978.

Farrelly, Maura Jane. *Anti-Catholicism in America, 1620–1860*. Cambridge: Cambridge University Press, 2018.

Fisher, Lillian Estelle. *The Background of the Revolution for Mexican Independence*. New York: Russell & Russell, 1971.

Flores, Antonio. "How the U.S. Hispanic Population Is Changing." *Pew Research Center*, September 18, 2017. https://www.pewresearch.org/fact-tank/2017/09/18/how-the-u-s-hispanic-population-is-changing.

Flores, Antonio, Gustavo López, and Jynnah Radford. "Facts on Latinos in America: Current Data." *Pew Research Center, Hispanic Trends*, September 18, 2017. https://www.pewresearch.org/hispanic/2017/09/18/2015-statistical-information-on-hispanics-in-united-states-current-data.

Florescano, Enrique. *The Myth of Quetzalcoatl*. Baltimore, MD: Johns Hopkins University Press, 1999.

Franchot, Jenny. *Roads to Rome: The Antebellum Protestant Encounter with Catholicism*. Berkeley, CA: University of California Press, 1994.

Galarza, Ernesto. *Strangers in Our Fields*. Washington, DC: Joint United States-Mexico Trade Union Committee, 1956.

Galvan, Juan. "Latino Muslims Leading Others to Enlightenment." *Islamic Horizons*, August2002.

Galvan, Juan, ed. *Latino Muslims: Our Journeys to Islam*. San Antonio, TX: Self-published, 2017.

Gamba, Laura. "Perdió el pelo y el nombre para encontrar su espiritualidad." *El Nuevo Herald*, August 23, 2016. https://www.elnuevoherald.com/noticias/sur-de-la-florida/article97421802.html.

García, Ignacio M. "Thoughts on Latino Mormons, Their Afterlife, and the Need for a New Historical Paradigm for Saints of Color." *Dialogue: A Journal of Mormon Thought* 50, no. 4 (2017): 1–29.

García, Mario T. "PADRES: Latino Community Priests and Social Action." In *Latino Religions and Civic Activism in the United States*, edited by Gastón Espinosa, Virgilio Elizondo, and Jesse Miranda, 77–95. New York: Oxford University Press, 2005.

García, Mario T. *The Gospel of César Chávez: My Faith in Action*. Lanham, MD: Sheed and Ward, 2007.

García-Ballester, Luis. *Medicine in a Multicultural Society: Christian, Jewish, and Muslim Practitioners in the Spanish Kingdoms, 1222–1610.* Burlington, VT: Ashgate, 2001.

Gerald, Rex E. *Spanish Presidios of the Late Eighteenth Century in Northern New Spain.* Museum of New Mexico Research Records 7. Santa Fe, NM: Museum of New Mexico Press, 1968.

Gonzales, Patrisia. *Red Medicine: Traditional Indigenous Rites of Birthing and Healing.* Tucson, AZ: University of Arizona Press, 2012.

Gonzalez, Gilbert G. "Mexican Labor Migration, 1876–1924." In *Beyond La Frontera: The History of Mexico-U.S. Migration,* edited by Mark Overmeyer-Velázquez, 28–50. New York: Oxford University Press, 2011.

González, Julio. *The Santuario de Chimayo in New Mexico: The Shrine of Our Lord of Esquipulas and the Holy Child.* Chimayó, NM: Sons of the Holy Family, 2013.

Goodykoontz, Colin Brummitt. *Home Missions on the American Frontier, with Particular Reference to the American Home Missionary Society.* New York: Octagon Books, 1971.

Green, Stanley C. *The Mexican Republic: The First Decade, 1823–1832.* Pittsburgh, PA: University of Pittsburgh Press, 1987.

Greenberg, Amy S. *A Wicked War: Polk, Clay, Lincoln, and the 1846 U.S. Invasion of Mexico.* New York: Alfred A. Knopf, 2012.

Gribble, Richard. "Roman Catholicism and U.S. Foreign Policy, 1919–1935: A Clash of Policies." *Journal of Church and State* 50, no. 1 (2008): 73–99.

Griffith, James S. *Folk Saints of the Borderlands: Victims, Bandits & Healers.* Tucson, AZ: Rio Nuevo Publishers, 2003.

Guardino, Peter. *The Dead March: A History of the Mexican-American War.* Cambridge, MA: Harvard University Press, 2017.

Gunnell, Kristine Ashton. "The Daughters of Charity as Cultural Intermediaries: Women, Religion, and Race in Early Twentieth-Century Los Angeles." *U.S. Catholic Historian* 31, no. 2 (2013): 51–74.

Gutiérrez, Gustavo. *A Theology of Liberation: History, Politics, and Salvation.* 15th Anniversary ed. Maryknoll, NY: Orbis Books, 1988.

Gutiérrez, Ramón A. "El Santuario de Chimayo: A Syncretic Shrine in New Mexico." In *Feasts and Celebrations in North American Ethnic Communities,* edited by Ramón A. Gutiérrez and Geneviève Fabre, 71–86. Albuquerque, NM: University of New Mexico Press, 1995.

Gutiérrez, Ramón A. *When Jesus Came, the Corn Mothers Went Away: Marriage, Sexuality, and Power in New Mexico, 1540–1846.* Stanford, CA: Stanford University Press, 1991.

Haas, Lisbeth. *Saints and Citizens: Indigenous Histories of Colonial Missions and Mexican California.* Berkeley, CA: University of California Press, 2013.

Hackel, Steven W. *Children of Coyote, Missionaries of Saint Francis: Indian-Spanish Relations in Colonial California, 1769–1850.* Chapel Hill, NC: University of North Carolina Press, 2005.

Hackel, Steven W. *Junípero Serra: California's Founding Father.* New York: Hill and Wang, 2013.

Hackett, Charles Wilson. *Historical Documents Relating to New Mexico, Nueva Vizcaya, and Approaches Thereto, to 1773.* Vol. III. Washington, DC: Carnegie Institution, 1937.

Hammond, George P., and Agapito Rey. *Don Juan de Oñate: Colonizer of New Mexico.* Edited by George P. Hammond. Vol. V and VI. Coronado Cuarto Centennial Publications, 1540–1940, Albuquerque, NM: University of New Mexico Press, 1953.

Handbook of Texas Online. "Census and Census Records," *TSHA,* June 12, 2010. https://tshaonline.org/handbook/online/articles/ulc01.

Hanks, Nancy. *Lamy's Legion: The Individual Histories of Secular Clergy Serving in the Archdiocese of Santa Fe from 1850 to 1912*. Santa Fe, NM: HRM Books, 2000.

Harrington, John Peabody. *The Ethnogeography of the Tewa Indians. Twenty-Ninth Annual Report of the Bureau of American Ethnology to the Secretary of the Smithsonian Institution.* Washington, DC: Bureau of American Ethnology, 1916.

Hartch, Todd. *The Rebirth of Latin American Christianity*. New York: Oxford University Press, 2014.

Harvey, Paul. "Civil Rights Movements and Religion in America." In *Oxford Research Encyclopedia of Religion*. New York: Oxford University Press, 2016. https://oxfordre.com/religion/view/10.1093/acrefore/9780199340378.001.0001/acrefore-9780199340378-e-492.

Hassig, Ross. *Mexico and the Spanish Conquest*. 2nd ed. Norman, OK: University of Oklahoma Press, 2006.

Henderson, Timothy J. *Beyond Borders: A History of Mexican Migration to the United States*. Malden, MA: Wiley-Blackwell, 2011.

Hendrickson, Brett. *Border Medicine: A Transcultural History of Mexican American Curanderismo*. New York: New York University Press, 2014.

Hendrickson, Brett. *The Healing Power of the Santuario de Chimayó: America's Miraculous Church*. New York: New York University Press, 2017.

Herz, Cary, Ori Z. Soltes, and Mona Hernandez. *New Mexico's Crypto-Jews: Image and Memory*. Albuquerque, NM: University of New Mexico Press, 2009.

Hester, Thomas R. "'Coahuiltecan': A Critical Review of an Inappropriate Ethnic Label." *La Tierra, Journal of the Southern Texas Archaeological Association* 25 (1998): 3–7.

Hieb, Louis A. "The Meaning of Katsina: Toward a Cultural Definition of 'Person' in Hopi Religion." In *Kachinas in the Pueblo World*, edited by Polly Schaafsma, 23–33. Salt Lake City, UT: University of Utah Press, 2000.

Hinojosa, Felipe. *Latino Mennonites: Civil Rights, Faith, and Evangelical Culture*. Baltimore, MD: Johns Hopkins University Press, 2014.

"Hispanic or Latino Origin by Specific Origin." *U.S. Census Bureau*, 2018. https://data.census.gov/cedsci/table?lastDisplayedRow=30&table=B03001&tid=ACSDT1Y2018.B03001&hidePreview=true.

Hispanic Summer Program. "Who We Are, and What We Do." *Hispanic Summer Program*. Accessed February 2, 2021. https://hispanicsummerprogram.org/whoweare.

Hispanic Theological Initiative. "The HTI Story." *HTI*. Accessed June 25, 2019. http://hti.ptsem.edu/about/history.

Hogan, Michael. *The Irish Soldiers of Mexico*. Guadalajara, Mexico: Fondo Editorial Universitario, 2011.

Hoopes, Tom. "Our Lady of Guadalupe and U.S. Immigration." *The Gregorian Institute at Benedictine College*, December 12, 2016. https://www.thegregorian.org/2016/our-lady-of-guadalupe-and-u-s-immigration.

Hurtado, Albert L. *Indian Survival on the California Frontier*. New Haven, CT: Yale University Press, 1988.

Johannsen, Robert W. *To the Halls of the Montezumas: The Mexican War in the American Imagination*. New York: Oxford University Press, 1985.

John Paul II. *Ecclesia in America*. Vatican City: The Holy See, 1999.

Juárez, José Roberto. "La iglesia católica y el chicano en sud Texas, 1836–1911." *Aztlán: A Journal of Chicano Studies* 4, no. 2 (1973): 217–255.

Juckett, Gregory. "Caring for Latino Patients." *American Family Physician* 87, no. 1 (2013): 48–54.

Kandil, Caitlin Yoshiko. "Buddhist Groups Increasingly Taking Root in Latinx Communities." *Lion's Roar*, November 21, 2018. https://www.lionsroar.com/buddhist-groups-increasingly-taking-root-in-latinx-communities.

Kanter, Deborah E. *Chicago Católico: Making Catholic Parishes Mexican*. Urbana, IL: University of Illinois Press, 2020.

Katz, Friedrich. "Labor Conditions on Haciendas in Porfirian Mexico: Some Trends and Tendencies." *The Hispanic American Historical Review* 54, no. 1 (1974): 1–47.

Kay, Margarita Artschwager. "The Florilegio Medicinal: Source of Southwest Ethnomedicine." *Ethnohistory* 24, no. 3 (1977): 251–259.

KEN Jewish Community. "About Us." *KEN Jewish Community*, n.d. http://kenjc.org/new/about-us.

KEN Jewish Community. "Bat Mitzvah Group." *KEN Jewish Community*, n.d. http://kenjc.org/new/bat-mitzvah.

Kessell, John L. *Mission of Sorrows: Jesuit Guevavi and the Pimas, 1691–1767*. Tucson, AZ: University of Arizona Press, 1970.

Kiev, Ari. *Curanderismo: Mexican-American Folk Psychiatry*. New York: Free Press, 1968.

Kim, Rebecca Y. "Religion and Ethnicity: Theoretical Connections." *Religions* 2 (2011): 312–329.

Knab, Timothy J. *The Dialogue of Earth and Sky: Dreams, Souls, Curing, and the Modern Aztec Underworld*. Tucson, AZ: University of Arizona Press, 2004.

Lake, Alison. *Colonial Rosary: The Spanish and Indian Missions of California*. Athens, OH: Swallow Press/Ohio University Press, 2006.

Lamkahouan, Carissa. "Latinos Mark 'Eid in America's First Spanish Muslim Center." *AboutIslam*, July 8, 2016. https://aboutislam.net/muslim-issues/n-america/latinos-mark-eid-americas-first-spanish-muslim-center.

Laso de la Vega, Luis, Lisa Sousa, Stafford Poole, James Lockhart, and Miguel Sánchez. *The Story of Guadalupe: Luis Laso de La Vega's Huei Tlamahuiçoltica of 1649*. Stanford, CA: Stanford University Press, 1998.

Latino Decisions. "Focus Groups with Latino Jews in Five American Cities." *American Jewish Committee and the Arthur and Rochelle Belfer Institute for Latino and Latin American Affairs*, December 11, 2015.

La Vere, David. *The Texas Indians*. College Station, TX: Texas A&M University Press, 2004.

Lee, Erika. "The Chinese Exclusion Example: Race, Immigration, and American Gatekeeping, 1882–1924." *Journal of American Ethnic History* 21, no. 3 (2002): 36–62.

León, Luis D. "César Chávez and Mexican American Civil Religion." In *Latino Religions and Civic Activism in the United States*, edited by Gastón Espinosa, Virgilio Elizondo, and Jesse Miranda, 53–64. New York: Oxford University Press, 2005.

León, Luis D. *La Llorona's Children: Religion, Life, and Death in the U.S.-Mexican Borderlands*. Berkeley, CA: University of California Press, 2004.

León, Luis D. "'Soy Una Curandera y Soy Una Católica': The Poetics of a Mexican Healing Tradition." In *Horizons of the Sacred: Mexican Traditions in U.S. Catholicism*, edited by Timothy M. Matovina and Gary Riebe-Estrella, 95–118. Ithaca, NY: Cornell University Press, 2002.

León, Luis D. *The Political Spirituality of Cesar Chavez: Crossing Religious Borders*. Oakland, CA: University of California Press, 2015.

León Portilla, Miguel. *Aztec Thought and Culture: A Study of the Ancient Nahuatl Mind*. Translated by Jack Emory Davis. Norman, OK: University of Oklahoma Press, 1963.

Levine, Irene S. "A Little Church in New Mexico with Some Big Healing Power." *Washington Post*, April 10, 2014. http://www.washingtonpost.com/lifestyle/travel/a -little-church-in-new-mexico-with-some-big-healing-power/2014/04/10/6989ca 34-b9bf-11e3-9a05-c739f29ccb08_story.html.

Levy, Jacques E., Fred Ross, and Jacqueline M. Levy. *Cesar Chavez: Autobiography of La Causa*. Minneapolis, MN: University of Minnesota Press, 2007.

Limonic, Laura. *Kugel and Frijoles: Latino Jews in the United States*. Detroit, MI: Wayne State University Press, 2019.

Lomnitz, Claudio. *Death and the Idea of Mexico*. New York: Zone Books/MIT Press, 2005.

Long, Carolyn Morrow. "Candle Shops, Botánicas, Yerberías, and Web Sites." In *Spiritual Merchants: Religion, Magic, and Commerce*, 159–185. Knoxville, TN: University of Tennessee Press, 2001.

López Austin, Alfredo. *The Human Body and Ideology: Concepts of the Ancient Nahuas*. Translated by Thelma Ortiz de Montellano and Bernard Ortiz de Montellano. 2 vols. Salt Lake City, UT: University of Utah Press, 1988.

López Pulido, Alberto. *The Sacred World of the Penitentes*. Washington, DC: Smithsonian Institution Press, 2000.

Lynch, John. *New Worlds: A Religious History of Latin America*. New Haven, CT: Yale University Press, 2012.

MacGregor-Villarreal, Mary. "Celebrating Las Posadas in Los Angeles." *Western Folklore* 39, no. 2 (1980): 71–105.

Machado, Daisy L. "Latinos in the Protestant Establishment: Is There a Place for Us at the Feast Table?" In *Protestantes/Protestants: Hispanic Christianity within Mainline Traditions*, edited by David Maldonado, 85–103. Nashville, TN: Abingdon Press, 1999.

Madsen, William. *Mexican-Americans of South Texas*. New York: Holt, Rinehart and Winston, 1964.

Martin, David. *Tongues of Fire: The Explosion of Protestantism in Latin America*. Oxford: B. Blackwell, 1990.

Martin, Patricia Preciado. *Songs My Mother Sang to Me: An Oral History of Mexican American Women*. Tucson, AZ: University of Arizona Press, 1992.

Martínez Boom, Alberto. "Evangelización e instrucción pública en el orden colonial español." *Revista Española de Educación Comparada*, no. 31 (2018): 55–86.

Martínez, Juan Francisco. *The Story of Latino Protestants in the United States*. Grand Rapids, MI: Eerdmans, 2018.

Martínez, María Elena. *Genealogical Fictions: Limpieza de Sangre, Religion, and Gender in Colonial Mexico*. Stanford, CA: Stanford University Press, 2008.

Martínez, Richard Edward. *PADRES: The National Chicano Priest Movement*. Austin, TX: University of Texas Press, 2005.

Matovina, Timothy. "Companion in Exile: Guadalupan Devotion at San Fernando Cathedral, San Antonio, Texas, 1900–1940." In *Horizons of the Sacred: Mexican Traditions in U.S. Catholicism*, edited by Timothy Matovina and Gary Riebe-Estrella, 17–40. Ithaca, NY: Cornell University Press, 2002.

Matovina, Timothy. *Guadalupe and Her Faithful: Latino Catholics in San Antonio, from Colonial Origins to the Present*. Baltimore, MD: Johns Hopkins University Press, 2005.

Matovina, Timothy. *Latino Catholicism: Transformation in America's Largest Church*. Princeton, NJ: Princeton University Press, 2012.

Matovina, Timothy. *Tejano Religion and Ethnicity: San Antonio, 1821–1860*. Austin, TX: University of Texas Press, 1995.

Matovina, Timothy. *Theologies of Guadalupe: From the Era of Conquest to Pope Francis.* New York: Oxford University Press, 2019.

McEvoy, Gráinne. "'Operation Migratory Labor': Braceros, Migrants, and the American Catholic Bishops' Committee for the Spanish Speaking." *U.S. Catholic Historian* 34, no. 3 (2016): 75–98.

Medina, Lara. *Las Hermanas: Chicana/Latina Religious-Political Activism in the U.S. Catholic Church.* Philadelphia, PA: Temple University Press, 2004.

Medina Gallo, César. "Magnetismo espiritual: Toribio Romo, sus reliquias y la expansión territorial del culto." *Espaço e Cultura*, no. 37 (January 2015): 195–217.

Migration Policy Institute. "Mexican-Born Population Over Time, 1850–Present." *migrationpolicy.org*, August 14, 2013. https://www.migrationpolicy.org/programs/data-hub/charts/mexican-born-population-over-time.

Miller, Howard. "Stephen F. Austin and the Anglo-Texan Response to the Religious Establishment in Mexico, 1821–1836." *The Southwestern Historical Quarterly* 91, no. 3 (1988): 283–316.

Miller, Robert Ryal. *Shamrock and Sword: The Saint Patrick's Battalion in the U.S.-Mexican War.* Norman, OK: University of Oklahoma Press, 1989.

Mora-Torres, G. Cristina. *"What's So Ethnic about Ethno-Religious Identity?: Contemporary Evidence from Latino Immigrant 'Conversion Narratives'."* In Conference Papers, Vol. 1, Great Divides: Transgressing Boundaries, American Sociological Association, Montreal, 2006.

Morales, Harold D. *Latino and Muslim in America: Race, Religion, and the Making of a New Minority.* New York: Oxford University Press, 2018.

Motolinía, Toribio, and Elizabeth Andros Foster. *Motolinía's History of the Indians of New Spain.* Westport, CT: Greenwood Press, 1973.

Mulder, Mark T., Aida I. Ramos, and Gerardo Martí. *Latino Protestants in America: Growing and Diverse.* Lanham, MD: Rowman & Littlefield, 2017.

Murphy, Joseph M. *Botánicas: Sacred Spaces of Healing and Devotion in Urban America.* Jackson, MS: University Press of Mississippi, 2015.

National Catholic Welfare Council, Social Action Department. *The Spanish Speaking of the Southwest and West.* Washington, DC: National Catholic Welfare Council, 1943.

National Conference of Catholic Bishops. *"The Hispanic Presence, Challenge, and Commitment: A Pastoral Letter on Hispanic Ministry,"* December 12, 1983. United States Catholic Conference, Washington, DC, 1984.

National Park Service. *San Antonio Missions, National Historic Park.* U.S. Department of the Interior, n.d.

Navarro, Armando. *La Raza Unida Party: A Chicano Challenge to the U.S. Two-Party Dictatorship.* Philadelphia, PA: Temple University Press, 2000.

Navarro-Rivera, Juhem. "Media Stereotypes and the Invisible Latino 'Nones.'" *Free Inquiry*, December2010.

Navarro-Rivera, Juhem, Barry A. Kosmin, and Ariela Keysar. *"U.S. Latino Religious Identification 1990–2008: Growth, Diversity and Transformation."* Hartford, CT: American Religious Identification Survey, Trinity College, 2008.

New Mexico National Guard Museum. "New Mexico National Guard's Involvement in the Bataan Death March," *New Mexico National Guard Museum*, 2014. http://www.bataanmuseum.com/bataanhistory.

Newcomb, William W. *The Indians of Texas, from Prehistoric to Modern Times.* Austin, TX: University of Texas Press, 1967.

Newell, Quincy D. *Constructing Lives at Mission San Francisco: Native Californians and Hispanic Colonists, 1776–1821.* Albuquerque, NM: University of New Mexico Press, 2009.

Nostrand, Richard L. "Mexican Americans Circa 1850." *Annals of the Association of American Geographers* 65, no. 3 (1975): 378–390.

Núñez Cabeza de Vaca, Alvar, and Enrique Pupo-Walker. *Castaways: The Narrative of Alvar Núñez Cabeza de Vaca.* Berkeley, CA: University of California Press, 1993.

Nuttall, Donald A. "Gaspar de Portolá: Disenchanted Conquistador of Spanish Upper California." *Southern California Quarterly* 53, no. 3 (1971): 185–198.

Oboler, Suzanne. "Citizenship and Belonging: The Construction of US Latino Identity Today." *Iberoamericana* 7, no. 25 (2007): 115–127.

Oropeza, Lorena. *The King of Adobe: Reies López Tijerina, Lost Prophet of the Chicano Movement.* Chapel Hill, NC: University of North Carolina Press, 2019.

Orozco, Cynthia E. *No Mexicans, Women, or Dogs Allowed: The Rise of the Mexican American Civil Rights Movement.* Austin, TX: University of Texas Press, 2009.

Ortiz, Alfonso. *The Tewa World: Space, Time, Being, and Becoming in a Pueblo Society.* Chicago, IL: University of Chicago Press, 1969.

Ortiz de Montellano, Bernard R. *Aztec Medicine, Health, and Nutrition.* New Brunswick, NJ: Rutgers University Press, 1990.

Ospino, Hosffman. "10 Ways Hispanics Are Redefining American Catholicism in the 21st Century." *America Magazine,* October 30, 2017. https://www.americamagazine. org/faith/2017/10/30/10-ways-hispanics-are-redefining-american-catholicism-21st-century.

Palmer, Anita K. "Sergio De La Mora: Turning a Generation." *OutreachMagazine.com,* November 2, 2015. https://outreachmagazine.com/interviews/13492-sergio-de-la-mora-turning-a-generation.html.

Parsons, Elsie Clews. *Pueblo Indian Religion.* 2 vols. Chicago, IL: University of Chicago Press, 1939.

Pavone, Frank. "Our Lady of Guadalupe and the Pro-Life Movement." *Priests for Life.* Accessed April 14, 2020. https://www.priestsforlife.org/articles/2791-our-lady-of-guadalupe-and-the-pro-life-movement.

Pedraja, Luis G. "Guideposts along the Journey: Mapping North American Hispanic Theology." In *Protestantes/Protestants: Hispanic Christianity within Mainline Traditions,* edited by DavidMaldonado, Jr., 123–139. Nashville, TN: Abingdon Press, 1999.

Peek, Lori. *Behind the Backlash: Muslim Americans after 9/11.* Philadelphia, PA: Temple University Press, 2011.

Peña, Elaine. *Performing Piety: Making Space Sacred with the Virgin of Guadalupe.* Berkeley, CA: University of California Press, 2011.

Peña, Elaine. "Time to Pray: Devotional Rhythms and Space Sacralization at the Mexico-US Border." *Material Religion* 13, no. 4 (2017): 461–481.

Pérez de Ribas, Andrés. *History of the Triumphs of Our Holy Faith amongst the Most Barbarous and Fierce Peoples of the New World.* Edited by Daniel T. Reff. Tucson, AZ: University of Arizona Press, 1999.

Pescador, Juan Javier. *Crossing Borders with the Santo Niño de Atocha.* Albuquerque, NM: University of New Mexico Press, 2009.

Pew Research Center. "A Portrait of Mormons in the U.S." *Pew Research Center, Religion & Public Life.* Accessed June 4, 2020. https://www.pewforum.org/2009/07/24/a-portrait-of-mormons-in-the-us.

Pew Research Center. "In U.S., Decline of Christianity Continues at Rapid Pace," *Pew Research Center, Religion & Public Life,* October 17, 2019. https://www.pewforum. org/2019/10/17/in-u-s-decline-of-christianity-continues-at-rapid-pace.

Pew Research Center. "Latinos, Religious Landscape Study." *Pew Research Center, Religion & Public Life*. Accessed May 13, 2020. https://www.pewforum.org/religious-landscape-study.

Pew Research Center. "Racial and Ethnic Composition, Religious Landscape Study." *Pew Research Center, Religion & Public Life*. Accessed May 13, 2020. https://www.pewforum.org/religious-landscape-study.

Pew Research Center. "Religion in America: U.S. Religious Data, Demographics and Statistics." *Pew Research Center, Religion & Public Life*. Accessed June 24, 2019. https://www.pewforum.org/religious-landscape-study/religious-denomination.

Pew Research Center. "The Shifting Religious Identity of Latinos in the United States," *Pew Research Center, Religion & Public Life*, May 7, 2014. https://www.pewforum.org/2014/05/07/the-shifting-religious-identity-of-latinos-in-the-united-states.

Phillips, George Harwood. *Indians and Intruders in Central California, 1769–1849*. Norman, OK: University of Oklahoma Press, 1993.

Pinheiro, John C. *Missionaries of Republicanism: A Religious History of the Mexican-American War*. New York: Oxford University Press, 2014.

Poole, Stafford. *Our Lady of Guadalupe: The Origins and Sources of a Mexican National Symbol, 1531–1797*. Tucson, AZ: University of Arizona Press, 1995.

Porter, Amy M. *Their Lives, Their Wills: Women in the Borderlands, 1750–1846*. Lubbock, TX: Texas Tech University Press, 2015.

Poyo, Gerald E. "The Canary Island Immigrants of San Antonio: From Ethnic Exclusivity to Community in Eighteenth-Century Béxar." In *Tejano Origins in Eighteenth-Century San Antonio*, edited by Gerald E. Poyo and Gilberto M. Hinojosa, 41–58. Austin, TX: University of Texas Press, 1991.

Poyo, Gerald E., and Gilberto M. Hinojosa, eds. *Tejano Origins in Eighteenth-Century San Antonio*. Austin, TX: University of Texas Press, 1991.

Privett, Stephen A. *The U.S. Catholic Church and Its Hispanic Members: The Pastoral Vision of Archbishop Robert E. Lucey*. San Antonio, TX: Trinity University Press, 1988.

Putnam, Robert D., and David E. Campbell. *American Grace: How Religion United and Divides Us*. New York: Simon and Schuster, 2010.

Ramírez, Daniel. *Migrating Faith: Pentecostalism in the United States and Mexico in the Twentieth Century*. Chapel Hill, NC: University of North Carolina Press, 2015.

Red, William Stuart. *The Texas Colonists and Religion, 1821–1836: A Centennial Tribute to the Texas Patriots Who Shed Their Blood That We Might Enjoy Civil and Religious Liberty*. Austin, TX: E. I. Shettles, 1924.

Reff, Daniel T. *Plagues, Priests, and Demons: Sacred Narratives and the Rise of Christianity in the Old World and the New*. New York: Cambridge University Press, 2005.

Rensink, Brenden W. "Q&A with Sujey Vega about LDS Latinos and Ethnic Religious Belonging in Arizona." *Borderlands History*, March 28, 2016. https://borderlandshistory.org/2016/03/28/qa-with-sujey-vega-about-lds-latinos-and-ethnic-religious-belonging-in-arizona.

Reyes, Raul A. "The Future of the Mormon Church? It's Latino." *NBC News*, August 22, 2016. https://www.nbcnews.com/news/latino/future-mormon-church-it-s-latino-n570621.

Ricard, Robert, and Lesley Byrd Simpson. *The Spiritual Conquest of Mexico: An Essay on the Apostolate and the Evangelizing Methods of the Mendicant Orders in New Spain, 1523–1572*. Berkeley, CA: University of California Press, 1966.

Rivera, Eric. "The First Mexican Protestant Loved the Bible." *Christianity Today*, February 18, 2019. https://www.christianitytoday.com/history/2019/february/first-mexican-protestant-bible.html.

Rodriguez, Jeanette. *Our Lady of Guadalupe: Faith and Empowerment among Mexican-American Women*. Austin, TX: University of Texas Press, 1994.

Romano V., Octavio Ignacio. "Charismatic Medicine, Folk-Healing, and Folk-Sainthood." *American Anthropologist* 67, no. 5 (1965): 1151–1173.

Romo, David Dorado. "My Tío, the Saint." *Texas Monthly*, November 1, 2010.

Rosales, F. Arturo. *Chicano!: The History of the Mexican American Civil Rights Movement*. Houston, TX: Arte Público Press, 1996.

Rosales, F. Arturo, ed. *Testimonio: A Documentary History of the Mexican American Struggle for Civil Rights*. Houston, TX: Arte Público Press, 2000.

Royal, Robert, and George Weigel, eds. *A Century of Catholic Social Thought: Essays on Rerum Novarum and Nine Other Key Documents*. Washington, DC: Ethics and Public Policy Center/Distributed by University Press of America, 1991.

Rubel, Arthur J. "Concepts of Disease in Mexican-American Culture." *American Anthropologist* 62, no. 5 (1960): 795–814.

Ruiz, Vicki L. "Claiming Public Space at Work, Church, and Neighborhood." In *Las Obreras: Chicana Politics of Work and Family*, edited by Vicki L. Ruiz, 13–39. Los Angeles, CA: UCLA Chicano Studies Research Center, 2000.

Ruiz, Vicki L. *From Out of the Shadows: Mexican Women in Twentieth-Century America*. New York: Oxford University Press, 1998.

San Francisco Zen Center. "Bienvenidos a City Center." *San Francisco Zen Center*. Accessed June 3, 2020. https://www.sfzc.org/practice-centers/city-center/bienvenidos-city-center.

Sanathavihari Bhante Bhikku. "Monje En La Modernidad." *YouTube*. Accessed June 3, 2020. https://www.youtube.com/channel/UCgX_kcAhHCuaDTdjejB1LZQ.

Sánchez, Joseph P., Robert L. Spude, and Art Gómez. *New Mexico: A History*. Norman, OK: University of Oklahoma Press, 2013.

Sánchez Walsh, Arlene M. *Latino Pentecostal Identity: Evangelical Faith, Self, and Society*. New York: Columbia University Press, 2003.

Sánchez Walsh, Arlene M. *Pentecostals in America*. New York: Columbia University Press, 2018.

Sandos, James A. *Converting California: Indians and Franciscans in the Missions*. New Haven, CT: Yale University Press, 2004.

Sandoval, Moises. *On the Move: A History of the Hispanic Church in the United States*. Maryknoll, NY: Orbis Books, 1990.

Sarat, Leah. *Fire in the Canyon: Religion, Migration, and the Mexican Dream*. New York: New York University Press, 2013.

Schwaller, John Frederick. *The History of the Catholic Church in Latin America: From Conquest to Revolution and Beyond*. New York: New York University Press, 2011.

Shellnutt, Kate. "On a Mission: Mormons Reach out to Hispanics." *Houston Chronicle*, May 6, 2010. https://www.chron.com/life/houston-belief/article/On-a-mission-Mormons-reach-out-to-Hispanics-1694354.php.

Sheridan, Thomas E. *Arizona: A History*. Tucson, AZ: University of Arizona Press, 1995.

Smith, Rosemary E. "*The Work of the Bishops' Committee for the Spanish Speaking on Behalf of the Migrant Worker*." M.A. Thesis, Catholic University of America, 1958.

Smithers, W. D. "Nature's Pharmacy and the Curanderos." *Sul Ross State College Bulletin* XLI, no. 3 (1961): 5–39.

Smithwick, Noah. *The Evolution of a State, or, Recollections of Old Texas Days*. Austin, TX: University of Texas Press, 1983.

Socolow, Susan Migden. *The Women of Colonial Latin America*. 2nd ed. Cambridge: Cambridge University Press, 2015.

Spears, Beverley. *Early Churches of Mexico: An Architect's View*. Albuquerque, NM: University of New Mexico Press, 2017.

Spicer, Edward H. *Cycles of Conquest: The Impact of Spain, Mexico, and the United States on the Indians of the Southwest, 1533–1960*. Tucson, AZ: University of Arizona Press, 1962.

Stavans, Ilan, and Steve Sheinkin. *El Iluminado: A Graphic Novel*. New York: Basic Books, 2012.

Stevens, Peter F. *The Rogue's March: John Riley and the St. Patrick's Battalion, 1846–48*. Washington, DC: Potomac Books, 2005.

St. John, Rachel. *Line in the Sand: A History of the U.S.-Mexico Border*. Princeton, NJ: Princeton University Press, 2011.

Stoll, David. *Is Latin America Turning Protestant?: The Politics of Evangelical Growth*. Berkeley, CA: University of California Press, 1990.

Tena, Rafael. "La religión mexica: catálogo de dioses." *Arqueología Mexicana* 30 (2009): 6–94.

Thiessen, Joel, and Sarah Wilkins-Laflamme. *None of the Above: Nonreligious Identity in the US and Canada*. New York: New York University Press, 2020.

Torre Villar, Ernesto de la. *La Independencia de México*. 2nd ed. Mexico City: Editorial Mapfre/Fondo de Cultura Económica, 1992.

Torres, Eliseo, and Timothy L. Sawyer. *Curandero: A Life in Mexican Folk Healing*. Albuquerque, NM: University of New Mexico Press, 2004.

Travis, Luke. "Man of God, Man of Business." *Fine Magazine*, August2012. http://www.finehomesandliving.com/August-2012/Man-of-God-Man-of-Business.

"Treaty of Guadalupe Hidalgo; February 2, 1848." *The Avalon Project, Yale Law School*, 2008. Accessed April 30, 2019. http://avalon.law.yale.edu/19th_century/guadhida.asp.

Treviño, Roberto R. *The Church in the Barrio: Mexican American Ethno-Catholicism in Houston*. Chapel Hill, NC: University of North Carolina Press, 2006.

Trotter, Robert T., and Juan Antonio Chavira. *Curanderismo: Mexican American Folk Healing*. 2nd ed. Athens, GA: University of Georgia Press, 1997.

United Farm Workers. "The Rise of the UFW." *United Farm Workers*. Accessed March 16, 2020. https://ufw.org/the-rise-of-the-ufw.

United States Conference of Catholic Bishops and Conferencia del Episcopado Mexicano. "Strangers No Longer Together on the Journey of Hope." *United States Conference of Catholic Bishops*, 2003. http://www.usccb.org/issues-and-action/human-life-and-dignity/immigration/strangers-no-longer-together-on-the-journey-of-hope.cfm.

University of New Mexico Curanderismo Class. "Curanderismo." *University of New Mexico*. Accessed January 31, 2020. http://curanderismo.unm.edu.

V Encuentro. "The Call to a V Encuentro." *V Encuentro*. Accessed October 1, 2019. https://vencuentro.org/encuentros/v-encuentro.

Vanderwood, Paul J. *Juan Soldado: Rapist, Murderer, Martyr, Saint*. Durham, NC: Duke University Press, 2004.

Vargas, Zaragosa. *Crucible of Struggle: A History of Mexican Americans from Colonial Times to the Present Era*. New York: Oxford University Press, 2011.

Vinson, Ben, III. *Before Mestizaje: The Frontiers of Race and Caste in Colonial Mexico*. New York: Cambridge University Press, 2018.

Vivian, Patricia. "Anthropomorphic Figures in the Pottery Mound Murals." In *Kachinas in the Pueblo World*, edited by Polly Schaafsma, 81–91. Salt Lake City, UT: University of Utah Press, 2000.

Wallace, Edward S. "The Battalion of Saint Patrick in the Mexican War." *Military Affairs* 14, no. 2 (1950): 84–91.

Weber, David J. *The Mexican Frontier, 1821–1846: The American Southwest under Mexico.* Albuquerque, NM: University of New Mexico Press, 1982.

Weigle, Martha. *Brothers of Light, Brothers of Blood: The Penitentes of the Southwest.* Albuquerque, NM: University of New Mexico Press, 1976.

Weise, Julie M. *Corazón de Dixie: Mexicanos in the U.S. South since 1910.* Chapel Hill, NC: University of North Carolina Press, 2015.

Williams, Joseph W. *Spirit Cure: A History of Pentecostal Healing.* New York: Oxford University Press, 2013.

Wright, Robert E. "How Many Are a 'Few'? Catholic Clergy in Central and Northern New Mexico, 1780–1851." In *Seeds of Struggle/Harvest of Hope: The History of the Catholic Church in New Mexico*, edited by Thomas J. Steele, Paul Rhetts, and Barb Awalt, 219–262. Albuquerque, NM: LPD Press, 1998.

Wright, Robert E. "Mexican-Descent Catholics and the U.S. Church, 1880–1910: Moving Beyond Chicano Assumptions." *U.S. Catholic Historian* 28, no. 4 (2010): 73–97.

Young, Julia Grace Darling. *Mexican Exodus: Emigrants, Exiles, and Refugees of the Cristero War.* New York: Oxford University Press, 2015.

Index

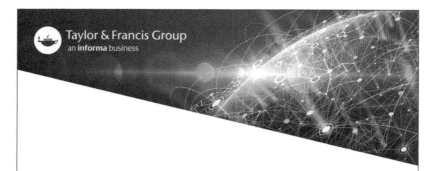